THE WOMAN CYCLIST

THE WOMAN CYCLIST

By ELAINE MARIOLLE
and Michael Shermer

CB
CONTEMPORARY
BOOKS
CHICAGO · NEW YORK

Library of Congress Cataloging-in-Publication Data

Mariolle, Elaine.
    The woman cyclist / Elaine Mariolle and Michael Shermer.
       p.   cm.
    Bibliography: p. 355
    Includes index.
    ISBN 0-8092-4941-3 (pbk.) : $10.95
    1. Cycling for women.   2. Cycling—Training.   3. Bicycle racing.
I. Title.
GV1057.M37   1988
796.6'088042—dc19   88-10339
                                               CIP

Published by Contemporary Books, Inc.
180 North Michigan Avenue, Chicago, Illinois 60601
Manufactured in the United States of America
Library of Congress Catalog Card Number: 88-10339
International Standard Book Number: 0-8092-4941-3

Published simultaneously in Canada by Beaverbooks, Ltd.
195 Allstate Parkway, Valleywood Business Park
Markham, Ontario L3R 4T8 Canada

This book is dedicated to my family and friends,
for their encouragement
and support for my cycling adventures,
and especially to Vance,
who never thought my dreams were impossible,
even from the very start.

—Elaine Mariolle

I would like to dedicate my contribution to this work
to the women who have played a key role
in my development as a person:

To Mom, for instilling confidence in everything
I have ever attempted in my life

To Christa, for unquestioned support and honest feedback
that kept me on the straight and narrow

To Karen, Shawn, and Tina, for unconditional love
and the acceptance that gave me strength to continue

To Ayn Rand, author, philosopher, and inspiration,
for clarifying the values in life.

—Michael Shermer

Contents

Foreword   ix

Preface   xi

Acknowledgments   xv

Introduction   1

1   Bicycles and Other Cycling Equipment   4

2   Safe and Self-Sufficient on the Road   44

3   The Feminine Physique   63

4   Weight Training and Stretching   83

5   Recreation and Touring   109

6   Cycling for Transportation   131

7   Competition   144

8   Mountain Biking   195

9   Endurance   206

10   Three RAAMs   251

11   Women in Sports   326

Appendix 1: Gearing   335

Appendix 2: Glossary of Bicycle Jargon   340

Appendix 3: Bicycle Periodicals   350

Appendix 4: Bicycle Associations   353

Appendix 5: Selected Bibliography   355

Appendix 6: Women's Cycling Records   359

Appendix 7: United States Cycling Federation Velodromes   366

Index   368

Foreword

Growing up watching football, I always counted myself a fan of the game, of its grace, power, courage. Then one day I heard an NFL player describe the field as a battleground of sorts and the athletes as fellow warriors devoted to each other as if to an ideal, committed to fight all odds, surmount all obstacles. The potency of friendship lifted them high above fear, up into a strata of fire-breathing desire. After that, I adored the sport of football.

Any sport is just a game, until it's elevated to a higher level by the player's imagination.

It was gliding across the moonlit surface of a vast and magical ocean that brought forth from me the dawning of an inspired athletic imagination. It happened in the process of the farthest swim in recorded history. An hour or so before dawn, after two days of nonstop swimming, my body switched to automatic pilot, and allowed my mind to open and drift. Egoless dialogues about mortality, godless visions of death and the meaning of life raced over the razor-sharp landscape of my mind. Freud, Amelia Earhart, Carl Sagan spoke their minds through my exhaustion. Then the first droplet of light eased up over the horizon into my goggles, and I was sucked back to left-hemisphere, race mode.

Athletes' bodies perform well; that's understood. But curiosity, mental energy, the perspective of humor, all can evolve from such physical effort, and that—the athlete's particular eccentricity—is what draws me to a sport.

For five years, as part of the "Wide World of Sports," I joined in filming the adventures of the Race Across AMerica. This is a grueling athletic event, one in which mere mortals raced mere bicycles 3,000 miles in eight days, sleeping no more than a couple of hours in any 24-hour period. The riders were interesting—some sweet, some funny, all gutsy. These men and women educated us about cadence, pit stops, winning, quitting, family sacrifice, and disk wheels.

Our crews chased these spirited souls up and down America's roadways, and, naturally, my favorite time to come upon them was early morning—an hour or so before dawn. Sometimes riders expressed themselves in the simple desire for a bowl of hot oatmeal. But there were two athletes we could count on, every time, for their fire-breathing brand of desire and mind-expanding philosophy.

Michael Shermer, seduced into the stream of consciousness flow, would theorize about the potential of the mind. He would offer unique possibilities to explain the different cultural pressures on women, as opposed to men. He was always mentally sharp, regardless of race position or physical state.

Elaine Mariolle would encapsulate the event as a grand life experience. She fascinated us with her revelations, like the connection between despair and determination. Her keen self-awareness enabled her to describe to us the point at which uncontrollable fatigue shifts briefly into eye-opening clarity. She would expound on the various elements of love—Love, capital "L"—like the sort gladiator football players might vow to each other.

It was Elaine and Michael who, for me, lifted the Race Across AMerica from an athletic event to a rich moment in time.

They are accomplished cyclists; you'll learn a great deal from their expertise. But they are thinkers. Fasten your toe clips—you might just get inspired.

Diana Nyad

Preface

Inspiring other people to get into cycling is the greatest reward I receive from bicycle racing. While training for the 1985 Race Across AMerica, I met a gentleman who told me that he quit smoking and lost 10 pounds after watching the 1984 Race Across AMerica on television. He figured that if I could ride 3,100 miles on a bike, he could go out and accomplish a few of his personal goals. During the 1986 Race Across AMerica, I received hundreds of telephone messages while I was battling the headwinds in Texas and Oklahoma or pedaling through Tennessee and the Appalachian Mountains. Many were friends and acquaintances telling me they had started riding to work or had posted their fastest time on a century ride. They were sending me their encouragement and support by becoming active themselves!

My hope is that this book will encourage more women to get out and ride. Cycling is a lifelong sport. Whether you're just starting, or you want to try racing or touring, there is something for everybody. Bicycling is a great form of recreation and exercise, and it's an economical and ecologically sound mode of transportation. Bicycle touring is a great way to see the world, enjoy the outdoors, and watch the seasons pass.

I started cycling when I was 25—the age when women are warned that, physiologically, everything starts to go downhill. I wasn't about to listen to that nonsense. For the previous three years, I had been lifting weights at the local YMCA, and I wanted to do something with my strength. Linda Skinner, a woman I worked with, and her husband Steve competed in triathlons, and since I was also interested in triathlons we got out and did a few rides together. They suggested I wear cycling shorts and a jersey to make riding more comfortable and told me about cleated shoes and how they are much more efficient. I was on a pretty tight budget and I couldn't afford to buy everything at once. Each week I found myself back at the Velo-Sport bike shop until I had all the basics. After a few weeks, Linda and Steve signed me up with their local bike club, the Grizzly Peak Cyclists, and took me on my first century ride, the Grizzly Peak Century. We were just going to do the first 50 miles, but when I finished, a friend told me I looked pretty strong and suggested I go ahead and do the second 50 miles. It only cost $1.00 more and I liked the nifty 100-mile patch, so I went for it.

The summer of '83 was one to remember. Everything was new. I was always improving, and although I wasn't breaking any records, there were lots of adventures and lots of fun. Since then, I have competed in many cycling federation races and events including three RAAMs, culminating in 1986 when I won the women's race and set a new transcontinental record. Now I have taken up a new challenge, road racing, but I still enjoy touring in the off-season.

I believe we are capable of accomplishing more than we think we can. Curiosity, good friends, and a little luck can lead you to places you never dreamed. I was, and am, fortunate to have friends who showed me the ropes, got me off to a good start, and are an important part of my life today. I hope that the information in this book and the profiles of successful women cyclists will help get you off to a good start too.

                                        Elaine Mariolle

For those of us in cycling, the world revolves around two wheels—a sort of "cyclocentric" view of the universe. But we insiders are biased. When I speak to bike clubs or write columns and essays for bicycle magazines, I know that I'm preaching to the converted. But when individuals outside of the sport become aware of its excitement, beauty, and potential for growth, then you know that "things are happening."

And happening they are in the world of women's sports, particularly in cycling. The majority of new entrants into the sport are women, and the size of the women's fields in racing has grown geometrically in just the last couple of years. In my research, I uncovered many facets of the sport I had never considered. There are many aspects of cycling other than racing, and *The Woman Cyclist* explores the options available.

Elaine Mariolle is the ideal person to coauthor this book. She wasn't groomed to become a professional cyclist from a young age but started cycling as an adult in her twenties, turning a hobby into a profession. Elaine went from being a "weekend warrior" to a world-class champion athlete. She did this through determination and willpower, characteristics we all share. Elaine is an inspiration to me and others because she was able to realize her potential and carve out a place for herself in the world of cycling. That is why this book is valuable for anyone in the sport—novice or expert. There's something here for every woman and for every man as well.

The gap between men's and women's performances is continuing to close. In the 1987 Ironman World Championships, the winning woman's time would have beaten the 1981 winning man's time by two minutes. Things have come a long way indeed. To the best within all who read this book—don't hesitate to reach for the biggest goal you can find. You may very well achieve it.

Michael Shermer

Acknowledgments

In many ways writing this book has been like so many RAAM adventures; it was truly a test of endurance and determination, with a healthy dose of humility folded in. There were many times the project seemed doomed and the temptation to quit was great. But just like RAAM, we made it with the help of friends, new and old, who contributed all sorts of talents, good energy, and hugs when we really needed them! I'd especially like to thank my coauthor, Michael Shermer, for approaching me with this project and putting the deal together. Mike helped keep *The Woman Cyclist* alive at critical points along the way.

There are many people and organizations that took the time to answer my endless list of questions and provided resources that enhanced the quality of this book. A special thanks to John Cornelison and Steve Gottlieb at the League of American Wheelmen; Greg Siple from BikeCentennial; Greg Snyder from the American Youth Hostels (San Francisco, CA); Lynn Jaffee of the Melpomene Institute; Diane Fritschner of the United States Cycling Federation; Georgena Terry of Terry Precision Bicycles; Mary Schmitz at the Courthouse Athletic Club; Lisa Gordon of ProServ; and John Marino of the Ultra-Marathon Cycling Association.

We have lots of terrific photographs and diagrams in this book and many people to thank for their generosity. In addition to all the photographers credited in the text, a special thanks to: RAAM photographer Dave Nelson for the wonderful cover shot and the many interior photos; Marina Fusco-Nims for opening her RAAM photo archives; Dana Davis for coming up with terrific product shots and portraits; Irene Young for doing a great job with the weight training and stretching section; Dave Dolson for the tire-repair shots he set up with Michael and Sara Neil; and the Coors Classic and Ore-Ida organizations for great race photos. A special thanks to Kathleen Jenkins for the wonderful drawing of a bicycle. Kathleen discovered a new talent and is now taking a graphic arts class!

I'd like to thank all the women who granted interviews and who answered the many questions we had for them. Their time, energy, and perspective on cycling are greatly appreciated. Other people who deserve mention: Patty Brink and Naomi Bloom for their thoughts on clothing and fabrics; Jill McIntire, Charlotte von der Hude, and Ray Orr for their suggestions on touring; Jennifer Peale for a handle on the fit-or-fat question; Dr. Joan Ullyot for her ideas on birth control; Tim Parker for his careful reading of bicycle basics; and Peter Rich for passing on some of the bicycling history and tradition.

When it was getting down to the wire, I needed a reality check, and there were many friends who read the drafts and revisions. I'd like to thank Lauren Agusta, Julie Anderson, Bob Kridle, and Janice Mariolle for their feedback and suggestions. Amy Smolens came up with some great one-liners, Susan Taylor went over many versions of the manuscript and made some suggestions that were invaluable, and Jan Kaufman proofread the final draft. A special thanks to my friends at MT XINU who let me tie up their Mac, laser printer, and copy machine for hours on end and never said a word.

I'd like to thank Diana Nyad for her encouragement and her suggestion that I approach this task like a sporting event. I appreciated Elizabeth Cunningham's knowledge of the publishing process and her support when I needed it. A special thanks to my training partners, Linda Skinner and Cindy Olavarri, who helped me keep my sanity and some semblance of fitness when the going got really rough!

I'm very grateful to Ginger Rodriguez for her editorial skill and courage with the original manuscript, and I'm indebted to Gigi Grajdura for making the many changes we wanted even though it wasn't convenient. A special thanks to our editor, Susan Buntrock, who had patience and heart for this project way beyond the call of duty. Finally, I want to thank Vance for rolling up his sleeves and wading on into a project that desperately needed some help. His editorial skills and sense of humor saved the day!

THE WOMAN CYCLIST

Introduction

"Let me tell you what I think of bicycling," Miss Anthony said, leaning forward and laying a slender hand on my arm. "I think it has done more to emancipate women than anything else in the world. I stand and rejoice every time I see a woman ride by on a wheel. It gives woman a feeling of freedom and self-reliance. It makes her feel as if she were independent. The moment she takes her seat she knows she can't get into harm unless she gets off her bicycle, and away she goes, the picture of free, untrammelled womanhood."

—Susan B. Anthony, interviewed by Nelly Bly,
New York World, February 2, 1896

Women and Cycling

Cycling was a major craze in America when Nelly Bly interviewed Susan B. Anthony. The arrival of the "safety bicycle" in 1885 and the development of the pneumatic tire in 1888 had made bicycles a practical form of transportation. Due to its relatively cheap price in comparison to a horse and carriage, the bicycle was well within the means of many Americans and they took to the roads in great numbers. Cycling pioneered new techniques of mass production and mass marketing. Cyclists were instrumental in getting roads improved and they invented road maps, street signs, and even weather reports. Americans were avid fans of bicycle racing and there was a large group of professional racers.

According to Robert A. Smith's *A Social History of the Bicycle*, the bicycle was a great "leveling influence" because anyone, regardless of class or social position, could ride down the same street or in the same park. The bicycle was recognized as a democratic and egalitarian form of transportation and recreation. It put the "human race on wheels" and reinforced the notion that "everyman was just as good as any other man."

Nowhere was the role of the bicycle as a vehicle for social change more apparent than with the status of women. An article in the *Minneapolis Tribune* reported: "Cycling is fast bringing about this change of feeling regarding woman and her capabilities. A woman awheel is an independent creature, free to go whither she will. This before the advent of the bicycle, was denied her."

These heady changes were not accomplished without resistance. There were heated debates about whether it was ladylike to ride a bike, and speculation that riding a bike would cause irreparable physical damage and even lead to miscarriages. But woman persisted and won many new freedoms in the process, including the all-important right to wear bloomers, which were referred to as more "rational dress."

In the 1900s, the car replaced the bicycle as America's transportation craze and cycling slipped into a long eclipse. Today, cycling is reemerging. There are estimates that 80 million Americans ride a bike at least once a year. Women are a major part of the new cycling boom. Statistics from the Bicycle Federation of America show that 55 percent of cyclists are women, and 70 percent of the new participants in the sport are women. Many of these women are coming into cycling from other sports such as running or swimming, and others are entering sport for the first time. Although cycling has changed a lot, the feelings of exhilaration, empowerment, and self-reliance enjoyed by women today have much in common with our predecessors of 100 years ago.

Photo courtesy of Terry Precision Bicycles for Women

Although bicycles have changed a lot in the past 100 years, the feelings of exhilaration and independence women experienced back then remain the same today.

Cycling is a lifelong sport that has something for people of all ages and abilities. It's simple and practical, and it is beautiful. There are lots of things you can do on a bike: run errands to the store or bank, visit friends, ride to work, tour in the country, race, get into better shape, and relieve tension and stress. Cycling offers the opportunity to meet new friends and to share adventures with old friends. It feels great to be outdoors under the sun and sky, with the cool wind blowing on your face and the rush of vitality cleansing and strengthing your body. There is freedom to be found in traveling under your own power and personal satisfaction to be found in completing a tough climb, or finishing your first century ride, or riding on the bike path in the park, and discovering you have muscles and that they work! You may start with simple rides around town, get "hooked," and discover that you are capable of feats you could never even imagine!

In this book, we introduce you to the variety of cycling, from riding to work to racing across the country. We begin with two chapters containing tips on how to set up your bike properly and a few pointers on riding in traffic and being self-sufficient on the road. In Chapters 3 and 4 we deal with some basic physiology and training and we discuss how your body responds to exercise. Each of the other chapters is devoted to some particular type of cycling.

Much of the material is in profiles and interviews with women cyclists, from commuters to world-champion racers. Their personalities are as diverse as their activities. I enjoyed working on this part of the project the best. Sometimes it was the stories, but always it was the sparkle in the eyes and the passion in the voice that told me these women's trusty steeds were more than just a few pounds of steel.

1
Bicycles and Other Cycling Equipment

There are many different types and brands of bikes. There are different kinds of bicycle equipment: wheels, tires, gears, brakes. And there is a wide variety of accessories for cycling: helmets, shoes, shorts, gloves, computers, rollers, and so on. This chapter gives you a quick tour through the variety of equipment and some hints to guide your shopping. We also discuss how to set yourself up to be comfortable on your bike and describe some common problems and potential cures.

Almost everything is a matter of opinion and nowhere is this more true than in cycling. Much of what follows is common knowledge, but I daresay that I could find someone who would dispute even the most benign comment. Keep in mind that you and your tastes and comfort are the final judge.

Types of Bikes

There are many kinds of bicycles of course: three-speeds, ten-speeds, mountain bikes, track bikes, tandems, clunkers, and recumbents, to name a few. The drawing on page 6 is of a standard 10-speed road bike with drop handlebars, two hand-operated caliper brakes, and two gear-shifters called derailleurs. This is the type most frequently used for touring, recreation, and racing on paved roads. It is specialized for efficient and comfortable travel on pavement. It has light,

narrow tires that roll efficiently. The handlebars allow several different riding positions for comfort and aerodynamics. Wind resistance
and weight are major factors in road riding.

The name 10-speed is an anachronism. Some years ago, most bikes
of this type had two chainrings in front and five cogs (or gears) in the
back. That gave 10 distinct gear combinations or speeds. Now, bikes
with 12, 14, 18, and even 21 gear combinations are becoming quite
common but they are all usually called 10-speeds.

Mountain bikes have much in common with the 10-speed road
bike, including the gearing system. They are "10-speeds" but they are
rarely called that. Mountain bikes are specialized for off-road riding.
They feature heavier rims and tires to survive knocking about in the
rocks and they have lower gears than most road bikes for riding
through dirt and gravel. Most mountain bikes have straight handlebars, resulting in a more upright riding position.

A choice between these two kinds of bikes obviously depends on
what kind of riding you intend to do. But people frequently ride
mountain bikes on the road and road bikes in the dirt. In particular,
mountain bikes are quite popular with many people who have no
intention of riding in the dirt. The upright riding position of the
mountain bike is less intimidating for some beginners. Its wheels are
sturdier and the low gears are great for getting up almost any hill
without strain. The trade-off is that you will work noticeably harder
to ride a given distance on pavement using the mountain bike than
you would using the road bike.

I'm lucky enough to have a track bike and a tandem in addition to
my mountain bike and several road bikes. I love to ride them all. But
this chapter focuses on the 10-speed road bike and mountain bike.
The next section takes you through the detailed anatomy of these 10-
speeds. The information on size and fit refers specifically to the road
bike. Much of the other information will apply to all types of bikes.

The other types of bikes are outside the scope of this book, but I
would like to say a good word for the tandem, or the bicycle built for
two. They are a lot of fun to ride. For one thing, you can go pretty fast
because you have the power of two riders without much more wind
resistance than one. But the main thing about a tandem is that it's the
great equalizer. You and your partner arrive at the tops of hills and at
the end of the ride at the same time, even when there is a large
difference in your riding strength.

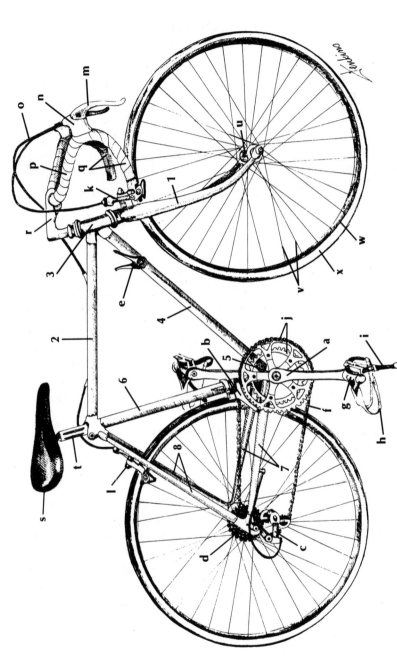

1. Fork, 2. Top Tube, 3. Head Tube, 4. Down Tube, 5. Bottom Bracket, 6. Seat Tube, 7. Chain Stays, 8. Seat Stays, a. Crank Arm, b. Front Derailleur, c. Rear Derailleur, d. Freewheel and Gear Cluster, e. Shift Levers, f. Chain, g. Pedal, h. Toe Clip, i. Toe Strap, j. Chainrings, k. Rear Brake, l. Front Brake, m. Brake Lever, n. Brake Hood, o. Brake Cables, p. Handlebars, q. Drops, r. Stem, s. Saddle, t. Seat Post, u. Front Hub, v. Spokes, w. Rim, x. Tire

Artwork by Kathleen Jenkins. Kathleen is an active cyclist who teaches a novice cycling class and works in a bike shop.

Anatomy of a 10-Speed

Even if you've decided on a 10-speed road bike or mountain bike, there is a bewildering array of brand names and models, and a very wide range in price. A local stereo store gives away a 10-speed with every purchase of a stereo system, some of which sell for about $200! At the other extreme, you can get a custom bike and pay as much as you want.

With all the variety, how do you choose? Just knowing a brand name does not suffice. Many manufacturers offer models ranging in price from $200 to $2,000. The price varies with the quality of the frame and the other individual bike parts. Worse yet, models tend to change from year to year. A model may be discontinued or different parts may be substituted on a given model. Perhaps you have access to a reputable bike shop with a large selection, where you can get good advice and help. But you might not and, in any case, it never hurts to know what you're shopping for. So here is a quick lesson in 10-speed anatomy.

You can think of a bike as a frame with a lot of components (brakes, gears, saddle, handlebars, wheels, etc.) added on. In fact, experienced cyclists frequently have bicycles specifically built for them. There are many framebuilders who will build a custom frame to your specifications. And many bike shops will "build" a bike for you using the frame and components of your choice. Each of these major components will be described here. But there are a few general principles that apply throughout.

Weight is a dominant preoccupation of the cyclist. This is especially true for people who race, but it also affects casual riders. Bicycles can easily differ in weight by five or more pounds. Next time you are climbing a hill, think about carrying a five-pound sack of potatoes up the hill with you. Careful bike selection can save you that work.

On the other hand, you can go to extremes to save weight. There is frequently a large gap between the price of two different components that work equally well but differ only by a few grams. Lighter components are a major factor in driving up the price of a bike. Getting rid of those last few ounces may be worth $500 to racers who finish long races inches apart, but it may not be worth it to you.

Wind resistance is another major preoccupation, and with reason.

On level ground at 20 mph, most of the work you are doing is pushing through the air. You will see aerodynamic everything, from the riding position to helmets and even aero spokes.

Cycling is growing and changing at an amazing pace. Not too long ago, serious riders purchased European bikes with Campagnolo equipment and wore wool cycling clothes that they might have had to import themselves. But today, cycling is different. Other manufacturers have jumped into the lucrative market with quality equipment. Japanese component manufacturers, led by Shimano, have introduced innovative, high-quality designs and there is fierce competition among companies. Today, the names to look to for quality equipment include Campagnolo, Galli, Mavic, Maillard, Shimano, and Sun-Tour. Tomorrow, there will be others.

Frame Geometry

There are some major variations in bicycle frames. Our road bike in the drawing is the standard men's frame or diamond frame. There are also ladies' frames, as pictured in Figure 3 on page 19. These are intended to allow women to ride while wearing skirts. They are a compromise, not as strong or efficient as the diamond frame. But if you are getting a bike to ride to work and you need to commute in a skirt, a diamond frame, for all its virtues, won't be usable. Another compromise is the mixte frame, also pictured in Figure 3. It is somewhat stronger than the ladies' frame and can be ridden wearing a skirt. Another advantage of the ladies' and the mixte is that it is easier to get on and off them, which makes a difference for some people.

The standard diamond frame has been around since the 1880s. But even here there are a lot of options and entire books are written about the details of frame geometry. Some of the variations are visibly different, like the "funny bikes" that have appeared lately in time-trial racing. But some frames that look identical to the untrained eye are actually different in ways that can make a difference to you.

A critical difference that may or may not be obvious is that frames come in different sizes. Getting the right size frame for yourself is the most important item in your selection process. Some people still think that there are two sizes of bikes: kids' bikes with 24-inch wheels and adult bikes with 26-inch wheels. Actually, almost all 10-speeds

Photo by Dana Davis

A mixte or ladies' frame bike is good for women who ride wearing a skirt. A mixte has a double sloping top tube and provides more support than the ladies' frame. A mixte is a nice bike for light rides or running errands. While it's easier to get on and off, most women prefer a standard road frame.

have wheels of approximately 27 inches in diameter and have frames that vary from about 19 inches to 25 inches (48 cm–64 cm). The size is measured from the middle of the bottom bracket (or axle that the cranks rotate on) to the top of the seat tube. Much more is said about frame size in a later section, "Fit and Position on Your Bike," but the quick test is to stand over the bike in front of the saddle, feet flat on the floor, straddling the top tube. You should clear the top tube by about an inch. People usually buy mountain bikes somewhat smaller.

One subtle difference you should know about has to do with "racing" geometry as opposed to "touring" geometry. There are some design trade-offs between comfort and efficiency and also between quick handling and stability. Racing bikes tend to be really stiff, which sacrifices comfort for efficiency. They also tend to have a short wheelbase for quick handling. Carried to extremes, this makes them less stable to the point where they are tricky (or even dangerous) to ride no handed. Hard-core racing geometries can rattle your teeth out and be very uncomfortable for long-distance riding. The differences are not easy to see. One clue is the fork. All forks tend to curve forward, but racing bikes have straighter forks than touring bike forks, which have a noticeable bend at the bottom. Ask the clerk!

Frame Materials:
Steel, Aluminum, and Carbon Fiber

A typical bike frame is made from tubing, which is brazed or glued together. There are usually lugs at the joints. Most frames are steel, but aluminum and carbon-fiber frames are becoming common.

Aluminum has the obvious advantage that it is lighter than steel. Less obvious is that it is a little "softer" than steel and it tends to absorb road shock and vibration more than a steel frame and hence makes for a more comfortable bike. Two arguments are commonly raised against aluminum. According to some, the very softness that makes it comfortable also makes it less stiff and efficient. This is really a fine point. I race on an aluminum bike and so do many professional European racers. People who are really serious may ride an aluminum bike most of the time, but have a special steel bike for events where they feel they need that last tiny percent of advantage. A more serious argument that is still heard is that aluminum bikes are unsafe in that they may fatigue and suffer sudden catastrophic failure. I don't know of any statistics one way or the other on this, but I have ridden my aluminum Vitus tens of thousands of miles.

Another material now being used for bike frames is carbon fiber. It has all the advantages of aluminum in that it is light and comfortable. It appears to have advantages over aluminum in that it is comfortable while maintaining stiffness and efficiency. Research findings on tennis rackets and golf clubs made out of carbon fiber confirm that it has a damping effect on vibrations and shock compared to conventional materials. This comfort is a significant factor if you ride extensively. Two negatives: carbon fiber is still very expensive, with bare framesets costing $1,000 or more. And it is a relatively new technology. How it will react to crashes and being jammed into the trunk of your car and other general wear and tear remains to be seen.

Steel is still the most common frame material. There is nothing wrong with it and good steel frames can be very light.

Gears and Derailleurs

Gears give your 10-speed its name. The gear system is operated by two levers or shifters typically placed on the down tube of the bike, as shown in the illustration, but sometimes placed on the handlebars. Each lever is connected by a cable to a derailleur. The front derailleur selects which of two or three chainrings the chain will run on. The back derailleur selects which cog on the cluster the chain will run on. You shift gears by moving one of the shift levers while pedaling. This causes the derailleur to "derail" the chain from one cog or chainring to the next. Shifting a 10-speed can take a little getting used to, but it quickly becomes second nature.

With most shift systems, you can set the derailleur anywhere and get in between gears so that the chain rattles or even jumps gears abruptly. You learn to make slight adjustments one way or the other so that the chain settles in one gear and runs quietly. Shimano introduced indexed shifting or click-shifting several years ago. With this system, the rear derailleur "clicks" into definite positions so that it is always in gear. Many reliable click-shift imitators are now on the market and the price is coming down. They are very convenient and the older systems are probably on their way out, although low-cost production bikes still tend to have the older systems.

If your bicycle has three chainrings and seven cogs on the cluster, then there are 21 different combinations possible. That's a lot of gears! What are they all for? Basically, of course, they serve the broad purpose of making it comfortable and efficient for you to pedal under a variety of conditions, especially going uphill and going downhill. There are different ways to set up gears depending on the intended use of your bicycle.

You will hear gears described in terms of inches, as in, "There were times on that downhill when I was completely spun out in my biggest gear, which is 108 inches, but when the wind hit me at the bottom of the hill, I had to gear down to my smallest gear, which is only 40 inches and I was having trouble turning that." (Appendix 1 gives you the formula that defines how many inches a particular chainring and cog give you. And there is a chart where you can look up the various combinations.) Now, most people don't have the vaguest idea how many "inches" their gears are. All you need to know for now is what is in that sentence. A big gear is like that 108-inch gear that you need if you want to hurry downhill and not coast. A 52-tooth chainring and a 13-tooth cog give a 108-inch gear. A small gear is like that 40, which you use when you're climbing hills or having trouble with fierce headwinds. A 39-tooth chainring and a 26-tooth cog give you a 40-inch gear. By the way, you might not find a range of gears this big on a production road bike, but even bigger ranges are quite common on production mountain bikes.

An ideal gear setup has a low gear that lets you maintain your spin or cadence while climbing hills and a big enough gear so that you don't have to spin too fast to keep up with your friends on downhills. The other gears are spread out evenly in between so that you can make fine adjustments for varying conditions to maintain your rhythm or cadence. (We talk more about spinning and cadence in the section, "Basic Bike-Handling Skills," in Chapter 2.)

Unless you are an equipment fanatic, your choice of gears will probably be dominated by what is available on production bikes in your price range. But you will find options and you should look for something suited to your intended use. For touring, you will want to have a wide range of gears, with a good low one for climbing long hills, especially if you are carrying all your camping stuff with you. Many a racer, on the other hand, probably wouldn't bother to have that 40-inch gear we talked about earlier, feeling that if she got to the point where she had to use it, she would be out of the race anyway. Instead, she would have a narrower range, giving her finer adjustments for dealing with the stress of competition. (But note that Jeannie Longo, winner of the 1987 Tour de France Féminin, caused a stir by using triple chainrings with very low gears!)

Pedals and Cranks

The pedals, of course, are where you put your feet! But what about those toe clips and toe straps? If you become serious about cycling, you will want some sort of pedal system that keeps your foot on the pedal. All most beginners can think about is being trapped on the pedal, unable to pull loose, and then falling over. But once you get past that idea and realize how to work the equipment, you will appreciate the added power and comfort.

Both the older toe clip and strap or the newer systems lock you onto the pedal so that you can constantly apply torque, limited only by your strength, without pulling your foot off the pedal. The toe clip and strap correctly position your foot on the pedal; with the strap tightened down, you can pull up on the pedal as well as pushing down, which gives you a continuous power stroke. Special riding shoes (see the section on shoes) have a cleat on the bottom so that when you tighten the toe strap, your foot is "locked" onto the pedal.

New pedal/shoe systems that do away with the toe clip and toe strap are now available. The pedal matches a mechanism on the bottom of a special shoe. You step into the pedal as if locking a ski boot into a ski binding. These systems, which are easy to use, also have the advantage that there are no straps squeezing and irritating your feet. (You lose all the advantage if for some reason you ride in your street shoes.) Aerolite, Campagnolo, Look, Mavic, Shimano, and Time all offer these pedal/shoe systems and others appear all the time. But what if you want to get your foot out? With the newer systems, you simply twist your foot to one side or the other to release it. With the toe strap, you have to reach down and flip it loose with your hand, which quickly becomes second nature. Some people ride with the strap a little loose so they can get their foot out in case of surprises.

Crankarms, or cranks, can be obtained in different lengths. Crank length makes a subtle difference in how efficiently you can spin and how much torque you can exert when standing to power up a hill. Most production ("off the rack") bikes come equipped with 170-mm cranks, but they are available as short as 155 mm or as long as 180 mm. Shorter people will tend to want shorter cranks, taller people longer cranks. Spinners will tend to like shorter cranks, while riders who like to torque up hills will like longer ones.

Wheels and Tires

A standard bike wheel consists of a hub, spokes, a rim, and a tire. As usual, there is variety right down to how many spokes are in the wheel, how thick the spokes are, and how they are laced. But the big decision with wheels is whether you will use clinchers or sew-ups.

Clinchers are by far the most common tire and they are what you are likely to get if you don't make it a point to get sew-ups. Fortunately, they are also just fine for most purposes. Clinchers are like car tires. There is a tube inside an outer casing that beads against the rim.

In a sew-up, the casing is wrapped completely around the tube and sewn up (get it?), so that the tube is completely enclosed in the casing. The casing is then glued onto the rim. That may seem like a lot of bother and it is. Clinchers are less expensive than sew-ups, and tend to be less trouble to maintain and to last longer. But sew-ups are lighter and saving weight on the wheel is paramount. An old saying that saving an ounce on the rim is worth a pound somewhere else on the bike is an exaggeration, but it has a grain of truth. The wheel has to accelerate forward, as well as rotate, so you do two kinds of work moving the wheel and that makes its weight doubly important. Fairly light clinchers are available and many people now race on them. There are still riders who prefer sew-ups, but many of them have a set of clinchers that they use for training.

Either type of wheel can be made lighter by using lighter rims and fewer spokes, but this can get extreme. Some wheels used in time trials have only 12 spokes. You probably won't want to go that far, but buying a lighter set of wheels is a good way to upgrade your bike, as you will really notice the difference with lighter wheels. But as they get lighter, they also become more fragile. You can go out on a club ride, hit a pothole, and damage or even destroy a wheel that cost $100. Even fanatics tend not to ride their precious superlight wheels except under controlled circumstances.

Wheels are a significant source of wind resistance and this is of critical importance in time trials. There are techniques to significantly reduce drag. One is the use of "aero" or bladed spokes, which are flat instead of round, and do have some advantage. Disk wheels are also aerodynamic and reduce drag even more than bladed spokes. They are constructed differently than spoked wheels, typically being a "solid" sandwich of some sort of foam between a thin and rigid outer skin. They are becoming quite common at time trials. You will not likely see one on a production bike as disks tend to be expensive, anywhere from $400 to over $1,000 for a single wheel. Covers that increase the aerodynamic advantage of an ordinary wheel can be bought, but these covers are not legal in many forms of competition.

If you want to own several different sets of wheels to use on your bike for different riding conditions, you need to be aware that there are some subtle differences between sizes 27-inch and 700C. They are *almost* the same, but are different enough to cause trouble with your brake adjustments. Most sew-up rims are 700C, but many clinchers on production bikes are 27-inch, so if you are going to switch back and forth, you will need to look for 700C clinchers.

One final note about wheels: many are attached to the bike by a skewer or quick-release mechanism that clamps the wheel to the bike. A simple flick of a lever allows you to remove the wheel in order to pack your bike in the trunk of your car. It also means that you don't have to carry special tools with you in order to change a flat tire on a trip. It really is quite convenient. But if you leave your bike locked up outside, it is also convenient for someone to remove your wheel and walk off with it. So you will need to consider a good lock that will secure the wheels as well as the frame.

Brakes

Essentially, all 10-speeds have a caliper brake on each wheel. The brakes are operated by levers on the handlebars and are connected to the brakes by cables. The details of the brake mechanism vary, but the general operation is the same. When you squeeze the lever, the brake mechanism closes and squeezes the rim of the wheel, slowing down the bike. When you release the brake lever, a spring opens the brake mechanism so that it stops gripping the rim. It is a good, simple, light system and there's not too much to know about it.

Shimano's recent innovations have added a spring in the brake lever. This reduces the tension and resistance in the system and results in a very smooth, easy brake action.

None of the caliper brakes work as well as you would like in the rain. Wet rims are slippery and the brake pads won't stop them as effectively as they will in dry conditions. In the rain, you will frequently notice a hesitation after you apply the brakes as the pads wipe the rim dry and start to get a better grip.

Typically, brakes are adjusted so close to the rim that the pads might bind on the tire as you remove the wheel. Most brakes also have a quick-release mechanism allowing you to flick a lever to open the brakes in order to remove the wheel more easily.

Brake levers can be obtained in different sizes. If your hands are small, be on the lookout for a bike with short-reach levers or ask if they can be installed on your new bike if the original levers are too big for you to operate comfortably.

Saddles

The humble saddle is one of the most critical pieces of equipment on your bike. If you and your saddle do not get along, you will not have fun riding. There are many different types of saddles, made of leather or plastic and other synthetic materials, on the market. Some have various kinds of padding added. Regardless of what type you select, make sure you break it in and give yourself a chance to adjust to it before you decide to change.

Some riders prefer the traditional leather saddle because over time it will conform to your shape. But this especially requires a long breaking-in period, sometimes of a season or more.

Synthetic saddles are more popular now because they are lighter. They won't conform as much as leather, but they come in a variety of sizes and shapes. Some of them are wide, specifically to conform to a woman's wider pelvis.

Some saddles have built-in high-tech foam padding. This might seem like an area where more is always better, but it's not true. As the saddle gets "squishy," you'll lose your feeling of control. And if the saddle is bulky, it starts to cause other problems.

Nowhere is the matter of individual preference more apparent than in saddles. I ride a Concor America, one of the narrowest of racing saddles. Some of my friends wouldn't consider it. I get sore on their saddles, they get sore on mine. Once you're used to something, any change is likely to cause problems.

The saddle is attached to the bike by a seatpost. The seatpost might seem like a pretty simple piece of equipment, but it makes adjusting your saddle possible: up and down, forward and backward, and tilt. The best ones can cost you over $40!

Handlebars and Stems

Handlebars are used to control and steer the bike, and they support the weight of your upper body via your arms and hands. Standard drop bars like those in the picture offer several options for where to put your hands and thus allow you to vary your position while riding. The bare metal of the bars is almost always wrapped with something, typically some sort of tape. Sometimes they are padded, or foam is wrapped under the tape to help absorb road shock.

Straight bars are common on mountain bikes, where they offer more leverage for control while raging through the mud and rocks in creek beds and other fun stuff like that. They are sometimes installed on road bikes for people who are uncomfortable with drop bars. (Sometimes you see a bike with drop bars turned upside down so the rider can sit up straight. This is pretty unstable and dangerous.)

Some newer shapes are now appearing that allow even more aggressive positions for cheating the wind. "Scott" bars allow you to get your back down parallel to the ground while supporting your weight on your forearms. They are becoming quite common on triathlon bikes, where aerodynamic position is much more important than bike-handling. Modolo has introduced an anatomical bar where the curved section of a normal drop is replaced by a straight section that makes for a more comfortable grip when on that part of the bar.

The stem connects the handlebars to the steering tube and forks. It comes in various lengths and angles. You can adjust your position on the bike, especially reach, by using different length stems.

FIT AND POSITION ON YOUR BIKE

Keep this in mind: you can spend a lot of money and get the best possible bike with a custom frame and the finest components but if it doesn't fit you, you are likely to be miserable. To get the proper fit, you must first select a bike frame that is the right size and then make fine adjustments with the saddle and handlebars.

Many people in bike shops can pretty much tell by looking at you what size bike you need. The trouble is, you can't always tell by looking at the person in the bike shop whether they know anything beyond that they want to sell you a bike. This section goes over basic information about choosing the right equipment and then adjusting it correctly.

A device called a Fit Kit is available at many stores. Using it allows a salesperson to take specific measurements of saddle height, reach, and other critical factors. It is fun to check out your measurements if one is available. If you are getting a frame built, having your measurements will be even more useful, as they will be a guide to tube lengths and other things you may want to specify.

It never hurts to test-ride lots of bikes as long as they fit you. Riding a friend's bike may be an unpleasant experience if it's too large or small for you.

FIGURE 1*

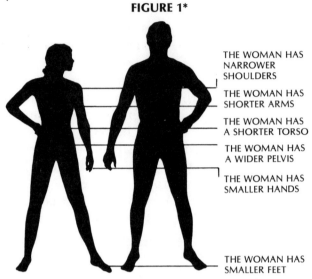

THE WOMAN HAS NARROWER SHOULDERS

THE WOMAN HAS SHORTER ARMS

THE WOMAN HAS A SHORTER TORSO

THE WOMAN HAS A WIDER PELVIS

THE WOMAN HAS SMALLER HANDS

THE WOMAN HAS SMALLER FEET

Women and Men: Different Sizes and Different Shapes

There are large differences among individuals that must be accounted for when fitting a bicycle. Looking at some of the differences in the way men and women are built will help to illustrate some of the most critical differences. Figure 1 compares a generalized woman and man. The woman will probably have narrower shoulders, shorter arms, a shorter torso, a wider pelvis, and smaller hands and feet than a man who has the same leg length or inseam. So the woman needs a bike smaller in some ways, but the same size in others.

Different frame sizes make it possible to fit people who are different sizes. But simply scaling the bike larger or smaller will not accommodate people with different proportions. Different frame geometries, different choice of components, and different adjustment of components make it possible to correctly position people who may be the same size but have very different proportions.

As far as height, our average man and woman could use the same size bike. But the woman's shorter torso requires a shorter reach,

* Figures 1-4 are from *The Fit Guide*, reprinted with permission from Terry Precision Bicycles for Women, Inc., Rochester, New York.

FIGURE 2

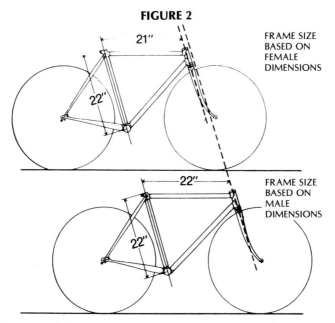

Two frames with the same seat-tube length, different top-tube length.

FIGURE 3

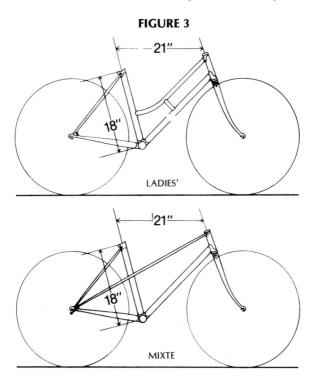

FIGURE 4

which can be accommodated by shortening the stem or shortening the top tube. Figure 2 shows two frames with the same height, but one has a shorter top tube, thus accommodating the woman's shorter torso.

If you need a bicycle that is smaller than a 19-inch frame, traditionally you would have had to resort to a ladies' bike or a mixte frame, developed mainly to allow riding a bike while wearing a dress. These are pictured in Figure 3. The problem with these designs is that they are not as stiff, strong, or reliable as the diamond frame. New frame designs have been developed that now allow diamond frames to be

The Terry Precision, one of the many frames built especially for women by Terry Precision Bicycles, provides a wider seat, shorter top tube, narrower handlebar spread, smaller toe clips and brake levers closer to the handlebars, all to accommodate a woman's smaller body.

constructed smaller than 19 inches. Figure 4 shows a radical design, the Terry 185SS, which features a small front wheel.

Georgena Terry, whose company makes "precision bicycles for women," has blazed a path in producing designs that accommodate women's proportions. Other manufacturers, mindful of the large number of bicycles purchased by women, are starting to follow her lead. In many cases, these smaller bikes also have smaller components: short-reach brake levers, shorter stems and crank arms, narrower handlebars, and smaller toe clips. Most also have a saddle that is adapted to a wider pelvis. In addition to Terry, other manufacturers producing small diamond frames include Bridgestone, Cannondale, Centurion, Fisher Mountain Bikes, Fuji, Lotus, Miyata, Nishiki, Palo Alto Bicycles, Peugeot, Raleigh, Shogun, Specialized, Sterling Cycle, Univega, and Vitus.

The following chart can be helpful in determining what size bicycle you need:

HEIGHT	SEAT TUBE LENGTH*	STRADDLE HEIGHT*	TOP TUBE LENGTH*
Shorter than 4'11"	16	26.1	18.9
4'11" to 5'1"	17	27.3	19
5'1" to 5'3"	18.5	28.7	19.3
5'3" to 5'4"	20	30.3	19.5–21
5'4" to 5'7"	21.5	31.8	21
Taller than 5'7"	23	33.2	21.5

* These measurements are all given in inches. Many bicycles are measured in centimeters.

Once you have selected the right size bike with the right components, you'll still need to adjust a few things.

Adjusting Saddle Height

To set up your seat height correctly, sit on the bike seat with both feet on the pedals. (You will need to have someone hold the bike up for you.) Position your pedals at 6 o'clock and 12 o'clock (straight up and down). With your foot on the bottom pedal parallel to the ground, your knee should just barely be flexed. You should not have to reach with your toe to get to the pedal. If you lock your knee, your toe should point up slightly. You adjust the seat height by loosening a binder bolt or nut that you should find near the top of the seat tube. Then you can slide the seatpost up and down where it fits inside the seat tube to achieve the right height.

Caution! Make sure that there is still enough seatpost inside the seat tube so that it is well supported. If in doubt, pull the seatpost all the way out—many seat posts have limit lines marked on them. Make sure that at least 2¼ inches remain in the frame.

Once you find the right height, lock the binder bolt down and go for a test ride. If your hips rock back and forth when you pedal, your seat is still too high. (See the section on knees for some fine-tuning advice.)

Adjusting Saddle Forward and Backward

Your saddle can be adjusted forward and backward as well as up and down. There is a general rule for this too. Get a plumb line (a piece of string with a washer or some other weight tied at one end will do).

Photo courtesy of David Dolsen Photography

Canadian National Champion Sara Neil shows how she adjusts the tilt of her saddle by using her tire pump as a level.

Ask your helper to hold the bike again and then get on the bike. Put your feet on the pedals and move the pedals to the 3 o'clock and 9 o'clock positions so that the cranks are parallel to the ground. Now use your plumb line to drop a straight line down the side of the forward leg through the middle of the kneecap. Ideally, the plumb line should hit the middle of the pedal axle. If it is behind the axle, move your saddle forward. If it is in front of the axle, move the saddle backward.

Adjusting Saddle Tilt

Your saddle should be approximately level. Different seatposts have different mechanisms for tilting the saddle. If you can't figure it out, ask a friend or someone at the bike shop. Once it's fairly level, try it out and make adjustments as necessary.

Adjusting the Reach

Get your trusty assistant to hold the bike one more time while you get on it. Sit on the seat, feet on the pedals, and put your hands down on the drops. Look down at the front wheel. For a racing position, you should not be able to see the axle, which should be hidden beneath the handlebars. (From your perspective, they will be in a direct line with each other.) If you see the axle in front of the bars, you need a longer stem; if it is behind the bars, you need a shorter stem. You may be able to achieve the same effect by moving the saddle forward or backward, as long as you don't have to move it so far that you mess up your relationship to the pedals.

Many casual or touring riders prefer a somewhat shorter reach, which is achieved with a shorter stem. They like to see that axle a little in front of the bars.

Handlebar Height

The handlebars can be raised or lowered by loosening a nut or a bolt and then sliding the stem up or down in the head tube. Racers set their bars below the level of their saddle by anywhere from 3 cm to 6 cm or even more. Most tourists also position their bars below the level of their saddle.

COMFORT IS THE KEY
OR SOME STANDARD DISCOMFORTS
AND WHAT TO DO ABOUT THEM

The Spenco 500 , a 500-mile bike race, has been held several times in Texas. Ironically, the halfway turnaround point has been in the city of Comfort, which most of the racers probably aren't in by then. But whether you're riding a 500-mile race or riding five miles for pleasure, you want to be as comfortable as possible.

Once you have made the basic adjustments to your bike, you should do some riding. Give yourself a chance to get accustomed to your position and the equipment. But if discomfort persists, your body may be telling you that your position or equipment or technique need further adjustment. The three big problem areas are the points of contact with the bike: rear end, feet, and hands. But your knees, neck, arms, and back may be telling you something, too.

Here are some general hints before you start making adjustments. Only change one thing at a time and give it a fair trial before you make another adjustment. Before you move something, mark or measure its original position for reference. That will save you trouble if you want to put it back where it was or if you get curious about how far you moved it.

Feet

Of course, you can have all the usual shoe problems while riding if the shoes don't fit, but only problems particular to cycling are discussed here. Two typical problems with the feet are arch pain and "hot foot." Arch problems generally stem from wearing tennis shoes instead of cycling shoes (see shoes). Proper cycling shoes, whether cleated or uncleated, have stiff soles to support your arch as you pedal. If you have arch problems even with cycling shoes, an orthotic insole may help.

"Hot foot" may be caused by the heat, but it can also be caused by shoes that are too tight or by structural problems with your foot that make it difficult to push against the pedal through a hard-soled cycling shoe. For some, the solution is a comfortable touring shoe. If you want to stick with cleated shoes, an insole can be used without too much compromise in efficiency, but you may have to get shoes a half-size larger. If you ride very long distances, "hot foot" can be caused by nerve problems in the foot. You need to pay attention and not allow this to become chronic: either cut your mileage or solve your shoe problem.

A final problem is swelling. You may need to consider shoes a size larger than normal if you find that your feet swell when you ride.

Buttocks

No one is exempt from saddle discomfort. It varies from actual saddle sores to that wonderful general soreness and aching feeling where you think your bones are bruised (they may be). Obviously, the more you ride, the more your muscles will adapt and firm up and your skin will get used to the activity. Of course, the more you ride, the more stress you experience and the more opportunities you have for problems, so there are precautions that you should always take.

Always wash your shorts after each use to help avoid sores and other nasty complications like yeast infections. And always get out of your riding clothes and shower as soon as convenient after you ride. If you have persistent problems with sores, try smearing antibiotic salves, such as Neosporin, around the general area of the problem. Some people work Noxzema into their chamois before they ride.

General discomfort is harder to deal with. You should definitely wear riding shorts (see the section on shorts). You can try different styles of shorts with more or less padding and you can try different styles and shapes of saddles.

Change your position frequently as you ride. Riding on the drops puts more pressure on your genitals. Give yourself a break and ride with your hands on top of the bars more. Stand up occasionally. Carry your weight more on your feet and hands. Change the angle of your saddle. Tilt the nose up a bit more. This may not seem logical, but it has the effect of making you sit up straighter and carry more of your weight on the bones of your pelvis. It doesn't work for everybody, so you can also try tilting it down slightly. Either way, the tilt should never be very large, only a few degrees.

Many times at rest stops on century rides, I have been approached by women whose expressions tell me what they are going to say. The look is a cross between wide-eyed amazement and terror. Sure enough, they are on their first serious ride and they have just gone to the bathroom for the first time. And it burned like crazy. This happens to a lot of women. It tends to be much less frequent as you become more accustomed to riding, but it still happens to me occasionally. It is aggravated by riding a lot on the drops. Again, Neosporin or Noxzema on the chamois may help.

If you can't find a combination of saddle, shorts, and technique to solve your soreness problems, high-quality saddle pads are available. These will at least provide you some variety and may provide you

Photo courtesy of Dave Dolsen Photography

When selecting a saddle pad for your bicycle, choose one that has a cushioning material with "memory." A pad with memory returns to its previous state after you've sat on it, while relieving pressure and absorbing shock.

enough comfortable riding time so that eventually you won't need them anymore. Steer clear of the sheepskins, which may seem comfortable at first but quickly lose their shock-absorbing effect. High-quality pads, such as those made by Spenco, distribute the shock evenly, have a foam that does not compress over time, and are not too bulky.

Hands

You can get blisters on your hands from riding. Cycling gloves plus a little riding experience usually solve this problem for most people. Varying the way you grip the bars can help too, just remember to move your hands around occasionally as you ride.

General soreness is harder to deal with. Again, padded gloves, padding your handlebars, and changing your position as you ride are the first remedies. But there are other things you can do. Tilting your saddle up or down changes the way you sit on the bike and can change the amount of pressure on your hands. The height of the handlebars and the reach also affect pressure on your hands. Try minor adjustments to your saddle tilt and see if this helps.

Numb hands are not uncommon and result from pressure on the nerves in the palm of your hand. The numbness usually goes away after you have been off the bike for a while and it can be treated by the same techniques as general soreness. However, don't tolerate it as a chronic condition: it can result in permanent nerve damage. Some riders have had to have surgery to correct nerve problems and if the damage is severe enough, it can be a career-ending injury. I damaged the nerves in my hands in the 1985 RAAM and they did not recover for four months. A neurologist warned me not to do that again.

Knees

The angle at which your foot rests on the pedal can cause knee problems. If the foot is turned in or out too much, it may cause the knee to follow through its circular motion at an odd angle and put stress on the tendons on either side of the patella, or kneecap. Most cleated shoes have adjustable cleats. (One of the things that the Fit Kit specifies is cleat positioning.) Or you can just try different angles until you find a comfortable position.

Knee problems related to incorrect seat positioning can easily be corrected. As a general rule, if there is pain behind the knee, then the seat is probably too high. If the pain is on the top or side of the knee, then the seat is probably too low. Move your saddle a bit and try it there. Never move it more than about a quarter inch and give it a fair trial (several rides of whatever distance you normally ride) before changing it again.

Neck

The reach of your bicycle (determined by your top tube length, saddle position, and stem length) affects the way you lean forward and can cause neck problems if not properly adjusted as previously described.

Beyond that, you can do exercises as you ride to keep your neck muscles loosened. When stopped at traffic lights, let your head drop onto your chest, then rotate it around in circles; you will feel tension disappear. Then rotate it in the other direction. You can trade neck and shoulder rubs with fellow cyclists and you can even do self-massages.

For persistent problems, you should consult a doctor or chiropractor.

Arms

The main problem for arms is fatigue. Fatigue in the arms also radiates into the shoulders and upper back. The cause of this problem is usually twofold: incorrect positioning on the bike and lack of upper body strength.

If the reach on your bike is too long, your arms are too stretched out and have to work too hard to support your torso. You may even tend to lock your elbows, which reduces the shock-absorbing properties of flexed elbows and can cause other problems. If the reach is too short, you tend to sit in a more upright position and to bunch up, leading to tension and tightness in the upper back, shoulders, and arms.

Determining the correct reach should help. Again, you can try variations which may better suit your individual needs.

Lack of upper-body strength is a common problem for women. Strength is obviously valuable for standing out of the saddle on a long climb, but it also helps with your general comfort on all type of rides. Weight lifting and sports such as swimming can help build this upper-body strength, which will increase your enjoyment of cycling. (See Chapter 4 for some weight-lifting exercises.)

Back

Bad position, especially bad reach, can cause tension that manifests itself as pain in the upper back. Much of the advice about arms and shoulders in the earlier sections applies here as well. Lower back problems can also be caused by cycling. Posture can be the culprit: sit with your back fairly straight, not unduly bent. Stretching exercises during your ride can help, along with a more extensive off-bike stretching program.

HELMETS

I strongly recommend using a helmet for all forms of cycling. More than 1,000 cycling deaths are caused each year by collisions with automobiles and in 80 percent of these, death is due to head trauma. Most of these people would still be alive if they had been wearing a proper helmet.

There is an old joke to the effect that it isn't the fall that kills you, it

There's no excuse for not wearing a helmet when riding. New designs have resulted in lightweight, comfortable, and protective choices. ANSI-approved helmets, like the hard-shell Bell or Vetta or the shell-less Giro, are required for all USCF races and organized century rides.

is the sudden stop at the bottom. A proper helmet cushions the impact of a collision with a car or the pavement and spreads that sudden stop out over precious fractions of a second, allowing you to survive with little or no trauma to your brain. Why do I keep saying "proper helmet"?

The Snell Foundation (named after Snell, a fellow who died of head injuries) notes that "the safety of many of today's bicycle helmets is a dangerous illusion. In a crash, the rider can suffer similar injury or death as if no helmet were worn at all." Both the Snell Foundation and ANSI (the American National Standards Institute) have established test procedures for helmets. When selecting a helmet, look for ANSI or Snell approval stickers. The United States Cycling Federation periodically publishes a list of helmets which have passed one of these tests. The most recent list has over 30 models by makers including ACI, Bailen, Bell, Brancale, Giro, Kiwi, Lazer, Monarch, Pro-Tec, and Vetta, so you certainly have a wide choice. But look for the stickers. Some manufacturers have models that pass and other models that don't pass.

A point to remember about helmets is that you shouldn't use them after they've helped you through a serious crash. The padding in helmets is designed to absorb energy by collapsing. It's not like rubber, it doesn't rebound (and bounce your head around even more)—it just stays crushed. So it gets used up in crashes.

In addition to being safe, an aerodynamic helmet, such as those seen in international competition since 1984, can mean enormous savings in time and energy for racers. As Dr. Chet Kyle, technical advisor for the US Olympic Cycling Team, noted in a paper presented at the World Cycling Congress in 1986: "In a 25-mile time trial, use of an aero helmet would mean about a 30-second improvement in time. Almost all winning time trialists in international competition use aerodynamic helmets."

There are still some cyclists who argue that helmets are too hot or too heavy. But heat lamp tests haven't confirmed any increase in internal temperature due to use of a helmet. And there has been a huge proliferation of lightweight helmets (some weighing as little as seven ounces) that are also aerodynamic, well ventilated, and cool. There is absolutely no excuse for riding without a proper helmet!

CLOTHING

Some people have a hard time accepting bicycle clothing and related accessories. They tend to shy away from the close-fitting black shorts and can't get past those funny cleated shoes. When I first started riding, I thought cycling clothes and shoes were just for racers. I planned to ride seriously, but since I wasn't racing, I didn't think I needed them. I didn't know that cycling clothes had a particular function beyond the look.

After a few days of wearing sweatpants and bulky running shoes, I knew there had to be a better way. Friends suggested shorts and cleated shoes, explaining the purpose of the clothing. I listened to them and made another trip back to the bike shop for Lycra shorts and cleated shoes. I have to admit, I was a bit self-conscious putting on those skintight black shorts. The saleswoman told me they should fit like a comfortable leotard: close fitting, but not restrictive or too tight. I had worn leotards in dance classes for years, but not out on the street. My

Photo by Dana Davis

Real women cyclists model a variety of warm-weather cycling apparel. Left to right: Amy Smolens is wearing mountain bike clothes: mountain bike shoes, touring shorts, a fanny pouch for snacks and extra items, and a cotton sweatshirt. Sarah Claus models the classic lycra skin suit worn in criteriums and on the track for short time trials. Chandra Tobey is wearing lycra bib-tights, a cotton T-shirt, and touring shoes. Ruth Tobey is wearing the classic lycra jersey and touring shorts with a hard-shell helmet.

apprehensions were soon put to rest. I was sold on the first ride! Those Lycra shorts were really comfortable and fun to wear. The stiff shank of the cleated shoes was much more efficient and made it easier to apply power to the pedal. Now, after years of riding in cycling clothes, even a short trip across town in jeans seems awkward.

Whether you're a recreational rider or a racer, cycling clothes will make riding more comfortable and fun.

In the last few years, cycling clothes have become more than acceptable—they are now a fashion statement. The triathlon has given cycling a whole new range of colors and fabrics. Triathletes, not caught up in the chains of tradition (they've only been around for slightly more than a decade), have come up with some of the most creative designs seen on cyclists. In addition to the fashion aspects, many triathlon cycling shorts and jerseys have incorporated mesh side panels that are excellent for warm-weather cycling and also look good. It's amazing to find ads for the "bicycle-clothing look" in the newspaper or fashion magazines. I guess this is what happens when sports like cycling and triathlon really take off.

Fit

Most of the major manufacturers make a women's line of clothing. They differ from men's in shape and fit to take into account a woman's curves. The color selection and style are sometimes different too. But you don't have to buy just women's clothes. Many women fit quite well into the regular unisex clothing. Size and fit are different with each manufacturer, so try on a lot of different styles and lines until you find what you like.

Fashion aside, the type of clothing you wear can have as much effect on speed, efficiency, and comfort as any other variable to consider in the sport. Chet Kyle reports that in wind-tunnel tests, "sloppy or loose-fitting clothing can raise the total wind drag by 10 percent or more; hence, more probably can be gained in choosing the proper clothing than by any other legal means in racing."

Fabrics

Until the 1970s traditional cycling togs were almost always made of cotton or wool. And if it was cold or wet outside, you definitely used wool. Wool provides warmth, maintains body heat even when wet, breathes, and can absorb up to 16 percent of its own weight without losing its insulating ability. Wool is "fuzzy" and the miniscule air pockets within the material hold heat. Wool is surprisingly comfortable even when it is warm. It wicks perspiration away from your

Patty Brink at Berkeley's Velo-Sport helps customers choose from a wide variety of styles and fabrics. Many bike shops are hiring women to assist the growing number of female customers.

body, allowing it to evaporate from the surface of your clothes, providing cooling in much the same way that evaporation does from the surface of your skin.

But wool does have its disadvantages. Colors run. Jerseys and shorts shrink if put in the dryer. They take a long time to dry. And they are usually very expensive. They also are not as formfitting and aerodynamic as modern synthetics.

Cotton was long the choice for warm-weather cycling because it conducts heat better than many other fibers and provides ventilation in the summer months. Cotton, on the other hand, is not so efficient for winter riding. Wet cotton transfers heat up to 200 times faster than dry cotton.

There are now many synthetics on the market that compete with both wool and cotton, if one has no objection to departing from nature's own. Polypropylene, for example, is an excellent insulator. It also breathes efficiently and is lighter than wool, even when wet. Polypropylene, or polypro as it is often called, is hydrophobic, which literally translated means "afraid of water." Water molecules do not mix well with the giant molecules of which polypro and other man-made fabrics are constructed. Polypro also dries very quickly, which is nice when it rains on and off or when the temperature fluctuates many times throughout a long ride.

Lycra is the new darling of the aerodynamically conscious rider. It is stretchy and smooth and really does make it easier to carve through the air. Many riders also like the form-fitting look.

Several combination fabrics are appearing. A combination nylon and polyester pile is similar to polypropylene in its ability to resist water. It dries quickly, is an excellent insulator, and is easy to wash and dry. Swisstex is another material that uses two layers to achieve dryness and warmth. It has a softer feel than Lycra and is generally found in clothing that is a little less form-fitting.

One of the finest wet-weather cycling fabrics is Gore-Tex. The material will shrug off water up to 110 pounds of pressure. No rainstorm will ever exceed that figure. But what makes Gore-Tex so special is that it is not only waterproof, but it also breathes. The pores of the fabric are larger than individual molecules of perspiration, yet smaller than the water droplets from rain. This allows some heat and moisture to escape (preventing overheating and sauna-like conditions inside your rain jacket) while keeping water out.

Color of clothing can also make a difference in temperature control. The rule of thumb is simple: light colors in the summer, dark colors in the winter. Research has shown that black material can absorb as much as 95 percent of the heat from the sun, while white material may absorb only 30 percent.

Shorts

If you are going to ride more than 10 or 15 miles, you will really enjoy wearing a good pair of riding shorts. The main characteristic of riding shorts is that they have a piece of material, usually called a "chamois" (pronounced "shammy"), lining the inside of the crotch.

The chamois provides additional padding, and it prevents chafing because it has no seams or stitching in critical places. It also helps keep your bottom dry and comfortable. In addition to the chamois, riding shorts are cut so that the legs do not creep up and the shorts don't bunch up in awkward ways and cause you grief. Riding shorts are worn without underpants, which really just get in the way and defeat the purpose of the shorts.

The name chamois is a holdover from a time, not too long ago, when virtually all chamois were actually made out of the hide of the chamois sheep, a particularly soft sort of leather. Nowadays you'll find a choice of real chamois, other sorts of leather, or various artificial fabrics. What you use is a matter of personal preference. I have used both types in training and in three RAAMs. I have found leather not as comfortable or dry as the synthetic types, but others disagree. Leather tends to offer more padding.

For those who have problems with yeast infections, the synthetics tend to stay drier and breathe better than leather. In any case, you need to wash your shorts between each use, and if you're on a trip, the synthetics are more convenient and quick-drying.

If you do a lot of riding, you'll probably wind up buying several pair of shorts. Try different types and see which you like better.

Bib shorts are a variation to consider. They have built-in suspenders, which eliminate elastic waistbands or drawstrings that are sometimes uncomfortable around your stomach.

There are times when Lycra shorts may not be appropriate. "Touring shorts" are made to look like hiking pants. The idea is that you can ride and then just get off the bike and go into a restaurant for lunch appropriately dressed. They are not as comfortable as riding shorts, but sometimes they are a good compromise.

Jerseys

Bicycle jerseys are essentially shirts specialized for bike riding. (The name "jersey" is yet another historical holdover from the time when most jerseys were made of wool jersey material.) They generally tend to be form-fitting pullovers with a short zipper at the neck and pockets on the back.

Pockets on the back? Yes! People who go on long rides frequently carry a lot of stuff with them, especially food. A couple oranges, some bananas, and a pound of fig bars can be carried in those back pockets since the weight tends to rest comfortably on your back when you ride in your normal position.

Beyond that, there are a wide variety of jerseys. Racers will often wear tight Lycra jerseys with no pockets for their aerodynamic properties. Skin suits combine jersey and shorts into one garment. More casual jerseys of Swisstex offer a variety of options for fit. And you can still get warm, heavy, long-sleeved wool jerseys for winter rides.

Shoes

Proper cycling shoes can save 10 to 20 percent of your energy and let you be more comfortable at the same time. They have a stiff arch that prevents your foot from flexing as you pedal. That helps prevent fatigue in your arch and is more efficient. They also tend to have a thin sole, which transmits power to the pedal more efficiently. (This is not an unmixed blessing, as some people develop sore feet from the pressure.)

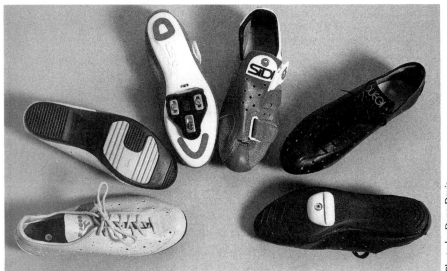

Photo by Dana Davis

Shoes for touring and racing (left to right): the touring shoe, like the Diadora, has a stiff shank and no cleat. Avocet and Cannondale also make good touring shoes. The "Look" compatible shoe by Sidi is predrilled to accommodate the ski-binding type cleat, thus eliminating the need for toe clips. At right, a traditional cleat to fit a cage pedal and toe clip system.

Many cycling shoes have cleats or other devices on the sole that attach to the pedal for ultimate efficiency. (Some of these shoes are really part of a shoe/pedal system and will only work with the particular pedal they are designed for. The section on pedals discusses such systems.) Cleats are awkward for walking. "Touring shoes" provide a compromise. They are more like a lightweight walking shoe, but have a stiffer, thinner sole. They are reasonably comfortable for walking and work pretty well on the bike. Pete Penseyres won two Races Across AMerica using Avocet touring shoes.

Cycling shoes tend to be very lightweight. Many are now made of synthetic fibers although leather is still common. The fit of the shoes is important. They should be snug without being uncomfortably tight. Sometimes a cyclist will have her shoe firmly attached to the pedal but will pull her foot out of the shoe. Leather shoes tend to stretch, so they have to be purchased a little on the tight side, which is a tricky proposition.

Gloves

Cycling gloves save wear and tear on your hands, which can suffer from constant contact with the handlebars. They are usually made of light leather or other comfortable material and help avoid blisters.

A variety of cycling gloves are available on the market (left to right): Standard full-leather glove with cotton mesh by Cannondale; Team LeMond and Serac lightly padded racing glove with Lycra or terry cloth back; and for those long rides on rough roads, the more fully padded Spenco glove.

Most of them have padding in the palms to absorb shock. The amount of padding varies from none to quite thick, so you have a choice.

Warm-weather gloves have a mesh back and no fingers for comfort in the heat. There are cold-weather gloves that provide more traditional long fingers for warmth.

Foul-Weather Gear

There is all sorts of gear to help you ride when you might prefer to stay indoors, from special booties to keep your feet warm to wool caps. And, of course, there is rain gear. All foul-weather bike gear is adapted to cope with special problems of cycling. When you ride your bike, you generate heat and you perspire, even when it is cold or wet outside. If you wear a rubber rain jacket, you will quickly get as wet from sweat as you might have gotten from the rain if you hadn't worn the jacket in the first place. And, if you just wear some monster down jacket, your torso may be too warm while other parts of your body are freezing.

So you'll find a lot of specialized foul-weather gear for bicyclists: wool tights with nylon panels on the fronts of the legs to keep the wind from blowing through, and jackets with windproof fronts and more normal knit materials on the backs. And rain gear frequently has vents and other special constructions to let water out without letting water in. Gore-Tex and other modern fabrics help to perform this magic.

Even if you don't ride in extreme weather, you will probably want a pair of tights. You really shouldn't ride bare-legged when the temperature is below 65 degrees.

Probably the single most important piece of foul-weather gear I own is a lightweight windshell. When the weather is at all iffy, I stuff it and some light tights in my pockets when I set out. That jacket goes a long way toward making me comfortable if the temperature drops or if it rains.

Fenders are more gear you might consider if you intend to ride much in the rain.

Photo by Dana Davis

Attire for cold-weather cycling. Left to right: Ruth Tobey models a full Gore-Tex rainsuit, long-fingered gloves, training shoes, and a hard-shell helmet. Underneath, she wears a light layer of clothing. Chandra Tobey protects her legs with Lycra tights and wears a light wind jacket over a Lycra/polyester jersey. Sarah Claus is prepared for cold-weather training with a wool turtleneck and a polypropylene jacket with windbreak material in the front. Amy Smolens is ready for cool spring rides with a long-sleeved Lycra and polyester jersey, Lycra tights, and booties.

MISCELLANEOUS EQUIPMENT
Essentials:
Spares, Pumps, Water Bottles

There are a few things that almost every cyclist does carry or should carry. You should make it a practice to carry sufficient equipment to fix a flat tire. If you ride on sew-ups, you'll need two spare tires and a pump. For clinchers, a spare tube or patch kit, some tire irons, and a pump. You will also want to carry one or more water bottles. Pumps and water bottles are usually mounted on the bike frame on special fittings. Spare-tire stuff is typically carried under the saddle, either in a small bag or just strapped to the frame of the saddle with an old toe strap.

Computers and Heart Monitors

A reliable bike computer is a lot of fun. It will tell you how long that ride really was, and you can keep track of how fast you go and how fast you pedal (your cadence). If you are training seriously, a bike computer is an essential tool to keep track of your training mileage and to monitor subtle changes in your performance.

There are a variety of computers with differences in the type of data they measure and what they display. Four things are commonly measured by computers: speed, distance, time, and cadence. Most computers now calculate other figures related to speed, such as

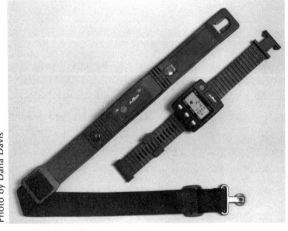

Photo by Dana Davis

The AMF Heartrate Monitor comfortably fastens around the chest and reads out on the watch unit. Using heart-rate monitors will enable you to train more accurately to your target heart rate.

average miles per hour and maximum speed. Typically, there is a trip distance that can be reset and a total distance that grows until the battery runs out. Cadence requires a second sensor and is not available on some models. Many computers display only one number at a time and you choose whether it displays time, distance, or another function. Others can display more than one thing at the same time.

Heart-rate monitors that allow you to keep track of how fast your heart is beating are now available. Some of them will record the readings for later analysis. Some people might find this amusing, but these are mostly an aid to serious training and are covered in Chapter 3.

Mirrors

Many riders simply glance behind them as necessary to keep track of what's back there. But you may want to consider using a rearview mirror. Two general sorts are available to cyclists. One mounts on the handlebars so that you glance down to see behind you. The other attaches to your helmet so that you glance up to see in the mirror.

Lights and Reflectors

If you ride at night, good lights are a must. You need to see and be seen. Lighting systems are discussed in Chapter 6, "Cycling for Transportation."

Carrying Stuff:
Bags, Racks, Panniers, Trailers . . .

There are all sorts of systems for carrying things on your bicycle. Small bags that attach under your saddle or on the handlebars are suitable for carrying some food and clothing on day trips or century rides. At the other extreme, you can equip a bike with racks and panniers that will carry 80 pounds of equipment for a self-supported multi-week tour. There are also trailers that are useful for making trips to the grocery store and special trailers for carrying children.

General advice on this is beyond our scope—find a store that sells bike accessories and check it out!

Riding in Your Living Room

If the weather or another factor is preventing you from getting out on your bike and you must have an exercise fix, there are several ways you can ride without leaving the comfort of your home.

Most people are familiar with stationary bikes, such as are commonly found in gyms. They usually have some mechanism for adjusting how hard it is to pedal so that you can vary the intensity of your workout.

There are also stands that will support your own bike while you pedal. Most of them require removing the front wheel and attaching the fork to the stand. The back wheel then rests on a roller that turns as you pedal. There are other types that don't require removing the front wheel. Many of these stands have a fan or blower that is driven as you pedal. This creates a work load and sometimes creates a breeze

Photo by Dana Davis

The Blackburn Trackstand windtrainer folds conveniently for travel. Windtrainers enable you to train on the bike when weather conditions are unfavorable. Try a workout routine that incorporates a warm-up, interval workout, and cool-down. Up-tempo music can help pass the time. For a rigorous workout, you'll probably want to use pedals with toe clips.

that cools you as you "ride." I have a small Blackburn stand that I take on business trips. If I can't get out for a ride during the day, I can ride in my hotel room at night!

Rollers are a real adventure. On rollers, you really ride your bike and you have to steer and balance, which is a bit of a trick. There are three drums, or rollers; the back two are about a foot apart and the back wheel rests between them. It tends to stay there as you pedal, unless you get too jerky or bouncy, in which case the bike will jump off the rollers, which is not good. The front wheel rests on top of the third roller, which is driven by one of the back rollers so that it also turns as you pedal. You have to see this to believe it. But riding rollers is one of the most effective ways to develop a smooth spinning technique. It's quite simple—you are either smooth or you fall! And once you get the hang of it, you can set the rollers up in front of your favorite TV show and watch while you get your exercise. Seriously.

Some rollers also have an attachment for generating a wind load. Kreitler is a long-time manufacturer of high-quality rollers and they offer a "killer headwind trainer." The front roller drives a fan that blows a breeze on you as you pedal. A little door adjusts the breeze, which adjusts the effort required to pedal.

A final note on staying sane until the good weather returns. A company recently introduced a system that links your indoor trainer to your personal computer. There is feedback from your bike to the computer so that you can race for the world championship in the privacy of your own home.

Bike Racks for Your Car

If you drive someplace with your bike very often, you should consider getting a bike rack for your car. Sure, you can put your bike in the trunk or the backseat. But you'll tend to take off some paint every other trip and you'll also accumulate those wonderful images of chainrings drawn in grease on your upholstery. There are simple racks that attach to the trunk lid of your car and will easily carry two bicycles. There are also more professional-quality racks that go on the roof and will hold five bikes and five extra sets of wheels for your bike racing team. They can be custom configured for extra wheels, tandems, kayaks, skis, and small sailboats. Yakima and Thule are two reliable manufacturers.

2
Safe and Self-Sufficient on the Road

"I've always relied on the kindness of strangers."
—Blanche Dubois, in *A Streetcar Named Desire*, by Tennessee Williams

Unless you are like Blanche, you will want to know a few things, like how to fix your own flat tires. Even Blanche might have liked a few clues about techniques for riding in traffic and climbing hills. And she definitely should have been familiar with the traffic laws.

SHARING THE ROAD WITH CARS
Traffic Laws and Rules of the Road

It's a cyclist's dream to ride on idyllic country roads, stopping only to marvel at the view or refill a water bottle. Unfortunately, you will almost always get to share those roads with cars, also known as "the heavy metal." For those of us who live in urban areas, riding in traffic is something we must do just to get out to the country roads. Dodging cars, dogs, pedestrians, and other obstacles can get your heart rate up faster than a good interval workout!

Laws and ordinances vary from place to place but, as a general rule, when you are riding your bicycle, you are subject to the same laws as cars. You should ride on the roadway in the same direction that the cars travel, definitely not against the oncoming traffic, the way you were taught to walk. You must stop at stoplights and stop signs, just like cars. You can be ticketed and fined for failure to obey any traffic law: in California and many other states, it is considered a moving violation, goes on your traffic record, and can drive up your auto insurance rates.

Techniques in Traffic

Although riding in traffic is challenging, and may even be intimidating at first, it is not an impossible situation to handle. You'll acquire the necessary bike-handling skills over time. It's also important to have the right attitude. You need to be confident and assertive, but not reckless and combative. A good way to learn the basic maneuvers is to ride with safe, experienced cyclists or to take one of the Effective Cycling classes taught by certified instructors from the League of American Wheelmen.

Following are some diagrams illustrating a few of the basic situations you will encounter on the road as well as some tips on defensive cycling.

Car doors are probably the most common cause of serious accidents in urban cycling. Much of your riding on city streets involves passing endless parked cars. A careless motorist opening the door on the driver's side without looking can take you out before you know what hit you. Ideally, you can ride far enough out in the street so that a door can't get you, but unfortunately this isn't always practical. When you are forced to ride close to parked cars, you must proceed slowly and carefully.

*PROPER POSITION ON THE ROAD**

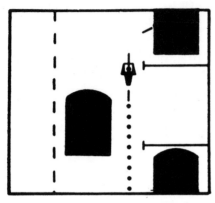

Ride in a Straight Line. Ride to the right of traffic, about a car door's width from parked cars. You will be more visible and avoid roadside hazards.

Maintain Your Position. When you are moving the same speed as motor vehicle traffic you should use enough of your lane so you can see the turn signal of the motorist ahead of you while avoiding the motorist's blind spot.

Ride in the Correct Lane. Change to a through lane if you are going straight and the right lane turns. Don't turn left from the right lane. Make lane changes the same way as an automobile. Begin your turn early, signal, watch for a clearing in traffic, and move over.

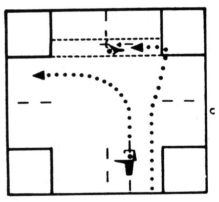

Choose the Best Way to Turn Left. There are two ways to turn left. 1. Like an auto: signal, move to just left of the center line, and turn left. 2. Like a pedestrian: ride straight to the far-side crosswalk and walk your bike across the street.

* Proper Position and Be Alert diagrams are reproduced with permission from the League of American Wheelmen, courtesy of U.B.A.

BE ALERT

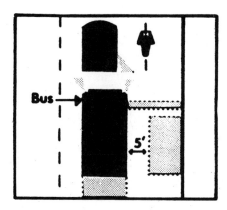

Avoid the Blind Spot. The shaded areas show the blind spots. If you are in a blind spot the driver cannot see you. Position yourself to avoid these areas.

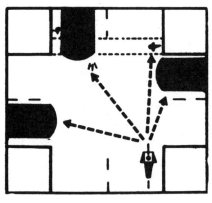

Scan the Road Ahead. Watch for left-turning vehicles, autos in intersections and driveways, motorists pulling out of parking spots, and pedestrians in crosswalks.

Scan the Road Behind. Learn to look over your shoulder without losing your balance or swerving. Some riders use rearview mirrors.

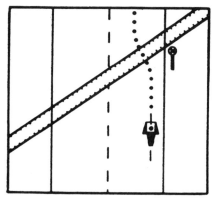

Cross Railroad Tracks at a Right Angle. Slow to a walking speed, raise out of the saddle slightly, and cross tracks at a right angle. Railroad tracks are especially dangerous in wet weather.

DEFENSIVE DRIVING

Defensive driving is especially important to bicyclists because of their vulnerability in an accident. The most common injury-producing accidents and how to avoid them are listed below. Remember: The most serious injuries are head injuries. A hard-shell helmet is the best protection for your head in case of an accident.

Potential Accident: A motorist turns left in front of an oncoming biker.
How to Avoid It: Watch for turn signals and vehicle slowing. Make eye contact with the driver. Prepare to swerve right or brake.

Potential Accident: A motorist turns right in front of a biker traveling in the same direction.
How to Avoid It: This often happens because the motorist misjudges the speed of the biker. Watch for rapid acceleration by the motorist and sudden slowing near the intersection. Avoid the motorist's blind spot. Prepare to swerve right or brake.

Potential Accident: A motorist, coming out of a driveway or side street, collides with a biker.
How to Avoid It: You'll be more readily seen and less likely to be hit if you are just to the right of the flow of traffic. Avoid riding too close to the curb or parked cars.

Potential Accident: A motorist collides with a biker not visible at night.
How to Avoid It: This accident is a leading cause of bicyclist fatalities. Use a bright light and red rear reflector at night. Leg lights and pedal reflectors are especially noticeable at night. Light-colored clothing or reflectorized material is also helpful.

Potential Accident: A motorist collides with a biker making an unexpected maneuver.
How to Avoid It: This occurs most frequently when the biker is making a left turn. Maintain proper road position, signal turns, and make eye contact with the motorist before changing lanes.

* Defensive Driving Tips are reproduced with permission from the League of American Wheelmen, courtesy of U.B.A.

SAFETY FOR WOMEN

Some women I know have ridden solo across the country and toured solo in foreign lands without problems. (But it does somewhat depend on what you think of as a problem. See the interview with Debra Harse in Chapter 5, "Recreation and Touring.") On the other hand, friends of mine have been seriously hassled on short local training rides. A lot depends on where you live, how well cyclists are accepted, and how well women are treated. Even if you set aside the possibility of being hassled, you can always have some sort of accident and if someone else is there, they can go for help or do whatever may be required. If you run off the road somehow while riding alone, it may take people a long time to find you even if they know where you were riding.

I do ride alone regularly and I like it. But I am more comfortable on long rides in the back country if I have company. If you do ride alone, it is best to let someone know where you are going and when you expect to return. That way, if you have a problem, they will at least know when to start looking for you and where to look.

BIKE MAINTENANCE

This book is not intended to be a complete self-help maintenance book. Many of the better bike shops offer classes in bike maintenance and repair. These classes are an excellent way to learn more about how your bike works and how to fix it when you have problems. And there are several good books on repair available. (see "Further Information" at the end of this chapter for titles.)

But there are a few things you should know. Your bike shouldn't squeak, rattle, or tick. If it does, fix it or get it fixed. You should also clean and inspect your bike periodically. Wash it with detergent and water, rinse it off, and lubricate the chain and derailleurs. Check the pressure in your tires. Look at the brake and derailleur cables to make sure they're not fraying. They should move smoothly and without grinding. Look at the brake pads and make sure they're not worn down. You should have your bike overhauled by a bike shop about once a year. They should repack the bearings in the bottom bracket, headset, and hubs, and lubricate and adjust other parts that you probably won't want to do unless you really get into it.

Your chain should be cleaned and lubed periodically, which can be a chore. A couple months after I first started riding, I ran into a local racer, Robert Wallace. He had a really nice orange Eisentraut bike, was friendly, and looked knowledgeable. I asked him how to clean the chain. He told me to remove the chain, melt some paraffin wax in a double-boiler, dip the chain in the wax, hang it up, and put the waxed chain back on the bike when it was dry. I had a helluva time, made a mess, and broke the chain tool in the process. Now I remove the chain, soak it in solvent, wipe and dry it out, put it back on the bike, and squirt some Tri-Flow on it. There are also systems such as Alsop that do a fairly decent job of cleaning the chain without removing it from the bike. (By the way, the paraffin process is used to get a clean chain that doesn't leave grease marks on everything it touches. Last time I checked, Rob doesn't do it anymore, either.)

Changing a Flat Tire

Sara Neil, Canadian National Time Trial Champion and 1988 Olympic hopeful, demonstrates how to change a flat tire. Sara's wheel has an aerodynamic cover so you can't see the spokes, but the procedure is the same.

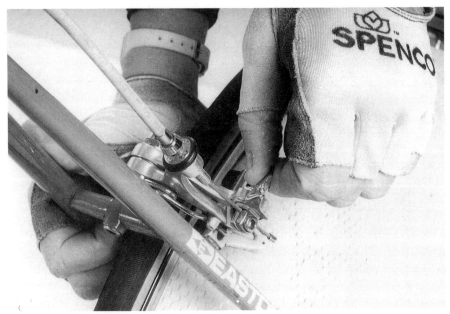

1. After you've shifted both gear shift levers to the forward position, putting the chain in the smallest cog, release the quick release lever on the rear brake.

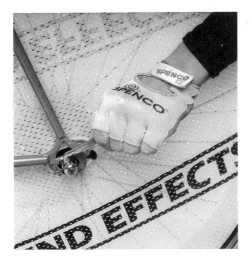

2. Release the quick-release lever on the rear wheel, and gently free the wheel from the drop outs.

 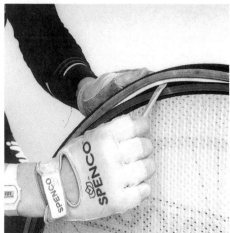

3. After you've removed the wheel from the bike, lay the bike on its side, with the large chainwheel side facing up, so you do not damage your derailleur. Remove one side of the tire from the rim by wedging a tire-iron between the bead of the tire and the lip of the rim.

4. Use a second tire-iron to release a larger portion of the tire from the rim. Continue along the tire with the second tire-iron, until an entire half is free.

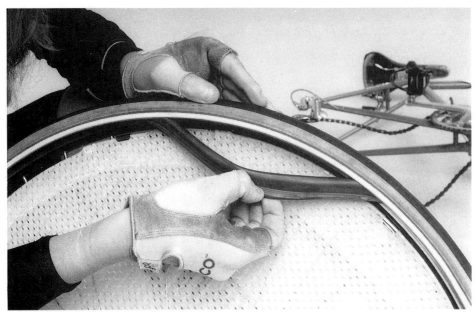

5. Next, pull the inner tube out from inside the tire. Gently pull the tire valve stem from the hole without tearing or damaging it. Depending on the severity of the puncture, repair the tube with a patch kit or replace it entirely if need be.

6. When replacing the tube in the tire, begin by putting the valve stem in the hole. Place the metal tire rim in front of you with the valve stem at the bottom. Position the tube back on the rim inside the tire, working around both sides of the wheel from the valve stem to the top of the rim. When replacing with a new tube, you may need to pump a small amount of air into the tube to give it shape.

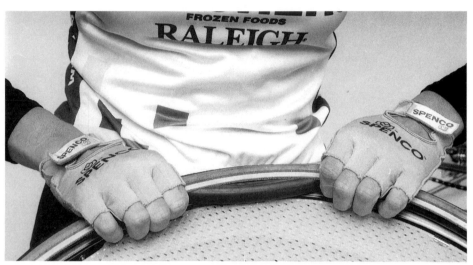

7. From the bottom, working upwards, place the tire onto the lip of the rim. You may have to use a tire-iron to help the tire onto the apex. Make sure the tube is not pinched between the tire and the rim.

All photos courtesy of Dave Dolsen Photography

Finally, when replacing the wheel onto the bike, you may need to pull the rear derailleur arm back as you guide the rear wheel into the drop-out position. Place the chain on the smallest cog for the least chain tension.

I remember when I got my first flat tire. I was out on a 25-mile loop in the Berkeley Hills with some friends. Peter Rich of Velo-Sport Cyclery was on the ride and offered to fix the flat. I had all the necessary equipment and even a photo illustration of how to fix the flat, but I hadn't actually done it before. After Peter got the tire off the rim and pulled out the punctured tube, he felt around the inside of the tire, and showed me a piece of glass that had cut clear through the cords. He then asked me for a dollar. I handed it over, thanking him for fixing the flat. He laughed, asked me to fold it in quarters, and then fitted it into the inside of the tire as a "boot" to cover the gash. (Dollar bills have lots of fiber, are quite durable, and make a handy protection for the tube.) "Besides," Peter said, "when you replace the tire, you'll probably have forgotten about the dollar and be surprised to have found a small down payment on the next tire." Since that time I've fixed many flat tires for folks out on rides. When the opportunity presents itself, I pass on the dollar-bill trick Peter taught me.

BASIC BIKE-HANDLING SKILLS

A major part of feeling comfortable on the bike is feeling confident about your basic bike-handling skills. When I first started riding, I used to fall down a lot for the usual reasons: road turtles, railroad tracks, going faster than I knew how to handle. I had a perpetual scab on one of my elbows. It was a joke between my riding partner Vance Vaughan and me—just as soon as it got better, I'd fall and nick it again. But I learned quickly and my skills have vastly improved over the years. Now I plow through gravel and speed through tight corners in criteriums with confidence. (Knock on wood. That is not to say that I won't fall again sometime.) Your skills will improve with time too. Here are a few hints to get you started.

Relax, Maintain a Comfortable Position

If you are having real problems with traffic or something, pull off the road and stop. Give yourself time to figure it out and gather your wits. Tension doesn't help anything. Breathe consciously and make yourself relax.

Even if you are just idling along on the flat, change your position frequently as you ride, perhaps every few minutes. There are three different places you can put your hands on standard drop handlebars: down on the drops, out on top of the brake hoods, or up on top a few inches away from the stem. If you are on the drops or the brake hoods, you can also stand up. (It's not a good idea to stand with your hands near the stem because you don't have the leverage to control the bike.) Moving your hands or standing up brings different muscles into play and generally helps keep you loose and relaxed.

You can also sit up and ride no-handed. It is very relaxing, but you have to know how to do it. It is dangerous under the best of circumstances and you must pay attention.

Your most stable position is down on the drops. Get down there whenever you foresee tricky handling coming up.

Road Hazards: Bumps, Railroad Tracks, Grates, Road Turtles

Don't just plant your butt on the saddle and sit there. Think of yourself as a spring—you can support some of the weight of your body on your legs and arms. This is especially important if you are riding over a rough surface or hitting bumps or railroad tracks. Consciously lift some of your weight off the saddle (but keep some contact with the saddle for stability and control). This saves you and your bicycle a lot of wear and tear. The bike can get over the bumps without lifting all your weight, and you don't get as much impact either. Your control is also better.

If you come to railroad tracks, line yourself up so you cross perpendicular to the tracks. This is especially important if they are wet. Wet tracks are very slippery and can simply wipe your wheels right out from under you. If traffic is bad or the situation is unclear, get off and walk. Bumpy tracks can destroy even the sturdiest rims.

Many storm drains are set up as grids, with narrow metal strips running parallel to the empty spaces in between. For your bike with its skinny tires, these are exactly the same as a big hole in the road and you must avoid them.

If it is wet, many otherwise innocuous objects can become hazards. Metal manhole covers are treacherous when wet, and painted places on the roadway are also suspect.

There are several species of road turtles, from the smaller Bott's

Dots used to mark lanes to sizeable pieces of cement used to enforce lanes. If you hit a bunch of them, or if it is wet or they are large, they can jostle you and threaten your control. Hitting a big one can definitely ruin your day. They are all over the roads and you just have to watch out for them.

You can actually jump over some small obstacles. If your feet are securely attached to the pedals, you stand up and use your arms and legs to lift the bike as it passes over the bump or whatever it was. People frequently do this when they are going fast downhill and want to avoid damaging a rim by hitting a ridge or something in the road. It does take practice to get it right. If your timing is off, you will come down right on what you were trying to miss, increasing the very impact you were trying to avoid.

Spinning and Cadence

Try to think of pedaling as moving your feet around in complete circles, not just stomp, stomp, stomping on each downstroke. Spin. Most experienced cyclists maintain a cadence (or spin rate) of 80 to 100 complete revolutions per minute under normal conditions.

Spinning slower and pushing harder fatigues your legs more than spinning faster and not pushing so hard. You have gears so that you needn't bog down and pedal too slow. You may sometimes choose to get into a big gear and torque, especially when you are climbing; but in general, think spin.

Climbing Hills

Funny thing—a lot of bike riders don't like going up hills! But with the right gears on your bike you needn't work any harder climbing a hill than you do riding on the flats. You will, of course, go slower. Somehow, many people wind up fighting the hill and exhausting themselves when they don't need to. You feel more pressure on a hill, because if you stop pedaling, you grind to a halt almost instantaneously, so it seems to require a constant effort that is not apparent on the flat. Of course, if you stop pedaling on the flat, you come to a stop too, but it takes longer and seems different.

One technique for climbing a hill is to treat it just as you would flat ground. Say you are spinning along the flat comfortably spinning

at 80 RPM and you encounter an increasing grade. Simply maintain
the same pressure on the pedals and start shifting down into smaller
gears to maintain your spin. Consciously avoid working harder than
you were working before you got to the hill. You will go slower, of
course, but if you have low enough gears, you can get up the hill
without working any harder than you did on the flat.

Most people tend to put out a bit more on hills, though. Getting up
hills fast is one of the things that serious racers have to do to be
competitive. And you will find otherwise friendly people kind of
looking around and picking it up a bit when they hit a hill even on
fun rides. Still, the choice is yours.

If you do want to climb faster, you basically have to work harder.
Many cyclists push big gears up hills and stand up as necessary to
torque the bigger gears, but sitting and spinning also works. Alternating sitting and standing allows you to maintain a high effort
longer because it changes the muscles you're using.

Climbing hills is where you really pay for any extra weight you are
carrying. The 1986 Tour de France winner, Greg LeMond, claims
that for every extra pound of weight, whether on his bike or his body,
he will lose about one minute in every 30 minutes of climbing.
Jeannie Longo, three-time world champion and winner of the 1987
Tour de France Féminin, has always been a good rider, but she used to
be a weak hill climber. Over the last few years, she has become leaner
and now she is a deadly hill climber, too.

A final note about hills—shift *before* you have to. If you find
yourself standing up and groaning with effort, and bogged down
with the pedals barely turning, you waited too long. You will have a
hard time reaching for the shift lever. And the mechanism will have a
hard time shifting—derailleurs shift more easily if you are spinning
and aren't exerting a lot of pressure on them.

Fast Descents, Fast Turns

Almost everyone would rather go downhill, or descend, than climb.
But you can get yourself into a whole lot more serious trouble going
downhill than you can going up. When descending, always ride at a
speed you can handle and at which you are comfortable. Know
yourself and your equipment. Some bikes will develop a wobble or

shimmy at high speed and that can ruin your control. Your bike shouldn't shimmy: if it does, have it checked. Shimmy is frequently caused by wheels that are out of true.

Slow down before you reach a turn. You shouldn't have to do a lot of speed correction in the turn, as braking increases the force making your tires skid on the pavement. If you lock up a wheel in a turn, you are guaranteed to slide, and if you are good enough to get out of that without falling, you don't need my advice.

On any turn, but especially when you are going fast, as on descents, it is best to have your hands down on the drops for maximum control. Don't steer your bike through the turn, *lean* it through the turn. Don't pedal through a fast turn unless you know you can do it. Your inside pedal may hit the pavement and throw you off your line. It is best to have the pedal on the outside of the turn down and to carry a significant amount of your weight on that outside foot where it is low to the ground and adds to your stability. As I said before, lift yourself off the saddle, but maintain contact with it for stability and control.

Be prepared to stop within the distance that you can see. Even if you are familiar with the road, unexpected obstacles may be just around that corner, such as gravel on the road or a car that is on your side of the road.

DON'T LEAVE HOME WITHOUT IT

Cycling is an equipment and gadget-oriented sport. Not everything found in a bicycle shop is necessary for every ride, but everything does have a purpose and might come in handy when you least expect it. There are some items that you simply can't or shouldn't leave home without. And there are a lot of options, which depend on the length of the ride and conditions you expect to encounter. Different people will take different things on the same ride, but the following list can give you ideas to help your planning.

Essential Items for Any Ride

Spare tube or two sew-up tires and pump
Patch Kit—complete
Water bottle—filled
Helmet, ANSI or Snell approved

Money
Personal items—identification, medication, ointments, and so
forth

50- to 100-Mile Ride

Two water bottles (an extra can be mounted on the handlebars
or stored in the back of your jersey)
Food in jersey pockets or in handlebar/frame bag
Bike computer, if desired
Rearview mirror (optional)
Bike bag for discarded food or clothes

100- to 150-Mile Ride (or Beyond)

Two large water bottles
Maps of the area
Extra food—such as a granola bar or a banana to save
through the entire trip in case you "bonk"
Liquid energy drinks such as Exceed, Unipro, or UltraEnergy
Saddle pad (optional)
Padded gloves
Change of clothes, if it is an overnight trip

Items for Special Riding Conditions

Hot Weather

Sunglasses or riding goggles
Sunscreen or sunblock
Two or more water bottles
An electrolyte replacement drink (many come in powder form
in packages you can carry in your jersey pocket)
Scarf or handkerchief to protect the back of your neck from the
sun

Cold Weather

Leg warmers
Arm warmers
Wool jersey
Wool warm-up jacket
Shoe covers to keep feet warm
Long-fingered gloves or glove liners
Bike cap under helmet (preferably wool)
Windbreaker
Handkerchief or scarf for neck or nose

Night Riding

Bike lights—front and rear
Reflective tape on bike, clothes, and helmet
Reflective vest
Small flashlight for map review, tire patching, and so forth

Rain Riding

Rain jacket
Booties or waterproof shoe covers
Fenders on bike, if available
Wool clothes (stay warm even when wet)
Extra socks

Optional Personal Items

Chapstick
Insect repellent (especially for tour camping)
Leg oil for cold-weather cycling
Soap or shampoo
Vitamins
Camera and film
Extra spokes
First-aid kit
Brake and gear cables
Tools: spoke wrench, two or three irons, Allen wrenches or
    open-end wrenches, and screwdriver

Sandals or tennis shoes for walking around on a break
  (especially when touring long distances)
Comb or brush
Swiss Army knife
Aspirin or other painkiller
Tampons, other "feminine protection"

RESOURCES

League of American Wheelmen
6707 Whitestone Road, Suite 209
Baltimore, MD 21207
(301) 944-3399

The LAW promotes safety through education and certifies instructors
for its Effective Cycling classes. For more information on certification
programs for instructors, or a schedule of Effective Cycling classes in
your area, contact the LAW. A complete description of the LAW and
its resources is at the end of Chapter 5.

Further Information

There are many books on bicycle maintenance and repair, ranging
from very simple to very complex and highly technical. A couple of
fun and readable books to get you started are *Anybody's Bike Book* by
Tom Cuthbertson, *Effective Cycling* by John Forrester, and *The
Bicycle Repair Book* from the editors of *Bicycling* magazine. You
might also check at your local bike shop to see if they offer a bicycle
repair class. You get to work on your bike in a clinic situation with
the help of experienced mechanics. It's a lot of fun and very practical.

3
The Feminine Physique

*"Let the world know you as you are, not as you think you should be,
because sooner or later, if you are posing, you will forget the pose, and
then where are you?"*

—Fanny Brice

BODY IMAGE

There are aspects of our physiology that affect the type of bicycles we
buy, the intensity and duration of exercise that we choose, and the
levels of performance we aspire to. But before we get into a discussion
of physiology and performance, it's important to take a moment to
think about how we feel about our bodies.

If you ask most women if they like their bodies, the typical answer
is an overwhelming no. There's always some complaint about looking
old or young; having the wrong texture or color of hair; being too
tall, too short, too fat, or too skinny; or having breasts and hips that
are either too small, too large, or, heaven forbid, a combination of
both! We live in a culture that emphasizes physical appearance, with
an ever-changing definition of what's fashionable. While lean and
athletic is in now, it wasn't long ago that the voluptuous Marilyn
Monroe look was the rage, or that the anorexic Twiggy image was
considered ideal. In many cases, a negative body image is related to
some arbitrary fashion or weight issue, rather than being based on a
realistic appraisal of our own body types and their unique physical
ability and beauty. For women with a variety of cultural, social,

political, and spiritual backgrounds, developing a positive body image that doesn't adhere to the rigid ideals set by the dominant culture can be a frustrating and losing proposition.

For women especially, how we feel about our bodies is often an emotionally charged subject that is related to more complex issues of control, esteem, and ultimately what it means to be a woman in this society. How we feel about ourselves affects the goals we set and in some cases it can even determine our ability to achieve those goals.

You may ask what a discussion of body image has to do with cycling and fitness. With the suddenly booming fitness craze, many women are becoming active—some for the first time—through aerobics and exercise classes, running, bicycling, and triathlons. According to Martha Nelson, journalist and past editor of *Women's Sports & Fitness* magazine, "Many women get into sports for overall conditioning and weight loss." It's important to identify why you're getting into cycling and physical fitness. Are you looking forward to enjoying the outdoors, to competing, or to losing weight? It could be a combination of reasons. Cycling can be an important tool both in losing weight and in becoming physically fit. But are you losing weight to improve your performance or so you look better? Are you trying to be fit or thin? Are you trying to improve your performance or your image of yourself? Madeline Brown, MPH (Master of Public Health), who studies the topic of women and body image at the Melpomene Institute, has found that:

> If a woman's motivation for exercise is to conform to an unrealistic weight or body image, exercise will not improve a poor body image. When her goal is to use exercise as a means of stress reduction and relaxation as well as to improve cardiovascular health and to tone her body, exercise can add to a woman's self-esteem and body image. This is especially true if she combines exercise with the support of family and friends, and a realistic expectation and appreciation of her own body type.

It may surprise you to learn that even some athletes who are in excellent physical condition can still have a poor body image. Researchers at the Melpomene Institute found that "weight issues often distorted the self-perceptions of even physically active women." Lynn Jaffee from the Melpomene Institute studies women's issues in exercise and fitness and finds that "some women lose weight to be thinner, not necessarily to be better in their sport." These athletes followed very strict diet and exercise regimens in excess of what was required for top performance in their sport, out of fear of being overweight. Although they were successful athletically, "their body image had not changed for the better." While I was road racing last season, I met a couple of national-caliber racers who told me that they got so preoccupied with losing weight in their training that it actually hurt their performance. While becoming leaner to improve climbing was a good idea, the obsession with losing weight was unhealthy and counterproductive in the long run.

Cycling and other forms of physical exercise are great ways to get in touch with your body. For me, being physically fit is not an end in itself, but part of a lifelong process of developing a strong, vital, and resourceful body and mind. I cycle for a number of reasons. The pure enjoyment of the exercise is important. But I also have a competitive personality and I like to improve my performance. Cycling does provide me with a tool and a framework for staying fit and maintaining my sanity. While no sport is a quick fix for life's problems, being physically active reinforces an "I can do it!" attitude that can help you deal with challenges in other areas of your life.

GETTING IN TOUCH
Keeping a Daily Journal

For some of you, getting out there on your bike for a few rides and discovering that you have muscles and that they work is something new. For others, regular exercise is already part of your life and you want to get stronger and improve your fitness level. Whatever your goals are, a good way to get in touch with your body and monitor your conditioning is to keep track of a few basic items. A good way to do this is to keep a daily journal.

You'll want to keep this simple. If there's too much paperwork you probably won't do it for more than the first couple of days. You can use the corner of a calendar, make your own log, or buy one of the cycling or triathlon logs available in bike shops and sporting-good stores. (Following is a sample format.)

The important information to include: waking pulse (before you get out of bed), standing pulse (after you get out of bed), weight, and subjective assessment of how you feel. I will give you a few tips on taking your pulse and its relevance to aerobic training. As far as gauging "how you feel," you can either jot down a quick note if you're the literary type, or simply assign a letter system A, B, C, or D (A is Absolutely feeling great, and D is for Doggone bad). You should also include daily activities: cycling, swimming, weight training, running, tennis, etc. Note the number of miles you rode, the type of terrain, and the intensity of the effort.

After you've done this for a few weeks, it'll be fun to look back and see if any patterns emerge. It's nice to have an idea of what's a normal resting pulse for you. An elevated heart rate could indicate stress, fatigue, or warn you of a cold even before you feel sick. How long does it usually take for you to recover after a hard ride? See if there were times when you woke up feeling a little down, but got out on your bike and rode great. You may find it interesting to note any changes in your body, how it looks and feels. If you exercise regularly, you'll probably find that your resting pulse decreases as you get into better shape.

Sample Daily Log:

Date: __/__/__

Waking Pulse: _____   Standing Pulse: _____

Weight: _____   How you feel (A, B, C, D): _____

Activity: _____

Miles: _____   Intensity, Terrain: _____

Time/Average Speed (optional): _____

Notes: _____

_____

_____

Waking Pulse and Standing Pulse

Monitoring your waking pulse and comparing it to your standing pulse (after you have gotten out of bed and walked around) is a good indicator of your fitness and general health. You may feel fine, but if your pulse is high, you could have a fever, or you might not have recovered from a previous workout. Take your waking pulse on the side of your neck or from your wrist in the morning when lying in bed. Don't use your thumb because it has a pulse of its own, and you'll pick up interference. I usually fall back asleeep if I try to count with my eyes closed for the entire minute, so I count for 10 seconds and multiply the result by 6. You could also count for 15 seconds and multiply by 4 or whatever works best for you. Keep track of this every day. The more fit you get, the lower your pulse will be.

Take your standing pulse a couple of minutes after you get out of bed and before you exert yourself with any exercise. As with your waking pulse, you will become familiar with what is a normal standing pulse for you. As you get into better shape, you will find that the difference between your waking and standing pulses will decrease. The difference between your waking pulse and standing pulse can tell you how well you've recovered from your previous workout. If your range is abnormally high one day, you may want to take an easy day and not push yourself.

Physiological Testing

If you're just getting into a regular fitness program, you may want to consider having a few basic tests done. Blood pressure is a pretty easy one, and a cholesterol check is a good idea to make sure your heart is healthy. I recently joined a health club and they suggested that new members do these tests. I think it's a good idea.

Many clinics offer sports testing. Consult an athlete or doctor who is familiar with sports testing in your local area for a recommendation. If you really get into training or racing you may want to be tested for body fat (covered in the next section), blood analysis, or VO_2 (oxygen volume intake) test. The VO_2 max test measures aerobic capacity. To a certain extent, VO_2 max is genetically determined, but most people can increase their aerobic capacity through training. Tests such as the VO_2 are a useful gauge of athletic ability, but remember that they aren't the determining factor in how well you will do in a race. Experience, skill, and savvy can compensate for raw strength and power—it's not always the strongest racer who wins.

WEIGHT AND FAT AND ALL THAT

Weight is important for a number of reasons, so let's talk about it first. Many women get into sport to shape up and part of that may include losing some weight. For competitive cyclists a good strength-to-weight ratio is particularly important. So what is the right answer? How much should you weigh? Why can't you just have no fat at all?

The muscles, bones, and organs comprise what we call lean body mass (LBM). Lean body mass supports obvious activities like getting around, and eating and digesting food. Lean body mass is the motor. It consumes calories to support your activities.

Fat has a role, too. Its main function is storing energy for the muscles. Covert Bailey notes that approximately 60–70 percent of the calories muscles burn while resting come from fat (either from a recent meal or fat stores). The other 30 percent is glucose from the muscles and blood. Medical evidence shows that a normal fat level maintains healthy skin and keeps you from getting sick, especially in the winter months.

The average American woman is about 25 percent body fat, while conditioned female athletes average 12 to 15 percent. Very few women have body fat under 10 percent, unless they are distance runners. If body fat gets too low, there are negative consequences for your health that could include early osteoporosis (a weakening of the bones) and amenorrhea (absence of menstruation). But conversely, too much body fat is bad because, among other things, it places a strain on your heart.

Estimating Percent Body Fat

There is no way short of cadaver analysis to measure your *exact* amount of fat and lean body mass. But this option is impractical and undesirable for most because it precludes the rest of your life! Fortunately, there are other methods available that *estimate* percent body fat. They include: (1) underwater weighing; (2) electro-impedence; and (3) skinfold calipers.

Studies have shown that underwater weighing is the most accurate way to estimate lean body mass, and hence percent body fat. The more dense you are, the more lean body mass you have, and the "heavier" you will be under water. This underwater weight is applied to a formula that takes into consideration sex and bone size (which varies by race). By approximating lean body mass and relating it to your dry-land weight and residual lung volume, percent body fat is estimated. Nancy Clark, R.D., notes that a subject could come up with a 3–5 percent higher body fat percentage if she got nervous and didn't expel all the air from her lungs. Intestinal gas and variations in scale calibration can also affect the results.

Electro-impedence is a computerized way of estimating percent body fat. A small and painless electrical current is sent through your body via electrodes attached to your wrists and ankles. Since only fat-free tissue contains water and conducts electricity, the computerized data can be factored into an equation that yields an estimate of body fat percentage. The test results vary considerably depending upon the subject's hydration level.

The most widely available method of estimating body fat percent is the skinfold caliper, or "pinch" test. Specific sites of the body are "pinched" and the millimeters of fat recorded. The test results can vary considerably depending on the experience level of the person conducting the test. If the measurer misses the standard site you could end up with an inaccurate body fat percentage. An individual's pattern of fat deposition can also affect the test results, especially if the fat is concentrated at one of the designated sites. Another limitation of this method is that it doesn't estimate intramuscular fat (fat inside the muscle).

Although these tests offer some useful information, they can be highly variable. Body fat tests are best used to gauge improvements in fitness over a period of time. The specific numerical percent may not be as important as a trend in becoming progressively more fit and lean. Probably the best method for gauging body fat is the most subjective. Go by how you feel, and what's practical for your fitness goals and particular body type.

Determining Your Ideal Weight

Your ideal weight depends on the type of activity you wish to undertake and your goals. As mentioned earlier, the average American woman is about 25 percent body fat. If you want to race it's probably ideal to have body fat between 10 and 15 percent. According to US Women's National Team Coach Sue Novara-Reber and former USCF

Olympic Sports Medicine advisor Dr. Edmund Burke, elite female cyclists keep their body fat somewhere in that range. Extra weight is dead weight if you repeatedly carry it uphill. It slows you down, tires you faster, and you have to work harder.

To a certain extent, the amount of body fat you have depends on genetics. Some women's metabolisms lay down more fat than others'. Each person's body metabolizes fats differently, some faster, some slower than others. Current thinking is that each person has a "set point," or an amount of fat at which her body feels comfortable. This set point can be lowered through a long-term program of exercise and diet.

While elite road racers need to keep their body-fat percentages low, it may not be practical for average recreational cyclists who work full time to do the same. Part of an elite athlete's ability to keep the weight off has to do with the long miles and high intensity of her training. Depending on your age and the type of riding you want to do, a recreational cyclist may want to aim for something between 17 and 22 percent body fat.

Adding LBM may be appropriate too. It makes you stronger and also results in an increased ability to consume calories. Muscle is more dense than fat, so if you lose a pound of fat and gain a pound of muscle, you will get stronger and smaller while staying at the same weight.

As Covert Bailey suggests in *Fit or Fat*, you should determine your ideal weight on what feels good for you, or how your clothes fit, and do away with the bathroom scale.

REACHING YOUR IDEAL WEIGHT: EXERCISE AND PROPER DIET

Weight control is a big subject and lots of books have been written on it. In the broadest sense, it involves balancing your food intake and your exercise to achieve your goals.

Fasting to reach an ideal weight is probably the most radical and unhealthy variation on the food intake and exercise equation. When you fast, calories and protein that would be used to repair and restore muscle tissue are used instead for energy needs. To meet basic energy needs, your body breaks down muscle tissue and you begin to lose your lean body mass—the very engine that burns the calories. Fasting puts your body in a starvation mode: the infrequency of calories encourages the body to lay down an extra layer of fat just in case it's a while before your next meal. It is better to eat five or six small meals throughout the day than to eat one or two large meals.

For women especially, proper nutrition is important. The active woman needs to include adequate amounts of calcium and iron in her diet to prevent osteoporosis and anemia. Generally, a diet that emphasizes fresh fruits and vegetables, whole grains, and minimal fats and processed foods will meet her nutritional needs. Most health-conscious women should strive to consume their daily calories in about the following proportions: 65 percent carbohydrates, 20 percent protein, and 15 percent fat.

Cindy Olavarri, fitness expert and former racer, recommends that competitive cyclists not get too lean too soon. It's the same thing as peaking too soon. Even elite athletes don't maintain very low body fat percentages all year-round. That would be too hard on the body. So it is important to lose weight slowly as part of a long-term fitness program.

The key to reaching your ideal weight is aerobic exercise. Aerobic exercise increases your basal metabolic rate and builds lean body mass (LBM). That causes you to burn more calories even as you sleep. As Covert Bailey says in *Fit or Fat*, LBM is the "engine" that burns the calories and determines how much you should eat. You don't want to feed your total body weight, just the lean body mass and essential fat. When you increase your LBM, you change the muscle chemistry, raising the level of enzymes that consume calories inside the muscle, and thus increasing the muscles' ability to burn fats. Good aerobic athletes are those who can burn fats steadily throughout the race and save their blood sugar for the final sprint.

Aerobic exercise should be steady, nonstop activity at your training heart rate for at least 20–60 minutes. (See the following section, "Training Heart Rate.") To maintain basic aerobic conditioning you should try to ride four to six times a week for at least an hour at a time. Century rides and long, steady distance (LSD) training for racers are the best "fat burning" rides. They are usually relaxing and can be a lot of fun, too!

Training Heart Rate

For any of you who have ever taken an aerobics class, the concept of a training heart rate is nothing new. A training heart rate is the rate at which you want to work to get the most efficient aerobic workout. Good aerobic training is steady and continuous, done at 65 to 85 percent of your maximum heart rate for at least 20 minutes to an hour. During aerobic exercise the cardiovascular system is challenged, but kept within a range where oxygen needs are continuously satisfied and exercise can be sustained for long periods of time. It challenges your heart muscle, which then becomes stronger so it can pump more slowly and still increase the amount of blood pumped through the heart. The more blood you can pump through your heart, the more oxygen that is available to your muscles, and the greater your aerobic capacity.

There are many ways to determine your training heart rate, and some approaches are more accurate than others. Researchers in the field and the American College of Sports Medicine consider the following approach based on the heart-rate range or reserve (difference between maximum and resting heart rates) the most accurate. We will begin with a simple calculation to estimate your maximum heart rate. If you have taken a VO_2 max test and know what your maximum heart rate is, substitute that into the equation.

220	Presumed Maximum Heart Rate for Humans
− 30	Minus Your Age
190	Equals Your Estimated Max. Heart Rate
− 50	Minus Your Resting Heart Rate (beats per minute)
140	Equals Your Maximum Heart Rate Reserve
× .65	Times .65 (Train somewhere in the range of 65%–85% of max. depending upon your goals)
91	Equals 65% of Your Max. Heart Rate Reserve
+ 50	Plus Your Resting Pulse
141	Equals the Low End of Your Training Heart Rate Range (beats per minute)

Using the above formula and the range of 65 to 85 percent of maximum, the full training heart range for this particular person would be 141–169 beats per minute.

Most of you are probably not going to want to stop and take your pulse every few minutes to see if you are riding at your training heart rate. If you're out to check out the sights and relax, you may not care about what your heart rate is, only that you have one. But if you *are* interested, the simplest test is to try talking to a friend, or if you're alone, talk to yourself. If you are sweating but are still able to speak without gasping for breath, that's fine. If you're wheezing and furiously sucking in air like a carburetor at high altitude, then you're going anaerobic (you're in oxygen debt) and you should throttle back.

Interval training is a variation of the theme of training heart rate. Instead of sticking to the 70 percent steady pace, bike racers like to experiment with how hard they can go, driving up their heart rate near maximum. Intervals are something that racers like to do (typically on Tuesdays or Thursdays). They gun their hearts up, suck in that air, and pedal in agony repeatedly for prescribed increments of time. Intervals are a quick, effective, and painful way to increase your aerobic capacity. Aerobic capacity comes in handy during races when the strong riders put the hammer down and try to burn up the rest of the pack. If you're serious about racing or triathlons, read Greg LeMond's book or Eddie B's book and do those intervals. There are lots of types to choose from (hill climbs, criteriums, time trials, etc.) so you'll never get bored. In Chapters 7–10, we'll talk a lot more about racing.

If you're serious about training, you may want to invest in a heart-rate monitor. That way you can make sure you're training at the correct heart rate. There are several good monitors on the market. Those that strap around your chest and read out on a watch unit are the most comfortable and the most accurate. They're great for interval and sprint training, and useful for time trials.

Overtraining: More Is Not Always Better

For some of us, exercise provides instant and reliable gratification. You can go out for a ride and even if it is physically demanding, it can lift your spirits and you feel great. There is a temptation to ride more and train harder to get better faster. More is not necessarily better. Rest is also important.

Listen to your body. Pay attention to how you feel. If you're training hard try to be a little more patient, and give yourself a break.

After you have a hard workout you need time to recover, and you should take that time. Cycling can be a lifelong sport, but you won't last more than a season if you burn yourself out. Signs of overtraining can include: elevated heart rate, chronic fatigue, loss of appetite, rapid loss of weight, frequent colds, and loss of enthusiasm.

WOMEN'S STUFF
Cycling and Your Period

In 1984, the US Olympic Committee studied menstruation and its effect on the performance of female athletes. The committee found that women competed and won medals throughout their menstrual cycles. Some athletes claim that menstruation helps their performance, while others say it has a negative impact. It varies from woman to woman.

The notion that all very fit women have regular cycles and don't experience cramps is a myth. Researchers at the Melpomene Institute studied the relationship between exercise and dysmenorrhea (painful menstruation) and found that an increase in exercise did not necessarily result in a decrease in menstrual cramps. Triathlete Joanne Ernst, for example, says that she experiences very bad cramps and takes ibuprofen, found in some over-the-counter and prescription drugs, for relief. Ernst has never had a bad problem with menstrual cramps during competition, mostly due to luck and the timing of the competitions. However, another cyclist said that when her period started on the day of the 1985 World Championships, cramps "ruined her race." She was advised to go on and off birth control pills to time her menstrual cycle around important competitions. For some women, problems with their periods are an added consideration in competing.

Nancy Clark, MS, RD, and nutritionist at Sports Medicine, Inc., estimates that 30 percent of female athletes also have problems with premenstrual syndrome (PMS). She suggests dietary ways to deal with PMS, such as cutting sodium, caffeine, and sugar out of your diet as much as possible. This may help with bloating and mood swings. (See "Resources" at the end of this chapter.)

Amenorrhea: Cycling and No Period

It is estimated that 20 percent of female athletes become amenorrheic (have no menstrual discharge) sometime in their careers. This condition is of particular concern because it can lead to early osteoporosis. When a woman becomes amenorrheic, her estrogen level drops and this affects her ability to retain the calcium that is needed to maintain bone mass.

Early studies linked amenorrhea to low body fat because the condition was most prevalent in women who participated in sports that placed a high premium on thinness (runners, ballet dancers, and gymnasts). However, researchers at the Melpomene Institute have found that dietary patterns (low dietary fat, less red meat), intensity of training, and psychological stress can all bring on amenorrhea. In most cases, amenorrhea is reversible, but it can lead to long-term problems with fertility over prolonged periods of time.

According to US Women's Cycling Coach Sue Novara-Reber, amenorrhea is not very common in most elite cyclists. Some women may become amenorrheic for a few months of the season when they are racing extremely hard and are their leanest, but they tend to resume regular periods in the off-season. For most women temporary amenorrhea is not a problem. However, if you become amenorrheic for long periods of time, you may want to consult your doctor.

Birth Control

For women for whom birth control is a relevant issue, I'm sorry to say that there isn't very much information on the best methods for women athletes. Dr. Joan Ullyot, sports physician, recommends the IUD, but cautions that the copper IUD has been withdrawn from the market. Dr. Ullyot did not recommend birth control pills on the basis of a study in Scotland that found that birth control pills resulted in a decline in aerobic capacity. Essentially, she said that leaves just the barrier methods such as the diaphragm.

Although Dr. Ullyot does not favor birth control pills, many top US cyclists use them and don't report any decrease in their performance.

Dr. Ullyot also warned that irregular periods are not a form of birth control since a woman can still become pregnant. A world-class runner stopped getting her periods and didn't find out she was pregnant until five months into her pregnancy.

Birth control is certainly an area of great concern for some women athletes, and more research is needed.

Cycling During Pregnancy

As more and more women adopt active lifestyles, the question of exercising during pregnancy comes up. Many physically active women want to continue enjoying the physical and psychological benefits of exercise, but they want to be safe, too.

Until fairly recently, women were advised to drastically reduce or stop all strenuous physical activity and exercise during pregnancy for fear of injuring mother and child. The jury is still out on what type and intensity of physical activity is safe for pregnant women. After reviewing studies with runners and women riding bicycle ergometers, Christine Wells, in *Women, Sport & Performance: A Physiological Perspective*, concludes that "strenuous exercise before and during pregnancy is not harmful to either the mother or the fetus and is generally beneficial to both." At the extreme levels of activity, some women have competed and won Olympic medals in the first trimester of pregnancy without even knowing that they were pregnant. Wells acknowledges, however, that many of these studies are outdated and that the training methods and levels of intensity for most of today's female athletes is much greater. She suggests more research, particularly on the effects on the fetus of increasing maternal body temperature. There are specific times during pregnancy when an elevated body temperature can affect the development of the fetus.

While most women do not care to exercise at high intensity during pregnancy, continuing some form of exercise can be beneficial. Most women find that exercise of some sort is a good psychological boost and helps maintain self-esteem. Some studies indicate that physically active women have faster and easier deliveries. However, this is primarily true for the second, not the first child. World sprint champion and current US Women's National Team Coach Sue Novara-Reber continued cycling during part of her pregnancy but didn't find delivery of her first child particularly easy. She now has two children and continued cycling through both pregnancies.

Novara-Reber mentions that "while some form of physical activity is desirable, you may not be able or desire to cycle completely through pregnancy." Continue your activity on the road for a few months, or until it becomes uncomfortable or difficult to balance. Crouching over standard road bars may be uncomfortable for some women. The upright mountain bike, with more stability, may be better. However, by the time cycling becomes uncomfortable, many women consider either riding a stationary bike or taking up walking to reduce the risk of falling off the bike and injuring child and mother. How much you cycle, or whether you cycle at all, should be based on what you and your doctor feel comfortable with. Pregnancy is not the time to take up cycling.

Some athletes find that their athletic performance is better after having children. Some claim a better psychological balance. When you have a child, small worries in training don't seem so big. Some claim that the pain in childbirth is much greater than anything experienced in training or competition so they are able to tolerate a higher threshold of pain in competition. Most studies indicate that childbirth doesn't negatively affect a women's athletic performance. Sheila Young-Ochowicz won a world sprint championship in her early thirties after having a child, and Maria Canins of Italy has twice won the *Tour de France Féminin* in her late thirties and she has two children.

Cycling or another appropriate exercise can be a positive element of your pregnancy. If you are considering cycling or some other type of physical activity during pregnancy, Valerie Lee, MA, of the Melpomene Institute suggests some guidelines. Listen to your own body. Each woman has her own history of physical activity and responds differently to pregnancy. What worked for your best friend may not work for you. Do what is comfortable for you with the consultation of your physician. Try to get a doctor who is supportive of your active lifestyle. Be flexible: be willing to cut back or even stop activity, if necessary. Be sure to get adequate rest and proper nutrition. This could be a good time to slow down and enjoy the scenery.

COMPARING WOMEN AND MEN

Why compare men and women? Well, like it or not, we do it all the time. Some women are embarrassed to go out on club rides because they're afraid they can't keep up with the guys. On the other side, some men get upset whenever any woman passes them. Women typically have separate categories in competition, but many of us, myself included, like to see how well we can do in the men's field. What gives? We're talking about a couple of issues here. There's some fairly straightforward physiology and then there are very complex questions centered on competition.

Physiology

There are definite physical differences between women and men, and some of them affect performance on the bike. In terms of skeletal structure, women are usually smaller and shorter than men. Frame builder Georgena Terry has found that women tend to have longer legs, shorter arms and upper body, a wider pelvis, and a higher center of gravity in comparison to men of the same height. She maintains that these skeletal differences don't affect a woman's efficiency on the bike, assuming the bike is fitted properly. For taller women, proportionately longer legs may even be advantageous.

However, the differences in body composition brought on during the adolescent growth spurt account for the variation in athletic performance between the sexes. Before puberty, girls and boys have similar strength-to-weight ratios. That's why girls can keep up and even excel before puberty. With the onset of puberty, the girls secrete estrogen and start to lay down fat in the breasts and hips for reproductive functions, and the boys secrete testosterone and gain most of their weight in muscle. So a man will tend to weigh more than a woman of the same height, and he will end up with more lean body mass and relatively less fat. In other words, he will have a higher strength-to-weight ratio.

Why can't you just get rid of all that body fat? Some amount of fat is essential to your health. If your fat percentage drops too low, you will stop menstruating and will develop health problems. The specific amount of essential body fat is somewhat genetically determined and depends on body type. For males the range is around 3 to 6 percent, and for females 8 to 12 percent. For comparison, the average American male is around 15 percent body fat, and the average female 25 percent. So, on the average, a man of a given weight is going to have somewhat more power than a woman of the same weight.

It was once thought that women would be much better endurance athletes because the fat would provide useful energy stores. However, exercise physiologist Dr. Christine Wells, in her book *Women, Sport & Performance,* finds that women don't metabolize fat any faster than men—so additional fat is not an advantage for energy supply. Fat provides additional buoyancy for swimmers, but it is a big disadvantage for cyclists because a good strength-to-weight ratio is critical for climbing hills.

Competition

Where does this leave us as far as competition is concerned? The biological analysis shows that males tend to have the advantage on the average, especially in sports where strength is a major factor. Christine Wells notes that "significant variations in physical characteristics occur within each sex that are often greater or as great as the differences between the sexes." What this means in cycling is that the top women can and do compete with strong men. It seems unlikely that the top woman will beat the top man in a sport that relies on power and strength, but both sexes are making incredible improvements in performance and the difference between top men's and women's times is decreasing.

As more people get into sports, the records continue to improve. As the percentage of womern in a given sport increases, their performance approaches that of the men. To take a spectacular example from swimming, when the legendary swimmer Johnny Weissmuller set an Olympic record of 5:04.2 in the 400-meter freestyle in 1924, the winning woman was 19 percent slower. In 1976, Petra Thuemer was only 8 percent slower than the winning man and her time was 4:09.89, almost a minute faster than Weissmuller.

Where this world-championship level competition between the sexes will end up is a matter of debate and speculation. Our generation is the first to see really open participation of women in all types of athletics. The next generation of women will have the benefit of our support and the support of fathers who are as proud of their daughters as men have traditionally been of their little-league sons. Diana Nyad, who holds the record for the longest distance swim, talks more about these matter in Chapter 11.

You don't have to be an aspiring world champion to enjoy competition. Many people who aren't even serious athletes get a kick out of seeing who gets to the top of the hill first or who finishes the century first. Most sports, including cycling, have age divisions and women's divisions precisely so that any individual can find a level of competition that is fun but not totally intimidating and impossible.

You may not give a hoot about competition. If you are simply afraid to go out and ride with a group for fear of holding people up and embarrassing yourself, the physiology has a message for you, too. There is a wide spectrum of ability and you can change where you are on that spectrum. If you apply yourself, you can get to a point where you hold your own in the group and have fun.

RESOURCES

Melpomene Institute for Women's Health Research
2125 E. Hennepin Avenue
Minneapolis, MN 55416
(612) 378-0545

Melpomene, the first woman marathoner, raced from Marathon to Athens to prove that she could qualify for the marathon in the first modern Olympics held in 1896. Although she qualified, the Greek officials did not allow her to compete, stating that such physical activity was not safe or proper for a woman.

The Melpomene Institute is a nonprofit research organization devoted to studying the impct of physical activity on girls and women throughout a lifetime. The emphasis is on recreational as well as elite female athletes. The research staff has long-term projects in the areas of: physical activity and osteoporosis, exercise and menstrual function, exercise and pregnancy, and physical activity and body image. Other related topics are added on a regular basis.

The Institute publishees *The Melpomene Report* three times a year and maintains a resource center with current bibliographies on research topics. You can support the Melpomene Institute by becoming a member.

Nancy Clark, MS, RD
Sports Medicine Brookline
830 Boylston Street
Brookline, MA 02167

Nancy Clark has information on a variety of topics related to nutrition, physiology, and performance. Many of her health and nutrition tips are reprinted in cycling and other sports-related magazines. For further information, send a self-addressed stamped envelope to the address listed above. Her book, *The Athlete's Kitchen*, is useful for women interested in sports and nutrition.

Women's Sports Foundation (WSF)
342 Madison Ave. Suite 728
New York, NY 10173
(212) 972-9170
(800) 227-3988

The WSF was founded to encourage women of all ages and abilities to become involved in sports and to enjoy the benefits of a physically active lifestyle.

The WSF promotes women's participation in sports through a variety of programs. The Women's Sports Hall of Fame, Speakers Bureau, and Public Service Announcements increase public awareness of women in sports. The Travel and Training Fund provides financial assistance to female athletes. Grants of up to $1,500 per individual and $3,000 for a team can be used for coaching, equipment, and experience in national and international competition. Internships are available to women interested in sports-related careers.

WSF maintains a referral service (including sports scholarship information) and a resource center. WSF is involved in many fund-raising programs and works closely with major corporations on programs that provide visibility and assistance to women in sports.

For women interested in sports and fitness, membership in the WSF is a great idea. You'll receive the quarterly WSF newsletter *Headway* and also *Women's Sports & Fitness Magazine,* the official publication of the Women's Sports Foundation. It's a great source of up-to-date information on women's issues in sports. The magazine covers topics ranging from physiology to psychology and provides an overview of many sports. Correspondence and membership questions should be directed to the Women's Sports Foundation.

Further Information

Covert Bailey's *Fit or Fat?* gives a clear, and at times, humorous explanation of the dynamic relationship between exercise and body composition. His emphasis is on building lean body mass and a strong aerobic "engine," balanced with proper nutrition as a way of reaching your ideal weight. Bailey explains some complicated physical and biochemical processes in a way that is easy for the layperson to understand. Christine Wells's book, *Women, Sport & Performance: A Physiological Perspective,* is an excellent and comprehensive source of information on women's physiology and sports. Wells covers all the bases with the latest scientific findings. Her book is in textbook format and very readable.

There is extensive literature on sports psychology, mental training, and visualization, a topic I only hint at in this book. A very readable and practical book by a woman who has extensive experience in the field is *The Athlete's Guide to Sports Psychology* by Dorothy Harris. Eugene Herrigel's books *Zen in the Art of Archery* and *The Method of Zen* are good reading. They are not sports psychology books, but I found the exercise of learning a sport in conjunction with the process of understanding zen particularly interesting. For an analysis of competition from a feminist perspective, *Competition: A Feminist Taboo?,* edited by Helen Longino and Valerie Miner, examines competition between women in a variety of arenas ranging from sports to workplace to personal relationships. Refer to the Women's Mountain Bike and Tea Society in Chapter 8 and the Women's Cycling Network in Chapter 9 for information on women's cycling groups.

4
Weight Training and Stretching

WEIGHT TRAINING: WHY IS IT IMPORTANT?

Whether you commute to work or compete in the World Championships, weight training is a good way to develop the basic strength you need to be a strong cyclist. Weight training is especially important for women, because in most cases, women haven't developed the overall strength that comes from an extensive athletic background. Until recently, most girls and young women didn't have the sports programs or the social acceptance of intense physical activity that boys and young men enjoyed from childhood to adolescence.

With the popular interest in aerobics and fitness, more women are comfortable working out and developing muscles. Since a woman's biochemical structure, in comparison to a man's, includes only trace amounts of the hormone testosterone, she can enjoy the shape and dimension that good musculature gives to the body without having to worry about bulking up.

The benefit of strength training for women goes way beyond the aesthetic. Cycling requires substantial upper and lower body strength. Most people know cycling demands strong legs, but who ever thought strong stomach, arm, and shoulder muscles were important? Does your lower back ever hurt on a long climb? In most cases, lower back pain is a result of weak stomach muscles that don't stabilize the back properly. Sore arms and shoulders are common for many female cyclists and can be remedied by strengthening the upper body. For advanced cyclists and racers, weight training builds the power required for intense climbing, sprinting, and time trialing. A strong musculature can also protect the bones and help minimize injury in the event of a crash.

Photo courtesy of Ron Shuman

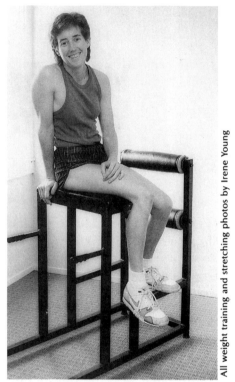

All weight training and stretching photos by Irene Young

Cindy Olavarri was a member of the 1984 Olympic Team and several World Teams.

Cindy Olavarri is a fitness instructor at the Courthouse Athletic Club in Oakland, California.

CINDY OLAVARRI
FITNESS INSTRUCTOR

Cindy Olavarri was born in Oakland, California, on March 23, 1955. She earned a BA, teaching credentials, and MA from the University of California, Berkeley (UCB). Olavarri has an extensive background in competitive athletics. She was a member of the 1984 Olympic Cycling Team and earned a silver medal in the 3,000-meter pursuit at the 1983 World Championships in Zurich, Switzerland. In 1983 she won three National Championships: 25-mile individual time trial; 3,000-meter pursuit, and the kilometer. Olavarri was a member of the 7-Eleven Racing Team, the US National Cycling Team, and several World's teams.

Before she got into cycling, Olavarri competed at UCB on the collegiate running and rowing teams. She won a silver medal at the 1976 National Rowing Championships as a member of the UCB Rowing Team.

Olavarri works as a fitness consultant at the Courthouse Athletic Club and counsels individuals at all levels of physical ability. Her other interests and activities include swimming, cross-country skiing, hiking, weight training, playing guitar, and reading novels and mysteries.

Olavarri recommends the following program for women cyclists who want to develop good overall strength and conditioning.

WARM-UP ACTIVITIES

Before you start lifting weights, it's important to warm-up properly. This will help prevent injuries to the muscles, tendons, ligaments, and joints. A good warm-up will elevate your heart rate and raise your body temperature, but shouldn't tire you out.

Suggested warm-up activities include jumping rope (5 minutes), cycling to the gym, riding a stationary bike (5–10 minutes), or an aerobics class. If you choose the aerobics class, make sure it's just the warm-up and stretching and not the dumbbell-weight exercises included in some classes. *Remember, this is a warm-up, not a workout.*

CLOTHING

You should pick *comfortable clothes* to work out in. This could be cycling or running shorts and a T-shirt, Lycra tights, aerobics outfits, or sweats. There are many options here since the only requirement is that the clothes are not restrictive so you can move freely and feel comfortable bending and stretching in a gym atmosphere.

A good pair of *supportive shoes* is important. Many companies make a good cross-training or aerobics shoe. Stay away from thongs and slippers. *Do not try to lift barefoot.* The better health clubs and gyms won't allow you to work out barefoot, anyway.

If you plan to lift weights beyond the basic conditioning stage, it's a good idea to use a *weight belt.* (You can see Cindy wearing one in some of the photos.) A weight belt is a wide leather support that is used to stabilize the lower back during a heavy lift. It is relatively inexpensive. Some health clubs will have them available for use.

NOTES BEFORE WE BEGIN

If you're lifting weights for the first time, or just getting back into the gym for winter training, it's important to *start off slowly.* Use a weight you can handle comfortably with the proper technique. *Work the large muscle groups first,* and then move to the smaller ones. Take the time to build the strength you need for more difficult lifts. If something hurts, stop and find out what's wrong. You can get injured if you try to lift too much too soon.

Maintain good form. Your moves should be smooth, controlled, and cover the complete range of motion. Make sure the muscles identified in the description of the exercise are the ones doing the work. *Don't strain, or jerk the weight.* If you find yourself swaying from side to side or back and forth, this is a sign that you are not using correct form. Lower the weight to an amount you can handle using the proper technique.

Breathing is an integral part of weight training. *Don't hold your breath during the lift!* You need to get oxygen to your muscles so you can lift that weight. Some people have a tough time coordinating their breathing with the exercise. A good rule of thumb is to *exhale with exertion.* Try not to feel self-conscious breathing in public; many of us do it all the time!

Remember to *get adequate rest.* Your body needs 48 hours to rebuild after working a particular body part. This means if you work your whole body in one session you should lift three days a week, at most. If you don't rest, you'll tear down the muscle, and it won't have a chance to rebuild. You will actually get *weaker*, not stronger.

WEIGHT TRAINING PROGRAM FOR OVERALL CONDITIONING

Work with an Instructor

You may want to use this program with the help of an instructor to make sure you're doing the exercises correctly. Pictures and narrative descriptions are helpful, but they don't give you the feedback you need to know whether you're doing the exercises right.

What if your gym does not have the same machine or weight selection? Maybe you prefer using Nautilus or Universal machines over free weights. In these situations, an experienced instructor can suggest alternate exercises you can use to work the same muscle group.

How Many Sets and Repetitions?

Start off with two sets of 12–15 repetitions for each lower-body exercise and two sets of 10–12 repetitions for each upper-body exercise. All repetitions in each set should be done continuously, without stopping, until the set is complete. Maintain resistance in the weights. Don't return them to a resting position until the set is complete. If you can't complete the set, stop and lower the weight.

After three to four weeks, you can start doing three sets of each exercise. You must listen to your body. Don't add the third set until you are recovering well and feeling stronger after each workout. Prolonged aches and fatigue are a sign that you need more recovery time. Remember, don't push too hard too soon.

A Note to Advanced Cyclists and Racers

Advanced cyclists and racers who are starting their winter training can use this program for the first six to eight weeks to develop good overall conditioning. After that you'll want to incorporate some more difficult lifts (i.e., squats, dead lifts, power cleans, lunges, etc.) and concentrate much more on power and speed.

Leg Exercises (4)

Leg Extension

Works the quadricep muscle group on top of the legs from the knee to the thigh.

Sit in the seat, secure the waistband, and hold onto the handles at either side. Place your feet under the padded lever. You may need to put a pad behind your back if the distance to the back of the seat is too far. Note the pad behind Cindy's back. Extend your legs out to an *almost* locked out position, then slowly lower the weight until your feet are farther back than your knees. Do not lock out to maximum; it's too much stress on the knees.

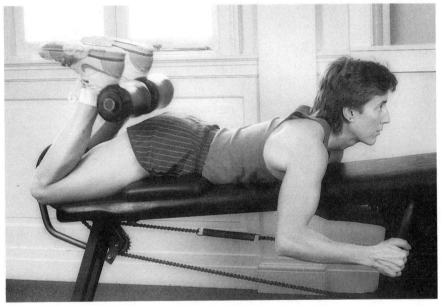

Leg Curl

Works the hamstrings and buttocks at the back of the legs.

Lie face down with a small pad under your abdomen. The pad will help keep your pelvis flat and your back from arching. Place your heels under the padded bar, hold onto the handles on either side of the machine, and curl your legs toward your buttocks. When your hamstrings are fully contracted, lower the weight down slowly.

Leg Press

Works the thighs and, to a lesser extent, the buttocks. This is a good beginning exercise to build basic strength in the legs and buttocks before trying squats. The leg press allows you to handle a lot of weight without placing stress on the lower back.

Sit in the seat with the back reclined, using a pad behind you if the reach is too great. Place feet on the plate in front of you, shoulder-width apart, with toes pointed fairly straight. Lower weight about halfway, or until knee is at a 90-degree angle. Do not go down any farther. It places too much stress on the knee.

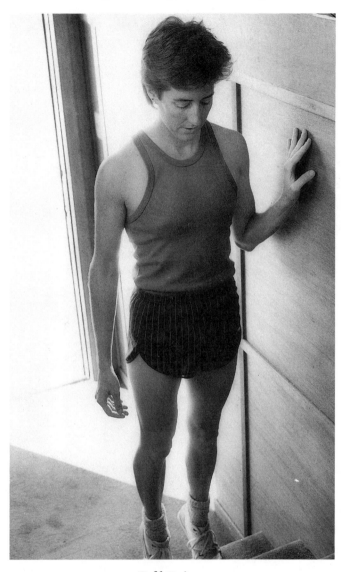

Calf Raises

Works overall calf muscles.

Stand on a step with toes straight ahead and heels extended off the end. Bend your knees slightly. Lower your heels as far as possible, then lift up on your toes as far as possible. Try to get a full range of motion. Start with two sets of 15 repetitions using just your body weight.

Chest Exercise (1)

Bench Press

Works the chest and, to a lesser extent, the shoulders and upper arms. (Pectorals, front deltoids, and triceps, respectively).

Lie flat on your back with your feet on the floor. If you are short and have difficulty reaching the ground without arching your back, place your feet at the end of the bench instead. Grip the bar with hands slightly more than shoulder-width apart. Lift the bar off the rack and hold it overhead with your arms fully extended. Lower the bar slowly and lightly touch your chest. Press the bar upward and fully extend your arms.

Back Exercises (2)

Lat Pull-Downs

Works the latissimi dorsi, or "lats." To feel your lats (right), wrap your left arm across the front of your body, hugging the mid-right side of your back. Tense the right upper trunk. These muscles are located on both sides of the back. They cover the ribs and extend from under the shoulder blades to the lower back.

Grasp overhead bar with wide grip, and sit on the seat with knees tucked under the support. Make sure your grasp is wider than your shoulders, but not so wide that the shoulder joint is hyperextended. Pull down slowly until the bar touches the back of the neck. Release the weight and extend the arms upward.

Back Hyperextensions

Works the spinal erectors in the lower back.

Lay face down over the Roman chair, and hook your calves under the padded frame. Place your hands behind your neck, and bend forward as far as possible, stretching the lower back muscles. Lift up until your torso is flat. Do not come up any higher than this, or you will start using the hip flexors instead of the spinal erectors.

Shoulder Exercises (2)

Dumbbell Press

Works the front deltoid muscles of the shoulder.

Sit on a bench with a back support. Rest your head and shoulders on the support. Start with the dumbbells at shoulder height with your elbows facing out and palms forward. Lift the dumbbells up and touch them together overhead, then slowly lower them back to the starting position.

Seated Rear Flys

Works the rear deltoids located on top of the shoulders.

Sit on a bench or chair with legs together. Bend over and pick up the dumbbells with wrists facing inward and arms slightly bent. Lift the dumbbells out to the side and up. Your palms should be facing the floor.

Arm Exercises (2)

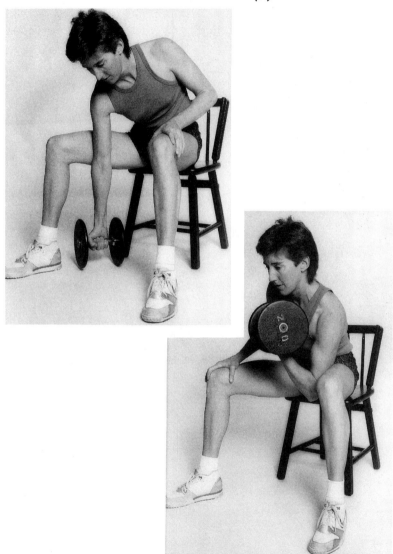

Concentration Curls

Works the bicep muscles in the front of the upper arm.

Sit on a bench or chair and rest the back of your upper arm against your inner leg. Hold the dumbbell at arm's length with your palms facing out. Curl the dumbbell up to your shoulder, then slowly lower it back down.

Tricep Press-Down

Works the tricep muscles on the back of the arm.

Stand with feet slightly apart and knees slightly bent. Press elbows to your side, with the bar no higher than the sternum. Press the bar completely down, keeping your arms and elbows tightly to your sides.

Abdominal Exercises (3)

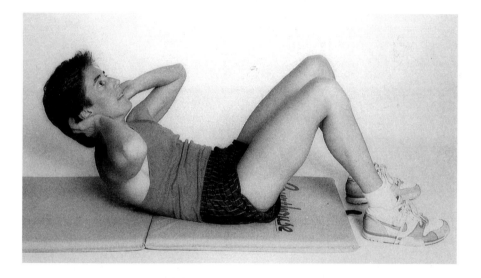

Crunches

Works the upper and lower abdominals.

Lie on a mat with your back flat and your knees bent. Place your hands at the back of your neck and, contracting your abdominal muscles, lift up four to five inches, then slowly lower one inch from the mat and repeat. Remember not to come up too high, and don't use your arms for momentum. Start with 15-25, depending upon how strong you are.

Alternating V-Ups

Works the oblique abdominal muscles on the side of your waist.

Place hands behind your neck. Lift head and feet a few inches off the mat. Lift up and touch left elbow to right knee; then slowly straighten out, keeping head and feet a few inches off the mat. Alternate sides, touching your right elbow to left knee. This will tire you out sooner or later. Start with 15–25.

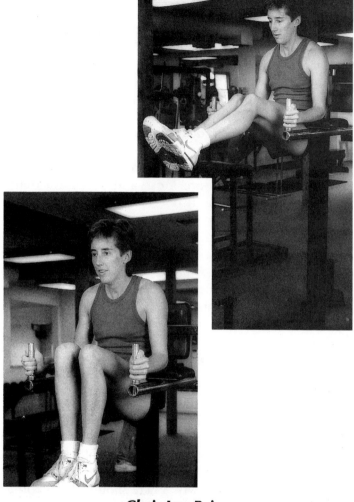

Chair Leg Raises

Works the lower abdominals.

Stabilize yourself on the chair using your arms. Keep your upper body steady, and rest your lower back on the back support. (1) Straighten your legs and lift them perpendicular to your torso, then slowly lower them. (2) Lift your knees to your chest, then straighten them to perpendicular, and then lower them back down. (3) Pull knees up to your chest, then lower them back down. Repeat steps 1, 2, and 3 in consecutive order five times each.

STRETCHING FOR OVERALL FITNESS
Why Should I Stretch?

Stretching is an important part of a cyclist's overall fitness program. The benefits are both physical and psychological. Stretching is a good form of relaxation. It improves circulation and helps keep the muscles smooth and supple. Stretching can also increase the range of motion in the joints. Good flexibility helps prevent injuries such as tears and strains to muscles, tendons, and ligaments.

Many people have trouble scheduling time to stretch. One suggestion is to incorporate 10 to 20 minutes of stretching into a regular weight-training session as a warm down. This is a good time to stretch because your muscles are loose and still have that warm, healthy glow. While stretching, think about how you're feeling both physically and psychologically. Pay attention to any twinges or pains. Use this time to evaluate your workout and your development. Acknowledge gains in strength and endurance. If you felt particularly tired one day, think about why. Are you getting enough sleep? Are you under additional stress? Development in any sport takes time. I've found that taking a few minutes to notice and appreciate the small advances helps keep me motivated to reach new heights.

How Should I Stretch?

The key to stretching is to be relaxed. Pick a quiet place. If you're at the gym or health club, find a stretching room or a quiet corner away from a lot of noise or activity. You should stay warm. If you worked hard in an aerobics class or in the weight room, make sure you don't get chilled. You can't stretch properly if you are cold. Stretch on a mat, carpet, or other comfortable surface.

Stretching should be done slowly. There should be no bouncing or jerky movements. Stretch to the point where you feel tension in the muscle, but not pain. Hold it for 20 to 30 seconds, then slowly release. Try it again, and this time go a little deeper into the stretch. Don't worry if you can't stretch very far at first; increased flexibility comes with practice.

Proper breathing is also very important. Throughout the stretch, your breathing should be slow and rhythmical. Exhale going into the stretch; inhale while coming out. Do not hold your breath. Breathe consistently during the 20- to 30-second stretch.

The following basic stretches are demonstrated by Cindy Olavarri. There may be other stretches you might want to incorporate into this program as you go along.

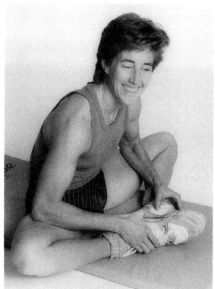

Groin

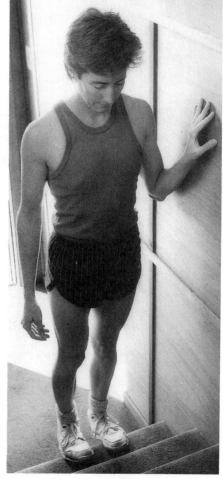

Calf

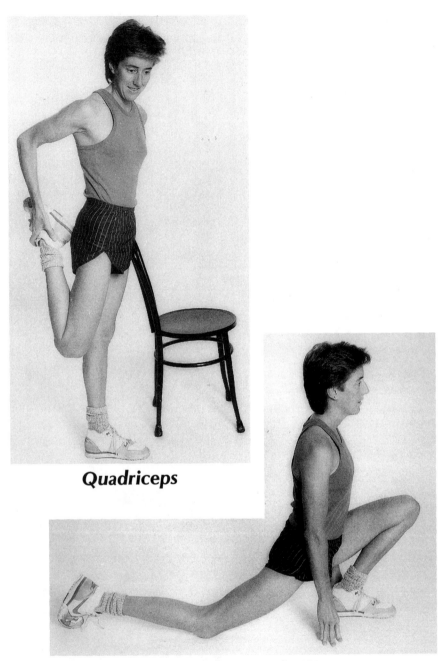

Quadriceps

Hamstrings and Hips

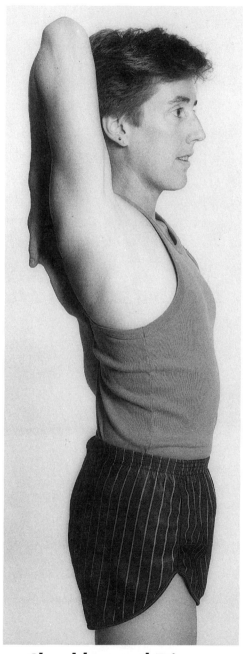

Shoulders and Triceps

Chest and Shoulders

Hamstrings

Hips and Back

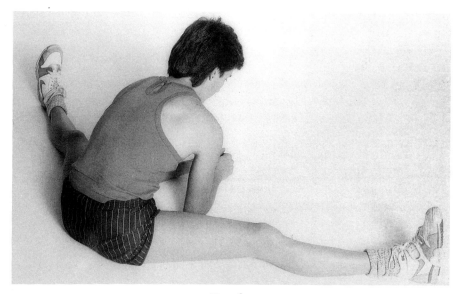

Groin

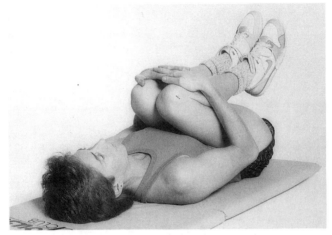

Back

RESOURCES

Weight Training for Cyclists by the editors of Velo-News has very good information on weight training programs designed specifically for cyclists. The book is for advanced cyclists, road racers, and track specialists who want to develop the strength and explosive power required in bike racing. The relevance of strength training for cyclists is discussed, and specific exercises and training programs are recommended. *Arnold Schwarzenegger's Encyclopedia of Modern Bodybuilding* is a useful reference if you can get past the fact that the emphasis of the book is on male bodybuilders. (Schwarzenegger also has a bodybuilding book for women.) The anatomical drawings, photo illustrations, and descriptions of how to do various exercises are very good. Bodybuilding is very different from weight training, and cyclists should be prepared to adapt some of the exercises and training routines to meet their particular needs.

In addition to stretching, massage is extremely important for the competitive cyclist. Massage helps keep the muscles supple, aids in the recovery process, and is very relaxing. We don't always have access to a good sports masseuse, so knowing a little self-massage, or having friends who are also willing to learn a few of the basics can really help. *The Massage Book* by George Downing is a good introduction to basic massage.

5
Recreation and Touring

"Travelers are always discoverers."

—Anne Morrow Lindbergh

RECREATIONAL RIDING

You don't have to have an athletic background to enjoy recreational cycling. It is a sport for women and girls of all ages, shapes, and sizes. In the same event you will see older women decorated with decades of ride patches, as well as a girl on her first ride with her family. Recreational cycling encompasses almost anything from a solo ride through the park to group rides, centuries, or tours. The emphasis is on having fun, not on competition.

You can use your bike as a way to combine fitness and the appreciation of nature. You can watch the seasons change, explore new places close to home or farther away, and enjoy the physical challenge of riding in varied terrain. One Saturday you might ride out to the ocean or over the hills to the country. You can pack a lunch and ride your bike to picnic in the park. If you walk, you can only go so far. Your bike gives you a greater sense of freedom and independence. It is a liberating feeling to travel under your own power, and that's good for the spirit.

One thing is for certain, you won't be alone! The largest segment of the cycling boom is that of the recreational rider. The Bicycle Dealers' Survey conducted by the Bicycle Federation of America estimates that there are approximately 80 million recreational cyclists in the United

States, and that 70 percent of the new participants in the sport are women. More than ever, women are joining clubs, participating in century rides, and enjoying the adventures of bicycle touring. Club rides, centuries, and tours are all great ways to meet a whole new network of friends.

Photo courtesy of Kevin A. Van Renterghem

KAY AND RUDY VAN RENTERGHEM

On September 15, 1984, Kay and Rudy Van Renterghem celebrated the completion of 50,000 miles on their custom tandem. They started cycling seriously in 1973 on single bicycles. In January of 1975, Rudy surprised Kay with a tandem for their 20th wedding anniversary. Since that time, Kay has cycled more than 100,000 miles, and more than 95,000 of that was pedaling in tandem. The Renterghems are charter members of the Tandem Club of America and members of the Greater Arizona Bicycling Association in Tucson, Arizona.

How to Get Involved

One of the best places to find out about clubs, rides, and events is your local bike shop. The better bike shops are hubs of activity. Usually the employees have cycling experience themselves and know what's going on in the local cycling community. Many bike shops let various cycling clubs post newsletters, membership information, and ride schedules. Posters for upcoming centuries and fun rides are also posted in shops.

Other very good sources of information are the various bicycle and regional sports magazines. The sporting or outdoor sections of many newspapers also list upcoming events, fun rides, and tours. In California, publications such as *California Bicyclist* and *City Sports* are free and widely available in bike shops, sporting-goods stores, loose gyms, and health clubs. *City Sports* began in San Francisco in 1973 and has since successfully expanded its operations to Los Angeles, San Diego, New York, and Boston.

Regional park departments are also a good source of information on local bike trails.

Other great resources are friends and other cyclists. Most cyclists like to share their adventure tales and tips on hot rides.

Club Riding

If you see a group riding along and all the riders are wearing the same jersey, it's probably a cycling club out for a spin. Club riding is a lot of fun. It's a great way to meet other cyclists in your area, learn new routes, and improve your bike-handling skills. Club rides are often casual, and you can pick up effective cycling tips and product and equipment reviews from fellow cyclists. If you want to be a stronger cyclist, riding with other people is the best thing you can do. Making an appointment to ride with others helps ensure that you'll really get out there. Most people find that when riding in a group, they ride harder and faster than they would if they were alone. Besides the pleasant company of new riding partners, most people feel more comfortable going new places in a group. There is safety in numbers: there's less of a chance of getting lost and almost always someone to help with mechanical problems, should they arise.

In club riding, the more experienced members teach the novices the bike-handling skills required for safe riding in a group. Stronger riders help the beginners by doing the things someone else once did for them. They urge novices to keep going on hills. They mix up the glucose when a newcomer bonks. They pass on tips.

If you are interested in joining a club, the first thing you should know is if it's a racing or a touring club. If it's a racing club, most of the rides will tend to be brisk training rides, and participants are expected to have excellent bike-handling skills. Although the touring-club rides tend to be more relaxed, you can definitely get a good workout. Club rides are usually designated by mileage, pace, and degree of difficulty. They range from novice rides for beginners, to touring, moderate, and brisk. Those who think all "tourists" are slow have another thing coming! Some of the toughest and fastest rides I've ever been on were those of a local "touring" club. Although most clubs are for either touring or racing, some, like the Davis Bike Club, in Davis, California, offer both. The Davis Bike Club has a first-rate racing team and also manages to put on one of the best supported citizens' events, the Davis Double Century.

Some clubs offer a novice series to teach new riders safe and efficient riding techniques. Some also offer group training for cyclists preparing for their first century.

Bike club activities also extend beyond the road. Typically, a club will meet once a month to discuss business, talk about future projects and rides, and enjoy entertainment. The meetings are social as well as educational. Often there are presentations on nutrition, winter training, and other cycling information. Club members and guests show slides of summer adventures and talk about their various accomplishments. Many clubs get together for holiday parties and annual celebrations. Bike clubs also work on issues relating to cyclists' rights, access to streets, legislation, and networking. Your club might help you keep track of your mileage on club events, provide discounts at local shops, or get involved with Christmas charity work or other projects.

Sound like fun? Timid about going out on your first club ride? Many people, women especially, have a hard time going out on club rides. They tend to be intimidated by riding in groups or they are afraid of not keeping up. I was intimidated at first. Friends signed me up with the Grizzly Peak Cyclists, which I'd heard was a really hard-core club. On one of my first rides, I got stuck in my toe clips and fell into the ride leader's wheel at a stop, which was not exactly a big confidence builder. But there were all levels of riders in the club and they helped me get strong and fast in a hurry. If you are nervous at first, try going on a club ride on the buddy system—make sure there's someone else out there at about your ability level and stick together.

Photo by Greg Siple/Bikecentennial

JEAN DUKES AND FAMILY

Jean, 46, her husband, Charles, and her daughters, Sara Beth, 16, and Caroline, 8, from Barnesville, Georgia, rode the TransAmerica Trail from Oregon to Virginia by way of tandem bicycles.

"The trip was harder than I expected it would be. We were in good shape physically before we left, but I don't think there is anything that can prepare you for long hours in the saddle for 90 days.

"It was a great adventure, and yes, I would do it again. Cycling with children on tandems definitely has its advantages: It's difficult for them to fight with each other!"

Novice Series

Many bike clubs offer a novice series for new riders. These rides benefit new riders because they help them learn cycling skills, and they also benefit the club by attracting new members and developing their skill level. Clubs that don't offer such classes should be encouraged to do so. Some bike shops also offer such classes. Again, this is good for the shop and the riders. They get to see the equipment other riders have. They can compare components, those funny shoes and shorts, gearing, and toe clips. They see helmets and computers and might decide to upgrade equipment or even buy a new bike. Novice class members often become customers.

Novice rides are usually about 10 to 30 miles long, and are slow and casual. They help riders learn how to handle the bikes by giving them practice going uphill and downhill and riding in a group. They can

Photo by Greg Siple/Bikecentennial

CYNDY BRAUN

Cyndy, 38, a high school Latin and French teacher from Missoula, Montana, bicycled 250 miles from Ennis, Montana, to Missoula. She rode most of the way alone.

"I've traveled alone on short trips of up to 10 days. I'm hooked on traveling solo. It's demanding but rewarding on a multitude of levels. It's physically challenging because I ride farther and faster when I'm alone. The sense of being independent and self-sufficient are what keep me going while I'm on the road."

also help novices learn to deal with public transportation. Some clubs show novices how they can make use of local public transportation. You can get to know routes and compare the difficulty of hills on other rides through novice rides. And someone inevitably gets a flat, so you'll learn how to fix and replace the tube and tire.

Some clubs also set up a series of rides before a club century. The goal may be to ride 50 miles or 100 kilometers. This gives new riders a chance to see the course, read the map, and gauge the difficulty of the climbs and the pace. These rides often have two experienced ride leaders, one for the front and another to bring up the rear, fix flats, and make sure everyone stays on course and no one gets lost.

Century Rides

Century rides, rides of 100 miles, are very popular all over the country. In some areas you might find one, or sometimes two, every weekend. Generally, the century is run by a bike club, which charges $10 to $25 as a fundraiser for charity or for profit or to pay for food at designated "feed stations."

Century rides are not races. Most participants are out to finish and have a good time. Some of them take these nonraces much more seriously, and try for the fastest ride. But generally, that's not the purpose of century rides. They're really for fun, so riders should go as fast or as slow as is comfortable and not be intimidated by others who want to ride for personal records. Most of the time, a ride such as the Chico Wildflower Century in Chico, California, follows beautiful routes, so it would be a shame not to enjoy the scenery along the way. Usually, centuries have 25-mile, 50-mile, 100-kilometer, and 100-mile options. On the other hand, they sometimes offer 200-kilometer and Double or Triple Centuries for those who can't get enough cycling to fill up the day.

Century rides offer a lot of support. There are rest stops every 15 to 25 miles where you can get water, refreshments, food, and encouragement. The sag wagon comes along to help with mechanical difficulties, injuries, or pooped-out riders. You'll get a route sheet and map detailing directions and sometimes providing a profile of the topography that can warn you when the next hills are coming up. Usually you'll also find signs posted or spray painted on the road indicating

Photo by Dana Davis

Most century rides award patches to participants upon completion of the ride. They're colorful and fun to collect.

when you have to turn. You might also get a T-shirt or patch at the end of the ride.

Centuries draw anywhere from a few hundred to a few thousand participants, of all ages and abilities. They are great places to meet others who share the same love of the outdoors, of being fit, and of riding a bike. You start to see the same people week after week, and a spirit of camaraderie develops that leads to many lasting friendships. Sometimes there is a barbeque or get-together at the end of the century, so the whole thing is a lot of fun.

Tips for Enjoying Century Rides:

1. *Come prepared.* Wear appropriate clothes, those you're comfortable in. Don't test-ride new shoes on a century! Take the weather into consideration. Eat a good breakfast. Get a good night's sleep (the day before, too). And take responsibility for yourself: learn to read the maps, so you'll be sure of where you're going and won't get lost.

2. *Check your bike.* Make sure your bike is in good working order. Don't wait until you get to the bike check at the century ride to notice that the tires are bald. Go to your bike shop or ask a friend to help you make sure everything—including brakes, chain, cables, and saddle—is in shape before the ride. Practice changing a flat tire. Ride your bike the day before the century to double-check it.

3. *Pace yourself.* Pace yourself so you can go the distance. Take into consideration how you feel and how much you have been riding. If you signed up for 25 miles and feel great, you might want to try to make 50 miles. Likewise, if you feel a bit tired after a late night, maybe you should do 100 kilometers rather than 100 miles. Going out too hard on one ride means it takes longer to recover and ride again. That takes the joy out of cycling and could lead to burnout faster. Riding to exhaustion also leads to errors in judgment and could cause accidents. You might find, though, that you'll be more likely to try to go the distance in century rides, like the Cinderella Classic in northern California, than on your own because there is backup and someone to look after you should you have trouble. That's part of the fee.

4. *"Eat before you're hungry; drink before you're thirsty."* Little meals and snacks at rest stops all day are the best. If you're cycling to lose weight, don't starve on the century ride. You'll lose water weight that will come back as soon as you drink liquids. If you don't eat enough, you'll just bonk, a cycling term that means you'll lose energy and feel miserable. It's best to carry food—bananas, dried fruits, nuts—with you to be on the safe side. Sometimes the mileage between the stops is off, rest stops run out of food, or other problems develop that keep you from eating when you expect to.

5. *Enjoy the scenery, the physical and psychological challenge, and the people around you. This is supposed to be fun!!!*

Tips for Riding in Groups:

1. *Relax.* If you're not used to riding in groups, it can be scary at first. The best advice is to relax and ride at the back until you feel more confident. Mass-start events—and there are fewer and fewer of them—let the hotshots go out first.

2. *Pay attention to the riders and traffic around you.* Avoid overlapping wheels. If you hit another person's back wheel, YOU will go

down. If there's someone who is squirrely or unpredictable, move away. Be especially aware at the beginning of mass-start events. People are excited as events begin, some are anxious to get a fast start, and there are frequently flat tires and other mechanical problems, with resultant crashes. When overtaking another rider, try to pass on the left, and say "on your left" so the other rider is aware of you. Hold a straight line. When going downhill, don't follow other riders too closely; leave plenty of space. Only pass downhill when you have to. In tight situations, a rider will sometimes touch another rider to let him/her know she's there. Don't be surprised if you get touched, and don't jump to the wrong conclusion.

3. *Drafting.* When I first started riding centuries I was training for triathlons, and drafting or riding in the slipstream of a front rider is a no-no in those events. After a few weeks, some friends showed me how much energy I could save and how much faster I could ride if I learned to draft, or ride a wheel. In the wake of another rider, there is less wind resistance, so there is a 10–25 percent energy savings at 20 mph, and at 30 mph, 30–40 percent savings. When you get the hang of it, a pace line (a line of riders who take turns riding in the front of a pack) can be a lot of fun. It feels good working together with other cyclists to post a fast time.

But drafting isn't for everyone. Someone may be strong but not a good bike handler, in which case drafting could cause a crash. Most experienced riders practice with people they know before following anyone closely. Try drafting only when you feel comfortable with your bike handling skills and your ability to ride in close quarters with others.

BICYCLE TOURING

Bike touring is one of the best ways to see the country, both the country near your home and foreign countries as well. Traveling by bike is a complete physical and social experience. You can hear the birds, smell the different flowers and grasses, and feel the wind, rain, or sun on your face as you pedal along. Wherever your tour may lead, you have the advantage of experiencing everything more closely on a bicycle than you could just buzzing by in a car. You can get to know the people and landscape better. Stopping at a café or grocery store to

Photo by Greg Siple/Bikecentennial

ANDREA COLNES

Andrea, 26, of North Caldwell, New Jersey, and her husband, Barry, traveled through 25 countries by bicycle, totaling 22,300 miles.

"We've said, 'We couldn't have done this trip alone.' Yet there is a strong sense of personal accomplishment. We have cycled all the miles on our own, overcoming our own battles with fatigue, weather, and mountains. It is quite a feeling to be able to say, 'I've cycled 22,300 miles around the world!' Would we do it again? You bet!"

talk with local residents is a great way to get to know a little bit more about how they think and what's important to them. The bicycle becomes a conversation piece. Most people have respect for the independence and effort it takes to bicycle from place to place. Even if you've gone only 30 miles, a common response is "Gosh, that's even a long drive in a car!"

There are a lot of different types of tours. Some travel only a few miles a day and allow for lots of time in museums or sight-seeing. At the other extreme, Lon & Sue Haldeman's RapiTours has taken groups 3,000 miles across the country in 14 days. Some tours are strictly for women. You can organize your own trip or sign up for a

Photo by Greg Siple/Bikecentennial

NANCY PRICE

Nancy, 37, an Australian, took an extended summer leave from her job in Victoria to ride the TransAmerica Trail from Astoria, Oregon, to Richmond, Virginia, with an organized Bikecentennial tour group.

"Riding along a country road out in the 'backblocks' of Kansas or Wyoming with not another human being in sight and letting your mind wander at will has a lot to be said for it. I think I was the only member of the group who actually enjoyed Kansas, hard as it was. Perhaps it reminded me of the wheatlands of northwestern Victoria."

commercial tour. A general rule of thumb is that the more you do for yourself, the cheaper it will be. There is a wide range of possibilities:

1. The fully loaded, self-supporting tour. You carry all your own stuff in panniers on the bikes and travel in low gears. Special considerations may include where you'll pitch your tent at night and whether you'll have enough water to make your morning tea.
2. The lightly loaded tour. This type relies on a support car to shuttle sleeping gear to a campground or a motel for the night.
3. The credit-card tour. In this type, you ride the bike and just tell the tour staff what kind of wine you want with dinner.

Whether you're planning your own tour or choosing a commercial one, there are a few things you should think about. You need to know how much time and money you have available and generally where you want to go. Do you want to use a road bike or a mountain bike; do you plan to buy a new bike or rent one? It's also important to consider your level of fitness, the terrain, and the number of miles you want to ride. Is this a training vacation or are you planning on cycling into shape? Do you want the emphasis to be on cycling or are there other activities such as sight-seeing or visiting museums that you'd like to incorporate into the tour?

After you decide where you want to go and how strenuous you want the tour to be, you need to consider logistics. If you're choosing a commercial tour, most of the logistics in terms of route selection, maps, and passport information will be worked out for you. When planning your own tour, routes, road accessibility, and traffic are all areas you will have to think about.

Your friends, club members, and other cyclists can recommend routes, specific tours, and hot spots to visit. Cycling and outdoor magazines, *Women's Sports & Fitness* magazine, and the outdoor sections of metropolitan newspapers are all good sources of information on commercial bike tours. American Youth Hostels, Bikecentennial, and the League of American Wheelmen are helpful, knowledgeable resources you can use when planning and selecting your next tour.

Photos courtesy of Debra Harse

Debra Harse relaxing on a pier during one of her cycling adventures in South America. Her $200 Panasonic is well traveled and reliable.

DEBRA HARSE
WORLD TRAVELER

Debra Harse is 31 years old, was born and raised in New York City, and has extensive touring experience. She works for half of the year and takes off with her $200 Panasonic 10-speed for the other six months, subletting her apartment while she is gone.

Debra's adventures have taken her to Europe, Africa, South America, Puerto Rico, and as I write, she is traveling in Nepal and Tibet.

At her home in Manhattan, I talked with Debra about her touring experiences abroad.

Q: How did you get into cycling?
A: For a long time, swimming was my main sport. I was just using the bike for transportation, riding to the beach and this and that. And then I just got an idea—I said, "A year from now I'm going to go to Europe." And I did. That whole summer before, I trained with the New York Cycle Club and AYH in transportation alternatives.

Q: Were you prepared for the cultural differences abroad?

A: I think being a Manhattan cyclist has me geared up for anything.

When I look back at all the places I've been, Third World cycling is so different from cycling in Europe. I've gone through Egypt, Morocco, India, Nepal, and Sri Lanka. These areas are so densely populated that a point of interest comes along every 15 minutes. There's somebody with a basket on their head or washing clothes in a stream. And there's animals, lots of animals, like monkeys and elephants. It was wonderful to ride along and see elephants, just hanging out by the road.

Q: Did you do this by yourself?

A: I traveled with a friend in India and Sri Lanka and again in Egypt, but I've traveled by myself in other countries.

Q: What are some things a woman should consider when traveling alone?

A: It depends on where you are. Before I went to India, I went to the tourism bureau and asked them point-blank, am I going to offend these people's sense of values and their culture if I am a white woman in shorts? And they said no. And sure enough, it was true. Since the British were there for 250 years, it's an English-speaking country. Even when I was cycling in the north en route to Nepal and going through small villages, there was always someone there who spoke English.

Q: Were you ever frightened as a woman traveling alone?

A: In general, if you are confident and matter-of-fact, you are less likely to be bothered. But, it varies.

Q: What clothes did you take?

A: I didn't take any specific bike clothes with me. In trying to travel light, I wanted shorts that I could wear to the beach and go sightseeing in as well as ride my bike in. I haven't gotten any rashes or anything from anything I've worn.

I never took bike shoes because I always wanted to wear sneakers during the day. I'd say you want to go low-tech, because if you want to tour these parts of the world, just by virtue of having bought a plane ticket, you are very wealthy to these people and that's not what you want.

Q: What kind of bike do you take abroad?

A: I take my $200 Panasonic clunker, which I love dearly.

Q: What kinds of bike parts and tools do you carry?

A: You see bike shops abroad but often they're for a different kind of bike. India has this whole autonomy thing, in every aspect. So they produce all their own equipment and it only fits their bicycles. I buy new tires before I go; tires are supposed to last about 3,000 miles, and they usually do.

Q: You don't take tires with you on the trip?

A: No. I've got a guardian angel that works overtime. I think, though, if it came down to it, I would probably be able to get a 27¼-inch tire somewhere, even if they had to order it and I was stuck somewhere for two weeks. I think that would be about the worst that could happen.

I have heard of people who took motorcycles and were stuck places for months waiting for spare parts.

Q: What kind of gearing did you use?

A: I have a granny gear, a 34. I think it's 40–52 in the front and a 14–34 in the back. I like to have some very low gears so I can ride up any mountain.

Q: So you can get up just about anything with that?

A: Sitting down even. You have to be able to use low gears, no matter how strong you are, because you're carrying a lot of weight, and often you didn't get enough sleep, or it's hot, or whatever.

Q: Have you also cycled through South America?

A: Yes, from January to June of '86. I lived for six months on something like $3,000 including taking internal flights when I really wanted to see something and my time was limited.

Q: You'd hop on a little local plane?

A: Right. The interesting thing is they don't charge you to fly a bike. It's usually a 25-kilo limit, and even my clunker is only 14 kilos. What I would do is take all my heavy things—my shoes, my sweaters, my books, and bottles of things like shampoo—and put them in my handlebar bag and carry that on the plane. Then I'd take all my lightweight clothing and check it. So, I would carry the heavy stuff on the plane and check the bicycle and the other stuff, and I'd never be charged for being overweight.

Q: Have you ever been to Western Europe?

A: Well, I traveled through Holland and it was a rough trip. The signs for the bike paths are ambiguous. Some crossings aren't marked at all. If the sun isn't shining, which it often isn't in Holland, you can't get any sense of direction. Also, Holland is flat, and the winds come sweeping across those plains. And all those picturesque canals are covered with insects. I remember coming to the end of a day of cycling, and I had bugs in my eyelids, in my ears, and along all the lines of my clothing. So don't be fooled by those canals; they're full of gnats.

And it rains. Sometimes I was going down the road and saw an exit or an entry ramp to a highway, and I just stood there with my thumb out.

Q: I suppose you need to be flexible and change plans if necessary.

A: Yes. For me, touring is not an athletic endeavor and I don't feel compelled to ride every mile. If it's not working I pack it in.

Q: What kind of cycling do you do in this country?

A: I go over the George Washington Bridge and up the Hudson, usually through Rockland County. That's usually all I do with the bike, some riding around 6 o'clock in the evening. And I also commute everyday.

Q: What are your thoughts on cyclists and commuting?

A: As of late, cyclists are taking a lot of criticism for being road hazards. Sometimes I come to an intersection and see someone who's on the defensive concerning cyclists. I just stop and I give them a big smile and they smile back. So I feel like I have to be a diplomat for cyclists. We're not all crazy and we do stop at the lights.

Commuting by bike enables me to maximize my day. I have three or four things I have to do in the course of the day, and my bicycle takes me directly from point A to point B to point C to point D. Whereas, if you're using public transportation, you have to walk, which is slower of course, to the station. Wait for the train. The train takes you to the next station, which is not exactly where you want to be, and then you have to walk from there. So, as extensive as the public transportation is here, it's still not as direct. You have to invest a lot more time.

Q: So what keeps you traveling?

A: I guess because I have so much fun all the time it makes me want to do it more. But it's also curiosity. I like going to different places. It's changed my life. It's made my political views pretty strong too. I think it's deplorable how ignorant Americans are. Not stupid, but very ignorant about the issues.

I've had some incredible experiences. I'll tell my grandchildren about the time I raced a Bedouin on a camel. I ran into him in the desert, and it seemed a natural thing that we should race. I passed the camel on an incline, but he passed me again on the descent. And then the Bedouin just took off back into the dunes and waved goodbye while I've watched the whole desert turn lavender at sunset.

Not everyone craves the extensive experience Debra has had with bicycle touring. However, I hope her story as well as those of the other women profiled will motivate you to consider touring on some level. Bicycle touring offers experiences and adventures not available through any other means.

Touring Resources

American Youth Hostels, Inc. (AYH)
National Offices
PO Box 37613
Washington, DC 20013-7613
(202) 783-6161

The purpose of the AYH is to promote a positive understanding of the world and its people by offering year-round housing accommodations to travelers of all nationalities. Hostels are located in urban and rural areas. Many of the hostel facilities are old farmhouses, converted hotels, renovated mansions, or old lighthouses. The hostels provide kitchen facilities, common rooms for lounging and socializing, and separate dormitory-style bunkrooms for men and women. Visitors are expected to help with the general housekeeping of the hostel by doing a brief chore each morning. Regional AYH councils also offer a variety of outdoor, recreational, and educational programs. These include various one- or multi-day bicycle trips and hiking adventures. There are also youth activities and an Elderhostel program for senior citizens. The accommodations and prices vary, but the usual rates range from $5 to $10 per night for members, with an additional $3 charge for nonmembers.

AYH membership benefits include: the *AYH Handbook, Knapsack* magazine, AYH local council newsletters, access to ride leader and hostel manager training courses, and discounts on various travel books and travel accommodations. The AYH is part of an international network called the International Youth Hostel Federation. AYH offices in large cities provide travel services for AYH members, including discounted air reservations.

AYH Publications

The *AYH Handbook* lists all the current hostels in the United States. There are 250 American Youth Hostels, mostly congregated on the East and West Coasts, and 5,000 hostels in 67 countries outside the United States. The handbook is updated annually.

World Adventure lists organized, low-cost trips put on by AYH throughout the United States and the world. This includes a variety of bike trips with various levels of support.

Bikecentennial
Bicycle Travel Association
PO Box 8308-S
Missoula, MT 59807-9988
(406) 721-1776

BIKECENTENNIAL'S NATIONAL BICYCLE TRAIL NETWORK

Bikecentennial started out as a transcontinental bicycle event celebrating the bicentennial in 1976. It had 4,000 participants. Since that time, Bikecentennial has served as a clearinghouse of information on bicycle touring of all kinds. Bikecentennial also offers a variety of 31 tours from fully loaded self-sufficient, to van supported, to light touring (involving staying in hotels). The tours range from 5 to 90 days in length. If you are planning your own trip, Bikecentennial can be a good source of routes and maps. Bikecentennial is also involved in advocacy on legal matters pertaining to cyclists.

Bikecentennial Publications

The Cyclists' Yellow Pages is a very useful resource. It includes a complete state-by-state listing of map and bike route information, an extensive bibliography of cycling books on a variety of subjects, a list of tour operators, information on mountain biking, and a listing of 15 established interstate Bikecentennial routes covering a 16,000 mile National Bicycle Touring Route Network. Canadian and overseas listings are also included.

BikeReport, the magazine of Bikecentennial, focuses on adventure stories of active tourists. It is published nine times a year.

June Siple, of Missoula, Montana, is seen here riding in the Andes Mountains of central Peru. June became the first woman to ride the length of the hemisphere in 1972–75 when she cycled from Alaska to Argentina with her husband, Greg. June and Greg are cofounders, with Dan and Lys Burden, of Bikecentennial.

Hemistour photo by Greg Siple

League of American Wheelmen (LAW)
6707 Whitestone Road, Suite 209
Baltimore, MD 21207
(301) 944-3399

LEAGUE OF
AMERICAN WHEELMEN
SINCE 1880

LAW, established in 1880 in Newport, Rhode Island, is the oldest national bicycle organization in the United States. Members of LAW were behind the Good Roads Movement that resulted in the first system of paved roads in America. The roads were originally paved for bicyclists, *not* motorists. In the late 1880s, LAW worked with New York City to ensure bicyclists access to Central Park.

For 108 years, LAW has been the largest advocacy group for cyclists. Currently, LAW has 500 clubs as members, representing over 160,000 individuals. LAW has a very strong grass roots base of support. Many LAW volunteers help staff the 73 time stations for the annual Race Across AMerica.

Activities and Services

Government and Advocacy. LAW has a lobbyist in Washington, DC and a strong grass roots network of volunteers at the state and local levels working on issues related to cyclists and their rights. LAW, along with other cycling organizations, recently sued New York City for bicycle access to three congested thoroughfares in midtown Manhattan during peak working hours. LAW has worked with the National Traffic Highway Safety Commission on federal funding for bicycle-related projects. LAW is currently working with the National Park Service on regional guidelines for bicycling in the national parks. At the state and local level, LAW has volunteers to help cyclists interpret the traffic laws in their particular state.

Touring Service. LAW maintains a network of volunteers in each state to help cyclists plan tours. LAW also helps foster camaraderie among cyclists through a network of hospitality homes in each state.

Effective Cycling Program. This service promotes safety through education. LAW certifies instructors for its Effective Cycling courses, which have been taken by approximately five to ten thousand people.

Historical Information. LAW maintains and makes available various doctoral and master's theses covering topics related to the history of bicycling.

LAW Publications

Bicycle USA, LAW's magazine, is published nine times a year. It covers a broad range of topics, including health issues, commuting, racing, off-road riding, and adventure touring. It also includes updates of LAW's lobbying and advocacy efforts, the largest ride calendar in the United States, and new product reviews.

Tour Finder lists all the commercial touring companies in the world. This publication tells you everything you ever wanted to know about touring, including information about off-road touring, touring with children, seasonal tours, and prices and accommodations. The publication costs $4.00, and is updated annually.

Almanac is LAW's yearbook of cycling. It lists all bicycle and touring clubs and volunteers in the United States, state by state. It provides specific information on each state's traffic laws, national organizations, and resources. It also recommends where to tour.

6
Cycling for Transportation

"I think I shall stick to my bike," said Christopher. "The bicycle is the most civilized conveyance known to man. Other forms of transport grow daily more nightmarish. Only the bicycle remains pure in heart."
—Iris Murdoch, *The Red and The Green*

Commuting by bicycle can be a rewarding experience. It's a good form of daily exercise, ecologically sound, and an economical form of transportation. A good ride to the office can make you feel energetic and productive. Statistics show that when the workplace is five miles or less from the home, commuting times for a bike and a car are about the same. If you normally use public transportation, the bike may actually be faster for short distances.

It is estimated that there are now over one-half million bicycle commuters in the U.S. Some communities are taking steps to encourage and enhance bicycle commuting by installing bike paths or routes. In San Francisco, the California Department of Transportation began to subsidize a shuttle to take bicycle commuters across the San Francisco Bay in 1977. Since then, 128,000 transbay trips have been made.

Although bicycle commuting is becoming more acceptable as a means of getting to and from work, it does have its drawbacks and it may not be practical for everyone. Coordinating child care, matters of dress, your working hours, and proximity to the job are all things you'll have to consider. In this chapter you'll meet two women who have successfully integrated bicycling to work into their active lifestyles.

131

EQUIPMENT

The purpose of good equipment is to provide comfort, safety, and reliability. Safety is a crucial factor when considering various types of equipment.

Many people use old bikes or clunkers for transportation purposes. These get more wear and tear than their weekend bikes and are set up with equipment you wouldn't normally need for a century ride or a race. On the other hand, I know women who use mountain bikes to accommodate both their daily commute and weekend rides.

Whatever bike you decide to use, you're going to want sturdy wheels and heavy tires. You'll invariably encounter potholes and glass while riding on city streets, and robust equipment will help avoid frequent flats and dinged rims. A basket or rack is handy for carrying clothes, lunch, and other items. A touring pannier made of waterproof material is a good way to keep parcels and clothes dry in case of rain. For wet weather, you'll probably also want fenders.

Probably the most essential equipment for the commuter is a good lighting system. Nothing is more important for you than to see and be seen. In most cases, motorists are not looking for cyclists so you have to let them know you are there. Pete Penseyres, winner of the 1984 and 1986 RAAMs and holder with Lon Haldeman of the transcontinental tandem record, commutes nearly every day. Pete recommends the Kearney Lighting System. It is quite expensive (in the several-hundred dollar range, depending on which system is chosen), but worth every dollar, according to Pete. It is a very reliable, rechargeable battery system which provides front and rear lights that some claim are nearly as good as an automobile. The Velo-Lux rechargeable that Ellen Fletcher uses is comparable. For those of you who don't want to spend that much on a lighting system, there are many generator systems such as the Sanyo and Union that work just fine. Union also has a great battery back-up pack that keeps your front and rear lights illuminated when you come to a stop. The battery even recharges itself as you ride. Cat-Eye makes strap-on front and tail lights, but they're only marginally adequate for the regular commuter.

In addition to a headlight and taillights, it's a good idea to use a lot of reflective material. Reflective tape on the rear chainstays, crank arms, in the wheel, and on your helmet and shoes is a good idea.

Reflective vests and a flashing belt beacon are also highly visible. When you get your system together, it's a good idea to ask a friend to observe you from different angles to make sure you're highly visible. Often drivers are looking for large objects and bright lights. Be sure they can see you clearly from a safe distance.

A good lock is an essential piece of equipment, especially if you can't take your bike inside. A sturdy lock like the Kryptonite or Citadel is worth every penny. An extra precaution is to buy a T-pipe from the local hardware store and slip it over the tumbler end to protect the joint. When choosing a lock, make sure that it cannot be cut easily with bolt cutters. Good bike locks are designed so that the bolt cutters needed to cut the lock would be so large that no criminal is likely to have it on hand!

CHOOSING A ROUTE

More likely than not, the route you take to work by bike is not the same as the one you'd take by car. Distance, traffic patterns, the type of road (highway versus city streets), and the terrain will all affect your choice of route. When trying to determine the safest and most pleasant route, talk to other cyclists and see what roads they recommend. Cycling club members and coworkers may be able to suggest the best roads to ride. Some cities have bike maps. Or look at a street map and find roads parallel to the major arterials. Occasionally a local automobile association like the AAA will have some useful information.

Before riding to work for the first time, try one of the routes you're considering on the weekend; ride an alternate route on the way back. This will give you a rough idea of the time you'll need, as well as familiarize you with the road and terrain. If you have a friend who also rides to work, try the buddy system.

ARRIVAL

Once you arrive at work, you need to think about storing your bike and getting yourself prepared for the job. While some companies offer bike storage lockers and special facilities in which to lock your bike, most don't, and few have even thought about it. Cyclists should ask about the option of keeping their bike in their workspace. If the only way to get there is by elevator, make sure it's OK to haul your bicycle in a passenger elevator. Perhaps a back room or a storage closet would be options if the company would rather not have the bicycle visible. Perhaps your employer would consider installing a bike rack. As a last resort, you can lock your bike to a tree, lightpost, or other sturdy structure. If you have quick-release wheels or a quick-release mountain-bike saddle and seatpost, taking your front wheel and saddle with you will reduce the chance of theft.

There are many women who commute by bicycle who can be role models. Two of them are Ruth Tobey and Ellen Fletcher.

Photo by Dana Davis

Ruth Tobey on her way to work. Ruth likes to commute on her "ladies' "-frame bike rather than a standard frame so she can wear skirts and dresses comfortably while riding. Notice the lock, reflectors, and headlight.

RUTH TOBEY
BICYCLE COMMUTER

Ruth has been riding to work on a bike for 18 years. She began commuting to work in April 1970 as part of the National Earth Day activities. It was a day to do something for ecology. Riding to work instead of taking the bus or driving the car seemed like a good idea. At the time, Ruth was living in Minneapolis, Minnesota, and commuted three to four miles to work. Since that time, Ruth has moved to the San Francisco Bay Area, where she continued commuting five to seven miles to downtown Oakland. Now she commutes a couple of miles to the University of California, Berkeley, where she works as the business manager for the Department of Electrical Engineering and Computer Science. Ruth is married and has two teenage children. She got her husband, Alan, into bicycle commuting a number of years ago, and the whole family enjoys recreational fun rides and centuries on the weekends.

Ruth commutes on a "ladies' bike" or "mixte frame" because her job demands that she wear a skirt and blouse. Ruth handles the wardrobe situation by riding slowly and giving herself plenty of time to get to work so she doesn't perspire too heavily. Ruth told me she has ridden to work in a three-piece suit, complete with heels and stockings, and handled it fine.

Ruth stays off the major arterial streets and does not take the bike if it's raining heavily. For lights she uses a Cat-Eye headlight and an ankle light, but is looking for a better system.

The morning commute is "better than a second cup of coffee and good for your health and your head." According to Tobey, "commuting is cheap and addicting." Ruth finds that she can save $1.50 a day in parking fees by riding two miles to work and having fun at the same time. When she commuted to work in Oakland, Ruth found herself stopping at intersections with fellow workers in their cars. A few minutes later, she'd see them again in the office elevator. "It was just as fast on a bike," she noted. "I'd see them out there hunting for parking places, and then again as we walked into the office together." Ruth keeps the bike in her office.

Ruth's final words: "I just wish more people would get out there and try riding to work. It's a lot of fun."

Ellen Fletcher campaigning by bicycle for Palo Alto city council in 1978.

ELLEN FLETCHER
COUNCILWOMAN AND
BICYCLE COMMUTER

Ellen Fletcher is a woman whose personal preference for cycling has led her into situations where she effectively improves cycling for an entire community.

Ellen Fletcher was born in Berlin, Germany. She came to the United States and received her education here. She now lives in Palo Alto, California.

A city councilmember, Ellen owns four bicycles, any one of which she might pedal 20 miles across town to a meeting. She also commutes to and from her job by bicycle. Her 27-year-old car is hardly ever used.

Ellen doesn't consider herself a competitive cyclist, but she did win first prize in her age category (over 45) in a bike-a-thon about four years go. She urges bicyclists to get involved in their local government as a way to improve conditions for commuting and recreational cycling.

We discussed her involvement in cycling at her Palo Alto home.

Q: *How did you get into cycling?*

A: I was born in Berlin, and my early years were spent in the Nazi era. Being in the middle of the city, I don't remember seeing bicyclists. Kids didn't have bicycles automatically the way they do now.

I left Germany when I was 10 years old. I was sent to a foster family in Yorkshire, England, in a suburban area where the kids had bicycles. Of course I immediately wanted a bicycle. My foster mother said "No, no, you can't have a bicycle, it's much too dangerous." But I did get some school pals to let me try their bikes, and I really loved it. My foster mother eventually did let me use her bicycle, and in essence it became my bike. I used that bicycle just for normal transportation. I'd go out in the evenings and take long rides in the English countryside. It gets dark quite late in England so I'd go to neighboring towns. I remember going to Beverly, going to Minster. It was very picturesque. Anyway, that was my normal form of transportation in England.

I eventually left England and went to New York City in May of 1946. My mother and stepfather had left Germany just before war broke out with the United States and settled in New York. I joined them in a crowded apartment building in the Bronx. I went to a job during the day and to high school at night since I had never been to high school even though I was almost 18 years old. I was just horrified at the crush of people in the buses and subways, and I thought that was so uncomfortable. So I decided I was going to use a bicycle in the Bronx. I bought myself a three-speed, a Raleigh, I believe. This was in 1947 or, '48, and it was very, very rare to see someone ride a bicycle. The cars weren't that numerous right after the war. You lived in the central city or on the edges of the city and there was good transportation, so I don't remember any particular traffic problems.

Q: *If there weren't many bikes, there were probably even fewer women riding.*

A: I don't remember that as being an issue. Actually, there were some other bicyclists although they were very rare, because the AYH (American Youth Hostels) ran bicycle trips, mostly day trips. I joined AYH, in fact, and went on some weekend trips. By that time I had a Holdsworth lightweight drop-handlebar bicycle. It was a 5-speed, had a 5-speed Strumey-Archer hub. I bought that from a bicyclist who made it a practice of going to England every summer for vacation, buying bicycles, and selling them out of his garage. I was really, really thrilled with my Holdsworth, and was really afraid of losing it. Eventually I got insurance for it from Lloyd's of London. This was in New York, maybe around 1950. I did lots of day trips after that, down into New Jersey, and through New England.

Q: Did you ride a lot by yourself? Or with AYH?

A: My recreational trips were pretty much with youth hostels, and during the week, I used my bike for normal utilitarian trips.

In 1958 I married, and my husband wasn't a bicyclist. Gradually my biking diminished somewhat. We moved to California, we had a baby and two others followed. The oldest is Linda, who has just turned 31 years old, and the youngest is Jeff, who is 25. The second one is Terry, who, I must say, is the only one of my children who is also a bike freak. She is the one who became a bike messenger in San Francisco, she's done extensive touring, and, of course, she uses her bicycle for commuting. What I was going to say is that once we were in California and had children, it didn't occur to me that bicycling was still practical. In a moment that I will regret forever, I traded my Holdsworth bicycle for a 3-speed man's bicycle. I thought my cycling days were over; after all, how could I ride a Holdsworth when I had three little kids? I just must have been insane for a few minutes. My husband did a little bit of very minor bicycling and to keep up I bought myself a bicycle. It turned out that I used it quite extensively.

Q: Were you using it to do errands and everything?

A: I was already getting active in politics and found that it was the most ideal way to do precinct work where you go knocking on doors. You could ride your bike all the way up the driveway, practically through the front door of each house. It wasn't like parking a car at one end of a block and then having to waste time going back to the other end to pick your car up when you finished. I got a little kiddie seat for one child and a tricycle for the next one up and so on.

But as I got back into bicycling more and more, strangely enough, I set limits for myself. I said well, I can go this far, like two miles, but nothing beyond that; that's too far to ride a bicycle. I'm sure all bicyclists who aren't really into bicycling yet, people who use their bicycles sporadically, set themselves limits to how far they can ride. But then, gradually, my limits got to be further. I think, to begin with, it was just curiosity on my part, wondering if I could get as far as Menlo Park, which is about six miles away. What got me really going was the gas shortage. In 1977–78, when people stood in gas lines, I thought it was ridiculous. Standing in a gas line is something that doesn't appeal to me at all. I decided I was just going to go by bike wherever I needed to go. I have quite a few meetings in San Jose, which is 15 miles away, and I found it was fun biking there. That really opened bicycling up for me.

Actually, before that even, I was a member of the Santa Clara Bicycle Association. I was more into the political aspect of bicycling. What happened was that when my little boy started elementary school, the PTA was looking for the safety chairman, and I thought this was an opportunity for me to have some impact on his route to school. He rode his bike to school and I wanted to be sure there were no danger points. So I volunteered to be safety chairman and became very active in the cause of bicycling safety. So I was appointed by the PTA council to be the PTA representative on the city bicycle advisory committee. Within a fairly short time, I was chair of the bicycle advisory committee and got into a lot of the bicycle parking issues.

Along with Mike Bullock, another member of SCVBA (Santa Clara Valley Bicycle Association), I wrote what was then known as the position paper on bicycle parking for that organization. That position paper went into several editions, the last of which was the sixth edition of 1983. When the city of Palo Alto became involved in upgrading its general plan for the first time in 20 years, I used that position paper very effectively to persuade the planning commission to require bicycle parking in all developments, just as automobile parking is required. That was the recommendation to the city council. But the city council weakened it by saying bicycle parking should be encouraged. When you put that kind of language in, you know it will never happen. I got so mad, I decided I was going to run in the next city council election.

I've been on the council for 10 years now; I'm in my third term. There's talk now about limiting council members to two consecutive terms. I hate the prospect of not having my finger in the pie any longer.

Q: So, your involvement started off trying to find a nice safe route for your son to go to school and ultimately led to you running for city council?
A: You could say that.

Q: Do you ride all year long yourself?

A: Absolutely—in all weather. When I was still in New York going to college, I would ride my bicycle even when it snowed. We had a cafeteria in the basement in the college and when it snowed, I would take my bicycle and put it in the basement hallway and go upstairs. I was called to the dean's office and reprimanded for bringing my bicycle inside. When I explained the situation, I was given a special spot in the basement to keep my bicycle. So it's nothing new for me to ride in bad weather.

Q: What kind of lights would you recommend?

A: I have a Union generator set on my three-speed, but I don't think it is adequate. What I have that I think is quite adequate is the Velo-Lux system. It is battery operated, but you can bring it home and regenerate it, plug it in. You could also have the Sanyo portable generator recharge it. The drawback is that the batteries don't last awfully long, and last even less long in cold weather. So I like the generator backup just in case the batteries give out. Also, if your bulb blows, you don't have to fiddle in the dark with it because you have your generator. The problem with the generator is that generally it's not as bright as you want it, especially in the rear where you want a really bright light. And when you stop, it goes off, which I found really nerve-racking.

The other thing I have is legbands. They're the best thing to have because when you're in motion you can be seen from all sides. They are really bright. Also, I have reflective stuff stuck on my handlebar bag.

Q: Do you have a special commuting bike?

A: I have many commuting bikes, from the smallest to the most deluxe. I have a Raleigh 3-speed with baskets and an elaborate lighting system. I also have a folding bicycle that I take on the train or bus when I go to San Francisco.

Q: What are some tips for somebody who wants to commute to work? What would you recommend as far as carrying clothes with them?

A: Very often, there are opportunities to leave your clothes at the office. You just take them in on weekends or whatever. But it's not difficult to carry clothes on a bicycle. There are panniers or baskets or

Ellen Fletcher commuting by train with her HON folding bike.

Photo courtesy of California Department of Transportation

various forms of bags that can be carried on the bicycle. It's best to attach it to the bicycle. A bicycle shop can give anyone advice on how to carry loads. Ideally, of course, it would be nice to have a shower at work. Some places do have them. In Palo Alto we require our new developments to have showers. But I've gone lots of places where you have to wash in the washroom. I can't stand where they have these blower driers where you can't dry anything but your hands. In any event, you'll have to allow for the extra time, but you don't have to take extra time to go jogging or to go to the racquet club or the health club if you've used your bike to get to work instead of your car. And you don't have to pay dues at one of these health clubs.

There's really nothing like commuting by bike. It costs less than driving your own car or taking public transportation. It also does away with parking hassles. There was a survey done in what we call the Golden Triangle in Santa Clara County. They found that 2 percent of employees there use public transit and 3 percent use bicycles to get to work. I was really impressed by that. It made an impression on the powers that be in the county and there was an editorial in the paper about it.

Also, you know it isn't really hot all year long. If you dress lightly, in a cotton T-shirt and shorts, you don't always feel the need for a shower. There are circumstances where you do get a little sweaty, and you do have to wash off in the washroom. Every place has a washroom.

Q: How do you pick a route? The route that you take by car is not the same as you would take by bicycle.

A: The best trick is to find bicyclists and ask them for advice. A lot of cities have bike route maps, which aren't always the best, but they do help. At least it gets you started. You look at the map and find parallel streets to the major, heavily traveled thoroughfares. Another source of information is local bike shops.

Q: Are there any other particular obstacles as far as commuting on a bicycle?

A: The traffic is intimidating if you're not used to it. In a couple of cities, local bike groups have set up bicycle day or bicycle week. They have set up a buddy system for riding to work. If you're timid on a bicycle and you know someone who rides a bike, ask them to escort you the first time or a couple of times to get you accustomed to riding. Of course, joining a club does more than just getting you recreational rides. You ride with people who can give you tips on how to ride safely. You meet people who ride bikes who can then also give you tips on routes and tips on equipment. I think joining a bicycle club has a lot of benefits. It's a learning experience as well as an enjoyment experience. You can get a lot of information that way. I joined the Western Wheelers when I started getting involved in cycling.

Q: What would you say as far as safety is concerned? Have you had any problems yourself?

A: Not really. Once in a while when a car goes really slowly behind me I sometimes worry that they're following me, but it turns out that they were just waiting to make a right turn and they didn't want to overtake me. Once I had a flat tire and I had to walk home, and I felt a lot more vulnerable walking than being on the bicycle. I didn't have any bad experiences, but I was nervous walking.

Q: Do you think that traveling on a bicycle gives you a better understanding of local politics?

A: I think of all the things that should be done that the legislators don't see because they don't see the neighborhoods.

RESOURCES

For some valuable information about bicycle commuting, I recommend John Forrester's book, *Effective Cycling*. Forrester's book is probably the best collection of information on just what the title says: effective cycling in all aspects of the term. It has sections particularly oriented to the bicycle commuter.

The Environmental Protection Agency (EPA) has produced an excellent 15-minute videotape entitled *Bicycling to Work*. In Los Angeles, The Human Powered Transit Association, Inc. (HPTA), not to be confused with the "cycling" association by the same name, is dedicated to making bicycle commuting a viable transportation alternative. HPTA presents noontime bicycle commuting clinics at employer's facilities. The clinic lasts about an hour and includes an excellent film by Iowa State University, *Bicycling Safely on the Road*. Michael Shermer has recently produced a video, *Sport Cycling*, which covers bicycle basics of all kinds, including riding in traffic and safe cycling. The bottom line, however, is to get out there and give it a try. Since every case is different, you don't know how or what the conditions will be for you until you try it.

7
Competition

"Cycling is a sport for everyone. Women of all ages, backgrounds, and abilities have excelled and found the freedom to express themselves through performance. There are events to fit each personality and physical attribute: long-distance road races, daredevil criteriums, time-trialing against the clock, the wide spectrum of track events . . . the choice is based on each individual's goals and expectations."

Sue Novara-Reber,
US Women's Cycling Coach

". . . the passion is what's important."

Inga Thompson-Benedict,
Racer

In 1984, many TV viewers saw Americans Connie Carpenter Phinney and Rebecca Twigg win the gold and silver medals in the first cycling event ever held for women in the Olympics. It was no accident. American women have been prominent in international cycling competition since 1969, when Audrey McElmury won the road race at the World Championships in Brno, Czechoslovakia. She was the first American world champion, male or female, in 57 years. Since 1945, Americans have won a total of 35 medals at the Worlds and 27 of them were won by women.

Photo courtesy of Coors Classic

At the 1984 Olympic Games, Connie Carpenter Phinney became the first American to win an Olympic Gold Medal in cycling competition, in the first-ever women's Olympic cycling event. Carpenter Phinney was a prominent figure in women's cycling in the 70s and early 80s. She was a three-time Coors Classic Champion, 1983 World Pursuit Champion, and won 12 American National Championships. Like so many other great American women cyclists (Sheila Young, Sue Novara, Beth Heiden, and Connie Paraskevin), Carpenter Phinney had a strong speed-skating background and competed in the 1972 Winter Olympic Games in Sapporo as a member of the American speed-skating team. Although she retired from competition after the 1984 Olympic Games, she remains involved in the sport, as the junior women's coach and as a journalist covering competitive cycling events.

How did these women do it? How do you go about getting involved in bike racing anyway? What are all those options Novara-Reber alludes to? This chapter answers those questions.

Even if you aren't thinking about racing, you may enjoy reading the interviews with prominent racers included here and in other chapters. They provide glimpses into lifestyles and motivation that I find fascinating.

Photo by Ed Bacon/Coors Classic

Sarah Docter, Connie Carpenter, and Beth Heiden at the 1979 Coors Classic. In 1980, Beth Heiden won the Coors Classic and became the World Road Champion. Connie Carpenter Phinney won the Gold Medal in the 1984 Olympic Road Race.

DIFFERENT KINDS OF RACING, DIFFERENT RACING ORGANIZATIONS

Bike racing varies from little informal races at county fairs to the Olympics and the World Championships. The events themselves vary from 200-meter match sprints held at special bicycle tracks called velodromes, to the 3,000-mile Race Across AMerica, held annually on the highways crossing the country.

Races are held under the auspices of all manner of organizations, from the local Elks' club to the *Union Cycliste International*, or UCI. Here is a list of the more prominent organizations involved in bicycle racing. Their addresses are given in Appendix 4, Bicycle Associations.

Each organization is involved in different areas or different types of racing and they perform valuable services for cyclists. Unfortunately, there are some turf wars hidden in this list. Competition at this organizational level is probably unavoidable and even understandable, but it is sad and unnecessary when it descends to a level where cyclists disparage or speak ill of other cyclists.

USCF—United States Cycling Federation

The USCF was founded in 1920, when it was known as the Amateur Bicycle League of America. It has tens of thousands of members and it sanctions and promotes a wide variety of amateur road-racing and track-racing events. It is affiliated with the United States Olympic Committee and the UCI. It oversees the selection of the Olympic cycling team and teams for international competition.

We will have much more to say about the USCF in this chapter, which is devoted to more details on some of its activities and interviews with four women prominent in USCF racing.

NORBA—National Off-Road Bicycle Association

NORBA was born of the mountain-bike craze. It is a fast-growing segment of the racing community and sponsors many off-road events, including a national championship for women. Chapter 8 says more about mountain biking and profiles two women prominent in NORBA racing.

UMCA—Ultra-Marathon Cycling Association

The UMCA was founded in 1980 by Michael Shermer, John Marino, and Lon Haldeman. It currently has over 1,500 members and women are a fast-growing component. UMCA sponsors the Race Across AMerica and its qualifying races, as well as other long-distance events. Since 1985, the RAAM has had a women's division. Chapter 9, Endurance, describes RAAM and profiles different women prominent in UMCA racing.

PRO—Professional Racing Organization

PRO does for American professionals what the USCF does for amateurs. Currently, there is no professional circuit for women.

GETTING STARTED:
LOCAL CLUBS

Your best resource for getting into any branch of cycling will be your local bike club. That is where you will find the expertise, camaraderie, and coaching that will give you a fast start, help you get wherever you aspire to go, and support you along the way. Riding with a group will really help you learn and make it more fun at the same time. (See the comments in the interview with Connie Paraskevin-Young about the value of a good club.) Your local bike shop may be able to help you find a club and you can check for bike clubs listed in local sporting publications. If you cannot find anybody locally, try contacting the national organizations for advice and clues.

USCF
UNITED STATES CYCLING FEDERATION
ROAD AND TRACK RACING

The USCF sanctions a wide variety of bicycle races. It sponsors national championships in nine different events for women and now it sponsors age-graded national championships. Age groups start at

Tricia Walters (center) earns first-place honors at the 1987 Ore-Ida Women's Challenge Junior Competition.

Photo courtesy of Ore-Ida Foods, Inc.

12 years old and a record is listed for women 65 or older. To give you some idea of the scope of USCF women's racing, here are brief descriptions of each of the National Championship events.

Road Race (70–110 Kilometers)

Road races are just about what you probably would expect: a bunch of people start and the first one to finish line is the winner—what could be more simple? But in fact, road racing is a highly complex and tactical event which calls on skill and teamwork as much as brute strength. You rarely see a road race won by an isolated rider, even after 60 miles of hard-fought competition. More often than not, a group of

Photo courtesy of Dave Nelson/PIW

Jeannie Longo of France is one of the most accomplished individuals in the history of women's cycling. In 1987, Longo became the first woman to win the Tour de France Féminin, Coors Classic, and the World Championship Road Race. She is three-time World Road Champion, World Pursuit Champion, and holds many time-trial records.

riders approach the finish together and the race is decided in a furious last-minute sprint for the line. This is due in large part to the effect of wind resistance.

Wind resistance is a major factor in almost all forms of racing. The basic fact is that if you are going 25 mph, you can save about 20 percent of your effort if you follow right behind another rider. Avoiding the wind by riding right behind another rider (or car or other vehicle) is called drafting. The effect that this has on a road race is that the group tends to stay bunched in large "packs" of riders. If you are in a pack, you can rest by ducking behind one of your fellow racers and drafting. A lone rider never gets any rest. Other things being equal, a lone rider cannot go as fast as a pack, at least not for long. Consequently, racers try to avoid being "dropped" from their pack at all costs, because once dropped they will rapidly lose ground. Even if you are staying with your pack, you have to watch for breakaways. Sometimes a small group of riders will do whatever it takes to get "off the front" of the pack and form a breakaway group. A breakaway group of strong riders who intend to work together can be more efficient than a large disorganized pack and can gain ground on them. If you miss a breakaway that turns out to be *the* breakaway, you may have to expend an enormous amount of energy to "bridge" up to it.

All of this results in team tactics, which are a recognized element of road racing. A group of racers who work together have a distinct advantage over a solo rider. The team can take turns chasing down breaks, or, if one of their teammates has broken away, they can foul up attempts to chase her down.

Hills are one of the places where packs tend to break up. Riders slow down, which lessens the advantage of drafting, and sheer power comes more into play. The ability to climb may get you and a few of your friends off the front for a successful breakaway.

Bike handling is another factor in road racing. Screaming through turns on a fast descent, elbow to elbow, with 30 other riders is a real rush.

Most road races are determined by a final sprint between the racers in the lead pack. After two or more hours of intense and exhausting racing, one more total effort that may last less than 10 seconds frequently wins a 50-mile race by inches. Some racers have a real talent for sprinting, and if they manage to stay with the lead pack, you'd better look out. Punishing and dropping the sprinters is a major objective of the strong long-distance road racer. Brains come into play, too. Other things being equal, the racer who has been most clever in not doing unnecessary work during the first 99 percent of the race will be fresher and stronger for the sprint.

Individual Time Trial (40 Kilometers)

In an individual time trial, a single rider is timed riding a prescribed course. Typically the competitors start off at one-minute intervals. If one rider catches another, they are not allowed to draft. The individual who records the fastest time is the winner. The result is a race that is more a test of strength and concentration than a test of derring-do and tactics. Aerodynamic position and equipment have become very important in all forms of time trials.

Team Time Trial (50 Kilometers)

This is like the individual time trial, except that teams of two or four people work together to ride the course as fast as they can. They form a "pace line" and take turns in front fighting the wind. With several people working together to overcome that pesky wind, times are faster than they would be for individuals.

Criterium (50 Kilometers)

Criteriums are a kind of road race where riders complete many laps around a short course, typically about one mile around. Many are held on city streets, which make for flat courses with right-angle turns. Criteriums tend to be very fast and very tactical, requiring a lot of teamwork. They are good spectator events because the pace is fierce, the racers come by frequently, and it is exciting to see a pack of 50 riders go through a sharp turn at 30 mph.

Cyclocross

Cyclocross is a winter sport. It features off-pavement sections and probably places where it is necessary to walk or carry your bike. Wet conditions, which are fairly common, result in a mudfest. Cyclocross is a real test of bike-handling skills.

Photo courtesy of Ore-Ida Foods, Inc.

The team trial awards celebration at the 1987 Ore-Ida Women's Challenge in Stanley, Idaho. The Ore-Ida Women's Challenge is the largest and most celebrated stage race for women. Left to right: Chemical Bank (5th), Weight Watchers (3rd), Lowrey's (1st), 7–Eleven (2nd), Winning Peugeot (4th).

Track Events

There are nine National Championship track events for women. These are normally contested on special bicycle tracks with banked turns. Tracks are also called velodromes (USCF velodromes are listed in Appendix 7).

Special track bicycles are used that have no brakes and have one gear which does not freewheel. You slow down by backpedaling or by dragging your (gloved) hand on the front wheel. In the tight quarters of a track, brakes would actually cause crashes since anyone who used a brake would probably be hit immediately by a rider following close behind.

Match Sprint

The match sprint eliminates the first 30 to 60 miles of fooling around that are prominent in road races and criteriums, and just concentrates

Bunki Bankaitis-Davis (right) and Katrin Tobin (left) blaze through a corner of the Parkcenter Criterium at the 1987 Ore-Ida Women's Challenge.

on that finishing sprint. Two riders usually race three times around the track, so the total distance is typically about a half mile or 1,000 meters. Only the last 200 meters are timed. Events are usually decided by a series of elimination heats between pairs of riders. Here, too, wind resistance makes for a highly tactical race. If one rider simply charged off the line, the other would fall in behind and draft. By the time they approached the finish, the lead rider would be exhausted and easy pickings for the following rider to pass at will.

Many times, these match sprints start out very slowly. It looks like both riders want to be in back and indeed most riders do prefer to be in back! They can watch the rider in front and control the race better from there. Sometimes, both riders will actually stop and balance, waiting for the other to go by.

But if the spectator looks away, she is likely to miss the race, which can be determined in the blink of an eye. If the lead rider doesn't watch her pursuer carefully, or gets caught with her cranks at a bad angle at a critical moment, the following rider will jump, or accelerate as fast as she can and achieve a speed advantage that she will maintain as both riders accelerate until they are both going as fast as they can possibly go. If she has timed it just right, her speed advantage will carry her past the lead rider before they hit the finish line. If she jumps too early, the other rider can tuck in behind her and rest and try to come back around before the finish. (See the interview with Connie Paraskevin-Young, who has been world champion at match sprints several times.)

One-Kilometer Time Trial

This is a really short time trial: accelerate from a standing start and just crank it out as fast as you can go. The pain will be over soon, in about 1 minute and 15 seconds if you are a world-class racer.

Three-Kilometer Pursuit

In the pursuit, two riders are started simultaneously on opposite sides of the track to ride the three kilometers. The first one to finish wins the heat, and events typically go through a set of elimination heats to determine an overall winner. You are racing that other rider on the track, but tactics are minimized since you cannot draft your opponent. Also, you can't really afford to glance over at your opponent because you have to maintain absolute concentration. In serious events, you will have a coach on the track who will tell you if you are on your schedule and let you know where you are relative to your opponent. (See the interview with Rebecca Twigg, who has been world champion at this event several times.)

20-Kilometer Points Race

This is sort of like a road race on the track. A whole pack races a given distance, with points awarded on specified laps for the leader at that time. The rider with the most points wins.

Stage Races

Stage races are an important form of competition even though there is no national championship stage race. The famous Tour de France is a stage race. Winning an important stage race may mean more to a racer than winning a world championship. A stage race consists of a series of events or stages. Typically, one or two stages are run each day

Photo by Ed Kosmicki/Coors Classic

Madonna Harris (c), a native of New Zealand, celebrates winning stage 5—the Copper Mountain road race. Katrin Tobin (l) was second, and Jeannie Longo (r) was third. Longo went on to win the 1986 Coors Classic.

for several days or even weeks. Each rider's time is recorded for each stage. The best total time for all the stages determines the winner. Stage racing is an incredibly tactical, team-oriented event. (See the interview with Inga Thompson-Benedict, who has raced the Tour de France, for some insights into stage racing).

The Ore-Ida Women's Challenge, held in Idaho in late June, is a premier stage race. Because it is not held in conjunction with an event for men, Ore-Ida gives the women center stage. It is contested annually by the top women racers in the world. The Seafirst Crown is another women's stage race, held in May in Redmond, Washington. The Coors Classic, held in early August in California and Colorado, is the most prominent American stage race and it includes a women's event.

SUPPORT FOR WOMEN'S CYCLING
USCF

The USCF has a paid staff including a women's coach. It sponsors many activities to help women cyclists. Three basic programs are currently offered:

A. Entry Level. Women just beginning in cycling can attend entry-level development camps and clinics conducted by the USCF. Held at the US Olympic Training Centers (OTC) in Colorado Springs, Colorado; Lake Placid, New York; and Marquette, Michigan; these camps provide classroom training in racing rules, nutrition, equipment, maintenance, and training schedules; also included are on-road drills covering pace lines, climbing, cornering, and time trials.

B. National Level. Promising women riders can participate in national development camps and clinics. Selected by coaches on the basis of racing results, these camps allow women an opportunity to work with national coaches and to be considered for major national and international competitions.

C. Track Program. The USCF assists coaching programs at several velodromes around the United States. Women have access to coaching expertise and equipment.

Photo by Ore-Ida Foods, Inc.

Women from all over the country come to compete and make new friends at the Ore-Ida Women's Challenge. Left to right: Sandy Meister, Laura Charameda, Sara Neil, Ann Sirotniak, and Sally Zack sing "Mothers, Don't Let Your Daughters Grow Up to Be Bikies" at the awards ceremony.

Women's Cycling Teams

There are several women's racing teams with commercial sponsors. Teams provide racers with various levels of expense money for travel, equipment, entry fees, and sometimes for training and coaching. It costs approximately $100,000 or more a year to run a national-level team which competes at all the major races. Many teams lack sufficient sponsorship to cover all expenses for their riders, but they will limit the amount of personal funds a serious woman racer has to contribute in order to compete.

Team sponsorship is an area in which more support is always needed.

SUE NOVARA-REBER
US WOMEN'S CYCLING DIRECTOR

Sue Novara-Reber, a native of Flint, Michigan, retired from competitive cycling in 1984. She has been the US Women's Cycling Director since January 1986.

Novara-Reber's achievements are many. She was the World Sprint Champion in 1975 and 1980; National Sprint Champion in 1972, 1974, 1975, 1977, 1978, 1979, and 1980; National Road Champion in 1982; world silver medalist in the sprint in 1974, 1976, 1977, and 1978; world bronze medalist in the sprint in 1979; and winner of five stages of the Coors International Bicycle Classic.

In addition, Novara-Reber was the first recipient of the Georgena Terry Award for an outstanding contribution to women's cycling in 1987. In 1982 she was the youngest inductee to the Flint Hall of Fame in Michigan.

Sue enjoys listening to music, hiking, and spending time with her husband and two children.

Novara-Reber was gracious enough to take time out of her busy schedule to grant the following interview.

Q: How did you get into cycling? How old were you? What were the circumstances?

A: I began cycling when I was 13 years old back in 1969 and used it primarily as a complementary sport for speed skating, which I did in the wintertime. I continued to do both sports until 1978, but gradually I had more interest in cycling and made that my primary sport.

Photo by Ed Kosmicki/Coors Classic

Sue Novara-Reber and Inga Thompson celebrate after a tough stage of the 1984 Coors Classic. Novara-Reber brings her experience and love of the sport to her new role as US Women's National Cycling Coach.

Q: You were world sprint champion and also involved in road racing—was the track your specialty? Why?

A: I think it was because the coach of the club I belonged to, the Wolverine Sports Club, saw a natural talent there and we worked to develop it. Sprinting was not to be included as an Olympic event in 1984, so I switched to the road in hopes of making the Olympic team.

Q: What was the highlight of your cycling career? What will you remember the most?

A: I think it was winning the World Championships back in 1980. I think that was the most memorable accomplishment in my career. It had been almost five years since I had first won the World Championships in 1975, and I realized that it wasn't as easy as I had originally thought to come back year after year. And also my father had passed away earlier that April of 1980, and he had been my coach/trainer for the most part and it meant a lot to me to win that year. I just wanted to prove to myself that I could do it, and I wanted it to be like a little memorial to my dad.

Photo courtesy of Rodale Press

Inaugural presentation of the Terry Award to Sue Novara-Reber by Georgena Terry, June 12, 1987, at the Lehigh County Velodrome, Trexlertown, Pennsylvania. The Terry is awarded to a woman who makes a great contribution to women's cycling.

Q: A lot of the successful women have had their own coaches. Does having that kind of support make a difference?

A: Thinking back to the 1970s, the ones that were doing well were people like myself, Connie Paraskevin, Sheila Young, and Connie Carpenter, and we had all come from speed-skating backgrounds. Now we don't see that as much. We see a wider variety of backgrounds. Many cyclists are runners who had injuries that shortened their running careers and now have gotten into cycling. We see triathletes getting into it. We see a wider scope as far as the type of talent that's coming into cycling. I think there's one thing that's common amongst all of them, and that is that they have someone who's very supportive, whether that be a club coach, or their family, or a very special friend who encourages them to go on and see what they can achieve in the sport.

Q: Do you think it's particularly true that women in sports need support?

A: I think so. We have not really been encouraged to go into sports as a whole in our society. For people to put that notion aside and go out and really try to achieve something athletically, they need some type of background that shows that there is a lot of support there.

Q: In 1986 you became the USCF national women's coach. That was the first time the women had had a full-time coach. Do you think your years of racing experience make you better able to understand the pressures and strains on the women athletes? What are your goals as coach?

A: First off, probably the love of the sport and having achieved what I wanted to while I was competing helps me get pleasure out of seeing other girls reach that. It's important for those of us who got positive things out of the sport to remain in the sport so that it grows. I feel that coaching is the best way I can help these girls achieve that. Connie Carpenter [gold medalist in the 1984 Olympics] is staying involved through other aspects of cycling and hopefully more women will return to the sport to help us out as club coaches or team managers. We know where the sport has been and we've seen it grow the last 20 years and we need to keep it going in a positive direction.

I want to establish a very strong US women's national program and raise these girls to become national team members. In turn, that will give us the most effective and strong team we've ever had for major competitions like the Olympics, World Championships, and Pan Am Games.

Q: Do you plan the training and competitions for our national teams?

A: My big plan now is to outline a series of races that the girls should attend in order to make the team. I want to make the competition stronger and develop a lot more depth, and that in turn will mean the girls are at a higher pinnacle once they get to training camp, and we can just go from there.

I think the biggest thing I may be able to provide these girls is the feeling of competitiveness; that once they get chosen for a team, that is not the end. That is only the start. If they have the confidence, once they get to a big event they can win. If you make a team, and then don't believe you can go further, then you won't have the concentration and the confidence for the training period that's building up to that event. Confidence is a good preparatory base. Make sure you're on the right schedule leading up to this event. If you do the right things in preparation, when the event comes, you'll be able to perform. There are no shortcuts in sports, as in anything else. If you do your homework, then you'll do well on the test. It's the same type of thing.

Q: Do you pick the national and the world teams?

A: The teams are picked partly on points scored in National Prestige Classic races. These are selected races around the country. Also, 50 percent of the team is picked at my discretion, so that if somebody's not real high on the points but she's a very good rider, I can select her.

Q: Is there a recruitment program to attract more women into the sport?

A: I think I'm going to start working on that. Part of that is trying to develop more of a regional coaches' network so that we have people all throughout the country who actively go out and look for talent, whether it means triathlons or high school sports or local clubs. So, having a network out there we'll reach more people. Also, if we can generate more success at the top level, it will help give the sport a lot more coverage. People who read magazines will read about our sport and will find out that, hey, that would be kind of nice to try.

We're also in the planning stages of using our national team for a lecture-type circuit to go around to various parts of the country and give talks and slide and video presentations on our sport and how you can get involved.

There are two or three development camps for newcomers. In the fall, it's Colorado Springs at the training center there. All through January, February, and March we hold three training centers for national team members who are aspiring to be better. Hopefully we'll be able to utilize the other training centers throughout the country and hold development camps similar to that, so that those who can't travel a long distance will get a chance to be looked at.

Q: Sponsorship seems to be a perpetual problem in women's cycling. Is there anything you can do to influence this situation?

A: I think it's just the opposite. I think there's better sponsorship among the women, especially in the elite ranks. Right now there are at least a dozen sponsors reaching women throughout the country who will allow them to race full-time.

Q: Will there ever be a professional league for women?

A: It's a possibility, though I don't think it will be within the next 10 years. Actually, I would like to see that happen, because, like in any sport, if you have professional ranks, it makes the amateur ranks aspire to greater heights. If it's done correctly, a draft situation will arise, where the professional teams will draft top amateurs. I think that type of formula would be very positive for both the professional and amateur organizations.

Q: Are there enough women to turn professional?

A: Well, I think it's getting to that point. I think what it'll have to take is a commitment from top cyclists that once they reach a pinnacle, like the Olympics, they then need to organize themselves into a professional circuit. I think if a professional circuit were to happen, it would have to be started here in this country. Possibly our federation will look into something like that in the future.

Q: Do you ever wish you were out there racing?

A: No, I think I got my fill when I was racing. I'm actually very happy not to be competing anymore.

Q: I read a study that was done prior to the 1984 Olympics on performance and the menstrual cycle. It concluded that there was no real effect on performance. Yet, when I talk to cyclists most say that their period affects training and competition. As coach of the women's team, do you think about these things? What advice, if any, would you give to women athletes? On the flip side, to what extent is amenorrhea a problem?

A: Well, I think everyone's menstrual cycle affects them differently, and because it's something that you can plan on once a month, you're going to have to deal with it the best you can. If you have a problem with it, many times girls can use contraceptive pills or something else and avoid the unpleasant effects they get from cramping during the time of their period. But if you've been training for an event and it happens to fall at around the time your period's going to start, you really have to put that out of your mind as much as possible, because you can't let that affect what you've worked so hard for all year. I think the top athletes can do that. They can find a way. They are so good with their own concentration and they have such control of their emotions and their thinking that they can really lessen the effects of the menstrual cycle.

Regarding amenorrhea, I don't think it happens that often. I don't think that, for the majority of the girls, their body fat gets down so low that it may cause amenorrhea.

Q: What's the ideal percent body fat for elite women cyclists?

A: The majority of the women cyclists may be closer to 15 percent body fat, but a few will come down as lean as 10 percent. Cycling is a very specific event, and I don't think it really encourages such a low body fat.

Weight should be a concern to all cyclists because the most effective riders are those who have the best power-to-weight ratio. If they build up their power, they're having to tow around extra pounds, especially if they are road riders who have to climb hills repeatedly with extra weight. It's going to tire them out. I stress that everybody should know what their ideal weight is and then try to maintain that weight. They shouldn't go much below their ideal weight because, again, it'll take away their strength.

Figuring out your ideal weight is difficult. Sometimes you can go on a height-to-weight ratio. By doing a body-fat test you can find out approximately how much weight, if any, needs to be lost. I would say that if a woman comes out between 10 and 15 percent body fat she's probably pretty close to an ideal weight for her.

Q: Do you test for VO$_2$ max (maximum oxygen volume)?

A: We do that periodically. There are good and bad points to it. If somebody is doing really well and then they get tested on VO$_2$ and it shows that maybe the VO$_2$ is not as high as somebody who isn't doing as well, then it may have a negative psychological effect on them. If you give the results only to a coach or don't compare results among the riders, it may be advantageous to their training program to see where they have weak points, but, usually, we can tell where their weak points are without the test.

If you have a VO$_2$ max up there in the high 60s, you would be pretty close to being an elite athlete, depending, again, on your type of competition. A road athlete who does many miles in a period of exercise at high levels is going to have a higher VO$_2$ than a sprinter, maybe than the world champion sprinter, because, again, it's a different type of discipline. You have to look at all the factors separately to find out if somebody is performing up to capability.

Q: Should results be compared?

A: I think where things like the percentage of body fat and VO_2 test results would come in handy is if you test yourself periodically and compare your results based on the time of year. You could compare VO_2 max and body fat in December, during the off-season—when you're doing a lot of alternate training—to your results in April or May, when you're getting into the height of your competition. Comparative results within the person are much more beneficial than comparative results between one person and another.

Q: Is age a factor in cycling?

A: Well, I think physically you can be competent from 15 or 16 years old all the way until you're 35. When you start you need to learn from mistakes and keep trying to improve. Then you can remain good for years to come, as long as you want to. Keeping mental freshness is very important. Usually you don't get too many injuries in cycling that would shorten your career, so you have the capability of remaining good for a very long time.

Q: Do you consider age when selecting teams for the Worlds and the Olympics?

A: I don't look at age very much at all. The only time I'd look at age is if I'm looking for the possibility of development. When someone is just getting into the sport, we realize that it takes a good three or four years before she understands what's going on out there and has the tactical savvy to be better. If it's between one person and another making the team, I don't look at age at all. I look at who I think is going to perform best.

Q: You had a child two years ago. Do you have any advice for cyclists who are pregnant?

A: Obviously, they should go with what their doctor thinks. I think if you've been used to cycling, then you can probably continue it. The biggest concern is that once you are pregnant, and the further along you get, there's the danger of falling off your bike. Probably the best alternative if you want to continue your cycling is to get on an indoor stationary bike where you're a lot safer. Just use good sense when you are doing things. I did a lot of cross-country skiing during the winter while I was pregnant, and I continued riding. I did ride the Turbo Trainer or Exercycle for quite a while during the winter. I stayed very active.

Q: *Are cyclists stronger after having kids?*

A: I think Sheila Young-Ochowicz won her third world championship after she had her first child. But I don't know of any scientific evidence to back that up.

Q: *Is having children a psychological help?*

A: Your priorities certainly change once you have a child. Also, in my case (I can only speak from my own experience) childbirth was such a painful experience, that by comparison the pain of an athletic event isn't as bad as you thought it was. Maybe some people can relate athletics to childbirth and can push beyond the pain better once they get back into competition.

Q: *How much traveling do you do with your job?*

A: I do quite a bit of traveling, actually. There are preseason camps that I attend and the Tour of Texas in March, which is a preliminary race series that I like to go to so I can scout for new talent and look for new riders who are possibly in a position for making international competition. The selection process for some of our European trips goes on here.

Q: *How do you juggle coaching and family and travel?*

A: I have a very understanding husband, and my daughter travels with me. Whenever I'm going to be away from home for a week or two, she comes with me and I have two younger sisters who alternate times being nanny.

Q: *What advice do you have for a woman who wants to race?*

A: I think the first advice is to try and find out if there are any local racing clubs in your area and get involved with them. Not only will they give you some coaching on the club level, but also they can introduce you to good training partners. That's always a plus because you can get better by training with people who are better than you. It also gives you an avenue for finding out about races that are going on in your area. Then you graduate to taking out a USCF racing license. The better you get on the local level, the more people take notice of you, and that can possibly lead to sponsorship on larger teams.

Q: *How would you make the transition from being a strong local racer to an Olympic hopeful?*

A: If you're going to become an Olympic sprinter, then you have to get into as many important sprint events as possible so that you make a name for yourself. The same goes for road riders: you have to schedule as many races as possible to be in competition, because that makes you better and because you can learn a lot from other people. The more experience you get and the better results you get, the more likely it is my regional coaches or myself will take notice.

Q: *Will you encourage your daughter to ride?*

A: If she wants to. I don't think she'll be able to stay away from it with me involved. She'll have the idea what it's all about and she'll be introduced to it at a very early age. I'd like her to get involved in some kind of sport. It builds confidence and self-esteem, that can carry over to many parts of your life.

REBECCA TWIGG
NO SECRETS, JUST HARD WORK

Rebecca Twigg was born in Honolulu and lived for several years as a child in the cycling mecca of Wisconsin, which produced Eric and Beth Heiden, Sarah Docter, and other cycling greats. She has spent the majority of her life dividing her time between her childhood home in Seattle, Washington, and the Olympic training camp in Colorado Springs, Colorado. She has a bachelor of science degree in biology from the University of Washington and as noteworthy as this is considering her athletic achievements, what makes it truly impressive is that she entered college in 1977 at the age of 14!

Rebecca started cycling the same year. Her first race was the 1977 state track championship, but since there were no girls entered, she was forced to race the intermediate boys. She then entered the road race against one other girl and won, thus beginning a long and varied career of winning.

She won her first national championship as a junior in 1979, on the track and in the time trial. This was to begin her mixture of road and

Rebecca Twigg on her way to a stage victory in the 1987 Ore-Ida Women's Challenge. Twigg is a three-time Ore-Ida Challenge winner, Coors Classic Champion, four-time World Pursuit champion, and was a silver medalist at the 1984 Olympic Games.

track racing. "I began racing Friday nights at the velodrome and Wednesday nights on the national championship road course. I recommend racing both track and road, particularly when young, or just starting out, because you aren't sure what you want to do, or what you will be good at. Also, the track quickens your reflexes, improves bike-handling skills, and helps you see situations faster. Actually, in terms of pure bike-handling skills, cyclocross is the best thing you can do. In fact, there was a time when I wanted to get every woman cyclist into cyclocross before they jumped in our races, to make the races safer for the experienced riders," says Twigg.

In 1980, talk of a woman's cycling event in the 1984 Olympics piqued her interest and revived her focus on racing. She began training for the Olympics in 1981. In 1984, the first Olympic cycling event for women was held, with Twigg taking a silver medal and Connie Carpenter a gold for the United States.

Michael Shermer interviewed Rebecca Twigg in her home in Pasadena, California. (She now lives in San Diego, California.)

Q: What motivates you to ride? What gets you going? What do you think about when you're riding?

A: In a race, all I think about is the race. In training however, I think about all sorts of things. The riding becomes second nature, like stopping at stop signs, riding in traffic. Sometimes I think about my competition, like when I'm riding up a hill I imagine one of my competitors next to me, and that really gets me going.

Q: What do you focus on in training?

A: The World Championships. Everything else is training, including all the other races. I aim to peak for the Worlds. It just comes naturally to me because I have been doing it for so many years. In March I don't ride that hard, but by June I am feeling stronger and in July I'm riding even better. So I just sort of grow into preparation for the Worlds.

Q: What was it like to have the 1984 Olympics on your home turf, the United States?

A: I don't really mind traveling to other countries—it is kind of exciting to go to new places—but there is a given amount of positive energy at work when racing at home as opposed to abroad.

Q: When the US took the gold and silver, the noise was deafening. It must have really been something to have been riding in all of that excitement.

A: We couldn't believe we had actually taken first and second. All of those great riders and we took first and second, and in America! It was really a relief when it was over.

Q: Was this the highlight of your career?

A: No, when I won the Worlds for the first time was the high point of my career. I just didn't expect to win, and even though the Olympics were a great thrill, winning is better than taking second. In terms of the race itself, however, being in the Olympic Road Race was the most exciting thing I have ever done. The crowd cheering just sort of pushed us along. You couldn't really feel the pain.

Q: What do you recommend for structuring a training program to prepare for racing?

A: I recommend starting to train in January. After six to eight weeks of rest from cycling through November and December, I'm usually ready to begin training after the first of the year. Even in November and December, though, I try to get out on the bike two or three times a week. I also sometimes use a little weight training a couple of times a week. Women don't have that much upper body strength compared to men and need to work on that aspect of it. Particularly arms and shoulders need concentration. I prefer free weights, though many people like the Nautilus machines because they can get through their workouts faster. The advantage of free weights for me is that I can work with them at home and don't have to go down to a gym after my ride.

I also recommend just doing sit-ups, push-ups, and pull-ups because you can do them anywhere, anytime, and they are quite effective in building upper-body strength. I even do them throughout the racing season just to keep the muscles toned and strong.

Q: Do you run for training?

A: I only run during the winter, and not more than five miles. Cycling is so much more fun than running and you can see more. When you go to another city, if you want to see the sights a bike is the best way to do it.

Q: What about other kinds of training on the bike, like alternating riding up a hill in an easy gear and then in a large gear?

A: I've heard that method works well for building strength. But new riders have to be very careful not to hurt themselves on extreme forms of training methods such as this. It is very easy to sustain an injury from overtraining in the early stages. A beginning rider shouldn't ride more than 200 miles a week in January and February. More experienced riders can go out and ride 250 to 300 miles a week.

For me, the weight training is primarily for staying in decent shape while taking time off the bike. I need that time mentally for recovering from so much racing, and the weight training allows me to do that without losing too much conditioning.

I also run stairs. Before hitting the weight room, I would warm up with approximately 20 minutes of stair climbing at the local university. Stair climbing is very hard on the legs, but great for conditioning. There is still a group up in Seattle that meets two or three times a week for stair climbing.

Q: *When you begin your training program in the spring, do you ride every day or take days off?*

A: I usually ride almost every day except when it rains, or it's a travel day. The more experienced you are, however, the less you need to train. You can rely on tactics and strategy to make sure you're in the right place at the right time. There's more to bike racing than just pure conditioning.

But when I was really nutso, like in 1984, I never, never missed a day of training. I would at least ride an hour, but even that would be considered a day off of training.

Q: *Do you feel that the more years of racing and training that go into your legs, the easier it is in the future to get back into shape, even when starting from an unconditioned state?*

A: Oh, definitely. I really think there is something to muscle memory. Also, people who have the experience of racing know how hard they can push themselves. They know what their body is going to experience and can work through the pain.

Q: *What about overtraining or stressing the body beyond its capacity? It seems like bike racers run a fine line between being extremely healthy and too weak and tired to resist illness and injury.*

A: A perfect example of that was the 1985 Coors Classic. It began only one day after the grueling Ore-Ida stage race. I was tired and a bit run-down, but was never given the opportunity to recover before the Coors started. I was getting pulled muscles; in fact, I even pulled a muscle in my wrist while sleeping one night! It's amazing what can happen to your body when you're that run-down. I wasn't even aware that it was happening to me until well into the Coors Classic.

Q: *Do you keep track of the miles you ride in a year?*

A: No, though many people ask me how many I ride. I would estimate that I ride 8,000 to 10,000 miles from January through August, then another 2,000 from September through December, which is generally the off-season. It averages out to approximately 250 miles a week for the first eight months, then around 150 miles a week for the remainder of the year. Though it's not infrequent that I may ride upwards of 300 miles in a week during the racing season, I would say that I typically ride 12,000 miles a year.

Q: Are there enough races that it isn't necessary to train once the schedule begins?

A: No, in neither America nor Europe are there enough races for women to avoid training. You still need to get in your miles during the season.

Q: Do you have to ride after a race to get in your miles?

A: Yes, particularly after the short races toward the beginning of the season. You should take two long rides a week, and a race can be part of one of those.

Q: What is a long day for you?

A: A long day is 60 to 70 miles, though I wouldn't recommend that for someone just starting out, or even for the first couple of years. Once you are a seasoned rider, I suggest doing this kind of mileage twice a week, though not more than 70 miles and not more than twice a week or your speed will drop off. Past that, you spend a greater amount of your energy on distance as opposed to speed. Even beginning riders need to work on speed, not distance.

Q: What is the typical distance of a woman's race?

A: Criteriums are 25 or 30 miles, and road races are about 35 to 40 miles. A 40-mile race is the equivalent of riding 60 miles on your own, though riding alone all the time is not a good idea because you tend to go slow. When riding in a pack you tend to ride faster and push yourself harder. Also, it is easier to practice your sprint in a group than alone. If you have to, you can do intervals and sprint to certain landmarks, but it is better to ride with others. I know a lot of good time trialists who can't ride in a pack because they don't practice this in training.

Q: When you are riding by yourself, how do you motivate yourself to train hard as opposed to just cruising around?

A: If I do intervals, I do them either by time or mileage markers. As for motivation, I just know that the only way to get better is to push yourself. I tell myself, "Hey, anyone can go this speed." So I go a little harder. I do this in time trials as well. I imagine what others can do, then push myself harder than they push.

Q: When you ride by yourself, how long does it take you to cover a 60-mile course?

A: Well, I usually don't push myself *that* hard on the longer rides. I save that for my speed days. But on a longer ride I usually average around 18 miles per hour.

Q: Do you keep a training log?

A: Yes, almost always. It's the best way to keep yourself honest and to get feedback. It's like checking in with someone—a psychological motivator. It is a visual method of seeing how much you did for the day. It helps you be consistent because you don't want to open the log and see glaring blank spots all the time. If you log weekly mileage, it becomes obvious how much it can hurt to miss a couple of days in a week. In addition to the mileage or time, I also try to record how hard I went out that day. For instance, I might record "30 miles—easy" or "25 miles—fast." And also what the terrain was like—flat, hilly, and so forth.

Q: When you train, do you train to peak?

A: Yes, I train to peak for certain races. However, you have to be in good shape most of the time.

Q: Why can't you train to peak early in the year, say March, and then hold it all year? Is it a physical barrier? A psychological barrier?

A: It's both physical and psychological. Physically, when you are stressing your body so much, it becomes weak and you are susceptible to injuries, colds, and illnesses. Mentally, it is difficult to maintain that level of training. The old European method was to log long, slow miles early in the season and then push really hard when the racing began. Eddie B.'s [Borysewicz, the former coach of the US Cycling Team] method is to push harder earlier to gain an edge over the competition. But I like to look forward to getting better later on in the season. I like to have that to look forward to throughout the early season.

Q: Do you use rollers or a stationary bike in the off-season to stay in shape?

A: I try not to. It's kind of boring, and it's always better to ride outdoors whenever possible. I do recommend rollers for the beginning rider to teach good balance and bike-handling skills. I also recommend riding a fixed-gear bike for learning to spin high RPMs. I will usually ride a 61- or 63-inch gear. [See the gear chart in Appendix 10 for the different combinations of front chainring and rear cogs to achieve this gear.]

Q: What time of the year, and for how long, do you do fixed-gear riding?

A: I usually ride a fixed-gear in the winter, for maybe an hour at a time.

Q: What about motorpacing (riding behind a motor vehicle)?

A: Motorpacing is really good for speed training, though I do recommend riding behind a motorcycle instead of a car so that you can see the road better and know what is coming. You can push yourself really hard motorpacing and not even know it because of the draft behind the vehicle. If you are going to motorpace, it is best in rolling hills. On the flats you go so fast that even in the biggest gear you may not be pushing that hard. But in the hills you can really get a great workout. I do know some cyclists that motorpace so much that they have become the type of rider to just sit in the pack and wait for the sprint, though. They typically end up missing the critical breaks. Ideally, you want to motorpace occasionally, in the rolling hills, and practice coming around the motorcycle and sprinting past it as if it were a break or the finish line.

Q: What level of physical conditioning do you think you are usually at if 100 percent were ideal, perfect conditioning?

A: Well, in the off-season I drop down to about 70 percent and stay there through a low-level maintenance program. But during the racing season I would say, oh, 90 percent!

Q: How can you get that last 10 percent?

A: That last 10 percent comes in the late summer when I peak for the World Championships.

Q: But what do you do to get that 10 percent?

A: Ride. And ride hard. Be very dedicated. Make sure you get a lot of rest and recovery so you are even stronger the next day. Maybe do double training sessions in the morning and evening. When I do my intervals I get to the pain threshold, go past it, and then hold it for maybe a minute or more. My goal is to get my heart rate up over 180 beats per minute and then hold it. When I recover, it drops back down to 120 beats.

Q: How do you measure your heart rate while riding?

A: I just put my finger up to my neck and feel the pulse through the major artery [the carotid arteries, located on either side of the front part of the neck]. The highest officially recorded pulse rate I have ever had was 186 beats per minute on an ergometer.

Q: To be a good road racer, you have to be good in the hills. How do you practice hill climbing?

A: I do hill intervals. Many times I will go out and ride the same hill over and over again. Any length will do, as long as it is *up*.

Q: How many times up and down the hill will you ride?

A: In my training program, I start off with just a couple of times, then later increase it to four, six, eight, and so on. Of course, it depends on how long the hill is. If it is a four-mile hill, a couple of times up will make for a good workout.

Q: What is a typical week of training like for you?

A: A: Monday is an easy day. Tuesday is a sprint day—maybe forty miles, sprinting for telephone poles, etc. Wednesday is a long day, say 60 miles. Thursday is an interval day, either by myself or with my team in a team time-trial fashion where we each take turns at the front. This will be for 40 miles. Friday is a 30- to 40-mile spin day, not too hard. Saturday is a 20- to 30-mile easy day, just staying loose. Sunday is race day.

Q: So you are sort of training each week to peak for Sunday, all of which is in order to peak for the year in August.

A: Right!

Q: Do you recommend training with men in order to get faster for the women's races?

A: Yes, if it is possible, and if you can stay up with the men, then it is a good idea. But many women, particularly when first starting out, can't keep up, and it becomes discouraging.

Q: Do you have any particular nutritional program that you maintain during the racing season?

A: Not really, believe it or not. I pretty much eat what I want, with the exception of sugar and caffeine in large quantities. I find that if I don't eat *any* sugar or caffeine, when I do have some, even in small amounts, it makes me ill; I usually catch a cold. So I take in small amounts now and then, just to maintain a certain tolerance level in my body. Caffeine in large amounts is now illegal in races, so you have to be careful anyway. It is very difficult to be on a special diet on the racing circuit. You are always traveling and on the road, staying in hotels, and eating at restaurants. It is hard to be really consistent with a diet on that type of schedule.

Q: Do you take any special vitamin or mineral supplements?
A: I've taken different vitamins. I think iron is good, particularly for women, though I'm not really on any special vitamin program.

Q: Since you don't seem to have any special program for eating off the bike, what do you eat on *the bike? What do you store in your back pockets?*
A: I usually eat raisins, or if it is really hot, maybe grapes because they have more water in them. Sometimes in my water bottle I put Gatorade or E.R.G. (Electrolyte Replacement with Glucose). But you have to remember that our races are fairly short. I don't even take any food with me unless the race is more than 45 miles long.

Q: What do you eat before the race?
A: If it is an early race, I don't eat. I'd rather get the sleep. I just eat a big dinner the night before and that supplies me with the energy I need. If I had a choice, I would want to be finished eating a full three hours before the race. If I did eat, it would be complex carbohydrates, such as pancakes.

Q: Do you ever drink alcohol?
A: I don't think it is good for cycling, particularly for endurance. I used to drink occasionally after the races, but I felt it hurt my performance. Maybe once a month wouldn't be too bad, but generally I don't recommend drinking any alcohol.

Q: Can someone who works a full-time job train to become a competitive racing cyclist?
A: Yes, that's what everyone does at the beginning since you can't get on a sponsored team right away. I used to work and train when I was starting out. I would do my interval and speed work during the week, and the longer rides on the weekends. It takes careful planning

of your schedule, and if you are married and/or have kids, it would be even tougher. Your riding has to be a bit more intense, though I wouldn't suggest just going out every opportunity and riding your brains out. You still have to be intelligent about it. You could essentially get by on 200 miles a week and still be competitive. Many women I meet are doing this and the competition at the races is really getting tough.

To be good in anything, though, is going to take some sacrifice. When you have a job it is just that much tougher. There are even little things—like walking, for instance. Walking uses different muscles and if you are really serious you shouldn't take long walks. If you want to be good, this is an example of what it's going to take to get to the top.

Q: What is it like to be a cycling celebrity?
A: It's nice to be recognized as an athlete, but it's more pressure. It's more pressure when people come up to you and say, "I know you are going to win the Olympics," or "I'm really rooting for you in the race." It makes you feel like you *have* to do well to meet their expectations.

Q: When did you notice your increase in fame?
A: After I won the Coors Classic in '83. That was also the year I was second in the Worlds, and there was a lot of pressure on that race!

Q: Are you well known outside of the sport of cycling?
A: After the Olympics were over and I returned to the university, people knew who I was. For a while, people would recognize me in the supermarket and on the street. I just wanted to put my sunglasses on and dye my hair! One guy at the university (in Seattle) just followed me around to my classes, waiting for me until class was dismissed, then followed me to the next one. He just wanted to be a friend, but I didn't even know him! For a while I got "love letters" from men I'd never heard of and even flowers once!

It is good for your confidence though. To know that there are people out there who care if I win or don't win, can really motivate you to try harder. Too much is pressure, a little bit is incentive. But the sport of cycling has been very rewarding for me.

Photo courtesy of Doug Conarroe/Coors Classic

Inga Thompson-Benedict winning a stage at the 1984 Coors Classic. After only six months of racing, Inga found herself competing in the 1984 Olympics.

INGA THOMPSON-BENEDICT
PASSION AND DISCIPLINE

I interviewed Inga at her home in Reno, Nevada.

Inga was born on January 27, 1964, in Salt Lake City, Utah. Her athletic background is strong: she was Nevada State Cross-Country Champion in 1979, 1980, and 1981, was fourth at the National College Cross-Country Championship, and was on a winning downhill skiing team.

Her most noticeable accomplishment was her incredible entrance into cycling in 1984. After only six months of competition, Inga was discovered by Connie Carpenter. She was signed onto the Levi-Raleigh team and then made the 1984 Olympic Cycling Team. Over the past four years Inga has emerged as one of the best US women cyclists. Her accomplishments include: third place, 1985 *Tour de France Féminin*; first place, 1987 Ore-Ida; second place, 1987 Pan Am Road Race; silver medalist at the 1987 World Championship Team Time Trial; winner of the 1988 Coors International Bicycle Classic, first place in the 1988 Olympic Trials, and eighth place in the 1988 Olympic Road Race in Seoul.

Inga started college and was studying physics and philosophy before she began racing. She has a red '57 Chevy pick-up and a great passion for flowers, particularly roses. The only problem with flowers, Inga told me, is that "I can only work in my garden in the off-season, which is winter!" Inga also enjoys woodworking and has a few pet rabbits.

Q: What is your cycling background? What was it like for you when you first got started?

A: I have 10 years of a competitive endurance running background. When I ran I was really slow. When I first started bike racing, I hated the sprints; I hated the tactics, hated the speed. In the last year, I got wrapped up in the sport and really began to respect women who can get in there and climb well in the hills like Jeannie Longo and Maria Canins. I developed such a respect for that, and that's where I got my desire to be able to climb well. Now that I can do that, I've developed new respect for the person who can do that plus get there at the finishing sprint. I've now lost my desire to just go out and do long miles. Now my desire is to do sprints too, to have the power and to have the speed. At first, I would do my sprint work out of duty; now I've got the passion for doing the sprint. To be in this sport you have to have the passion.

Q: You've told me that one of the things that really inspired you to start bike racing was the prospect of the Tour de France Féminin.

A: The reason I first started racing my bike was the dream (of a women's Tour de France). Some guy would tell me, "Oh, in bicycle racing you have to climb mountain pass after mountain pass. It's too hard for women!" I thought, "I'll do it!"

So that's the reason why I started the women's Tour de France because I heard that there were all these mountain passes and the climbing, and I thought that was the type of racing I wanted to do. Once I was in it, I was almost climbing with Canins but not quite because I don't have the years that she's got. But I couldn't get rid of Longo. I could drop her, but then she'd turn around and kill everyone in a sprint. That's when I decided if I want to be great I'd have to refine my technique.

Q: When you first started cycling, people made the comment that you had only been on a bike for six months and made the Olympic team. Many people didn't understand that you had such an extensive background in running. Did your background—training your body for over a decade or more—contribute to your success?

A: The only reason I did well my first year was because of my background. The only strength I had was endurance. In the Olympics there were some hills, and the race was long, and those were the only things I had going for me. As far as running is concerned, I was maybe national class, but I didn't have speed, and I was just too big. I don't think I would have been great at it or even good.

Q: You told me that you do a lot of stage races. Do you consider yourself a stage racer over a one-day road or criterium racer?

A: This is the first year that I've done a lot of stage racing. Just comparing how I do in stage races versus single day races, I would

Inga Thompson-Benedict wins the mountain jersey and overall first-place title in the 1987 Ore-Ida Women's Challenge stage race.

Photo courtesy of Ore-Ida Foods, Inc.

have to say that stage races are what I do best. I'd hate to call it my specialty because I didn't want it to be. Because of my background in endurance, I recover better than others do. During the first week, everyone is racing the same, but when you get into the second and third weeks, I'm recovering better than they are.

Q: So it's your endurance background that gets you to the point where you can pull it off?

A: Yes, and attitude in the sense that I love to go day after day after day. When the girls start to slow down, I start to become stronger, attacking more and becoming more aggressive, and mentally that really starts to affect them. They're hoping that things will slack off as their attitude slacks off as they become more tired, and that's when I start putting the pressure on, and most people can't stand up to that.

Q: Do you see yourself as talented?

A: I see myself as having a really strong background and the natural ability. I try hard, but I see my biggest weakness as my lack of discipline. When I have a conference with myself, I say, well it's good, but considering what I've done, I could do a lot better. Discipline and maintaining the passion is what's important.

Q: What's your training like in the winter and during the season? Do you work with a coach?

A: I had a guy who coached me for a year, but we were always knocking heads. He put all the discipline there, but the passion was gone. In 1985, I was very disciplined, but I didn't like riding my bike.

Q: Do you lift weights?

A: I lift weights in the winter, both for my upper body and legs. I think this year I'll put a lot more emphasis on power, and maybe not quite so much emphasis on upper body training. I do some mountain biking. I always used to ski in the winter—I was an instructor—but I don't anymore because now when there's an off-season I want it to be an off-season. I'd like to do more cross-country skiing, though. I get pretty lazy.

Q: Do you find that you need a physical and psychological break from all the training, competition, and traveling?

A: Ever since I was in fifth grade I've been competing year round. I've found that over the last couple of years I need to take time off to be a human being and have a normal life. I've also found that whenever I do take a break it brings back a lot of passion. The first time it happened to me, I was injured. I had been competing year-round for eight years, and I took off about a year. Then after I started riding in February, I made the Olympic team by June.

Q: *Do you have to make yourself back off and rest?*

A: I've learned that the most important thing is rest. The whole time that I was running, I'd never take a day off because of the guilt trips. I'd think, "Oh, if I take the day off, it's going to hurt my training." When I started riding in 1984, I did the same thing. I'd ride mountain pass after mountain pass sometimes for six or seven hours a day and never take a day off. When I started training in 1985, one day a week no matter what, feeling great or feeling bad, I'd take a day off. I'd put the bike in the garage one day a week and I wouldn't touch it. This year I did the same thing, plus, after a hard tour, I'd get off my bike for a full week. I'd be flat for a week or so and then just peak myself back up. Now I'm a real believer in rest. I discovered through experience that rest is just as important as training. You can't really train hard if you're not rested. Mentally, it's important to get off the bike for a while.

Q: *When you race in Europe, do you find that the European women have the same level of support American women enjoy?*

A: I don't think so. In all the races I've been in, I've never seen a European women's trade team. Most of their teams are national teams. In America, women are just about equal to the men in their sports. In Europe, bicycling is the main sport for the men, and it's encouraged from a young age. Whereas in America, cycling is not the main sport for men and it's not really encouraged. In America, bicycling for women is supported more than it is in Europe. In Europe, women cyclists are regarded as second-class citizens in the sport and they aren't supported. That's why you see so many strong American women. Europe has their great athletes, but we have much greater depth. The women that you see racing in the United States are there because they want to be, not because their parents pushed them into it at a young age.

Q: *Does women's racing get the respect it deserves, here and in Europe?*

A: If you're just a girl out there riding, you're fair game. You should have been in France; they were terrible over there. You'd be up there on the starting blocks, with these old leches up there who are supposed to be holding onto the bike, and instead they hold onto your butt. You slap them and they pretend not to speak English. The only time I got mad about it was when I'd come by in the women's race and they'd start laughing. It's the women, they'd be saying it in French. "It's Le Femme" and they'd start cracking up. I think for the support that we have and for what's demanded of us we're out there racing just as hard as the pros. In the '86 Coors Classic, I beat a lot of the guys. Out of a 30-minute time trial I think I was only 45 seconds down on Bernard (Hinault). I was 20th overall in the men. I also beat Eric Heiden. I think more women could be top racers if they had the support.

Women don't really have the coaching. The USCF tries. Since they've gotten Sue Novara-Reber, it's definitely taken a step upward. She's done an excellent job. But before she came, I seriously feel that no one cared about the women's racing. If they don't have support, how are these women supposed to advance? Take football. You have the Pop Warner leagues in junior high school and high school and college with scholarships, and then they can go on and be pros and make a couple million. In women's bike racing, the only thing that gets them in is the desire because there is no money. This year will be neat because there are a lot of new sponsors coming in, but I have the feeling that it's another one of these Olympic things. In 1983, a bunch of sponsors came in but from what I understand, as soon as the Olympics were over, all the sponsors dropped their women and said as soon as the Olympics come around we'll pick you up again. I don't respect that at all. That's why I like 7-Eleven, because even though the Olympics were over they still supported their women.

Q: Will you still race for 7-Eleven in the future?

A: Yes, I'm going to stay with them because they are truly interested in the sport. I have never been asked to do anything besides race my bike for them. They don't put a lot of ties on me. To have a major sponsor do that is pretty good. It seems like when you get with a smaller sponsor, people who don't have quite as much money, they get very petty.

Q: Is the lack of substantive support, both financial and developmental, the really big issue in women's cycling?

A: It's really hard when you're racing for somebody and your gut feeling is that they don't really care. When you're training hard and racing hard, especially if it's the middle of the winter and you're training in a raging snowstorm, and you don't have a lot of money, you wonder why you're doing it.

Q: Do you think that the women's races should be longer, more challenging? What would you like to see?

A: The races should be more challenging as the men's. The courses that they gave us were not as challenging as the men's. In the Tour, the races weren't as long, but they were challenging as the men's. For example, the men would go out and climb three mountain passes, and we'd climb two. What was neat was that we were climbing the same mountain passes. But in the Coors, a couple of times, we didn't get to climb mountains that the men got to climb. It's too bad because you can have this long race, but when it gets fun is when it gets difficult. Then the colors start to come out, things break up, tactics start to happen.

Q: What advice would you give to a woman who wants to get into racing?

A: I would ask if she wants to do it for fun or if she wants to be one of the best. If she says, "I want to do it for fun," then I'd tell her to keep it as fun. Do all the other things you want to do in life but don't make bike racing first. Make it something you enjoy doing. If you want to be one of the best, or be your best at it, then expect to become disciplined, expect to go through a lot of hard times, and expect a lot of things, not just the training, to be hard. Be ready to deal with everything that comes with bike racing because that's where you make or break it. I got all the support that I needed and that was great because if I didn't have that support I don't think I would have done quite as well. I don't think I could have handled it without the support of my family. Not many women are going to have that support.

What I've also found is that when you train with a group, you should keep it fun. At a certain point you're going to have to separate yourself and do what you have to do. Some things that I hated but knew I had to do were intervals and sprint workouts. I think the difference between the good and the great is who goes out and does the dirty work when she really doesn't want to.

Photo by M. Chritton/Coors Classic

Jeannie Longo, Inga Thompson-Benedict, and Rebecca Twigg after the Estes Park stage of the 1985 Coors Bicycle Classic. Longo was the stage winner.

Q: *Do you keep a training diary?*

A: This last year has been really bad. I used to fill the thing out every single day—how much I weighed, how much sleep I got, how many sit-ups or push-ups I did. After France, I haven't even touched it. You know what's really important: you should list your weight, how many hours you slept, and your heart rate—waking and then after you've been up for a couple minutes. You should list your workout. You don't have to go into any great detail; I put down what my workout was in a very simple block form. I have a separate column where I put down how I felt physically and mentally— nothing in great detail unless I'm in a sarcastic mood and then I talk about running over snails with my bike. When I look back the next year, I don't look for the detail stuff, but I want to see the building. When I look back a month later, I look at how hard I trained, my heart rate, and my attitude. If I notice that I'm doing the same workout but I'm going slower, my attitude's bad, or my heart rate's higher, I know when to back off a little bit. Attitude is really important; I keep track of my attitude for my own good. In some ways, I really should have kept track of the time between the Tour de France and the Coors because I think that's been the most interesting part of my whole athletic career because of the things I had to go through. I didn't keep track of it, but I would be really interested to look back and see an entire month of nothing but cussing.

Q: What kinds of stress did you have to deal with during that period?

A: A lot of it was physical because I never had to put that kind of stress on my body. A lot of it was mental because I was with a new team. Also, I was about to get married and you put a lot of time into relating to somebody. So between developing a relationship that's really new, being about to get married, racing, and feeling physically and mentally the stresses of racing, I couldn't tell you which way was up. A couple of times, I thought I was going to have a severe physical breakdown because of the stresses.

Q: Is having a good relationship a real strain, or is it a support, or is it some of both?

A: I think it's a real support. I'd have to say I think one of the reasons I did much better this year was having my husband to tell me what was going on. He's not my coach but he knows me. I think that's where I've gotten my change of attitude. As far as the bicycling goes, there's been nothing but support. Where it's been hard is when it comes down to two people and both people need equal time. My whole life has revolved around bike racing. Now I have to take half of that and put it into this person. But that's the way a relationship for me should be—equal. I don't deserve anything more because I'm out racing my bike; he works too.

Q: I get the feeling that you have discovered a lot about yourself and that you're much more aware of what your strengths and weaknesses are and how to improve and that you're really coming into your own.

A: I think that's true. The first couple of years that I was racing, you could say that I was just in the pack. The only time you ever saw me was when something individual happened, like if there was a hill, because I just didn't have confidence in the pack. It hasn't truly been until this year that I started to say, "Hey, this person isn't invincible," and then it becomes exciting.

Q: What are your future goals both in cycling and beyond?
A: If I have a goal, it is—just because of what I have learned from Longo—to always be there in the finishing sprint. To be in contention, to be somebody that people watch. I just want to give the best. It's just being there—I think that's my goal.

Q: Some people would say their goal is the Olympics or the Worlds. What you have said is that it's a quality and it's a state of mind, not something that you can hold up as a trophy or medal awarded at some distinctive point.
A: Sure I want to make the Olympic team and win a gold medal, but when you're racing with the best, then it's either luck that day, or it's who's feeling the best. If you look at swimming, everyone is a tenth of a second off, and the winner maybe wins by 1/100th of a second. To me it all comes down to who's feeling the best on that particular day, and there are so many variables. You could get a cold or the stomach flu, or maybe for women it's that time of the month. It's just one of those things—I'm going to go for it, but all I can give it is what I have that day. In some ways I'm discouraged with the Olympics and the attitude that the Americans have toward it. You can go off and win the World Championships and no one really pays attention, but it's different if you have a gold medal. The public always wants somebody to have a title; race promoters want to call you "The winner of the Tour de France" or "an Olympic gold-medal winner." Well, I hate to have my achievement all come down to one day. Sure I'd love to win a gold medal for myself, but I want satisfaction out of my racing.

CONNIE PARASKEVIN-YOUNG
WORLD CYCLING CHAMPION

Connie Paraskevin-Young, a resident of Indianapolis, Indiana, joined the competitive cycling and speed-skating ranks at the early age of 10.

Photo courtesy of ProServ

Connie Paraskevin-Young. Connie was a member of the 1980 and 1984 Olympic speed-skating teams, was World Match Sprint Champion in 1982, 1983, and 1984, and was a bronze medalist in the 1988 Olympics in Seoul. She is also a 10-time National Cycling Champion.

Paraskevin-Young was a member of the 1980 and 1984 Olympic speed-skating teams. She was the World Cycling Champion (match sprints) in 1982, 1983, and 1984, winning bronze medals in 1985, 1986, and 1987. In 1988 Connie Paraskevin-Young won a bronze medal in the first-ever Olympic Match Sprint competition for women. She is also a 10-time National Cycling Champion.

In addition to her role as an athlete representative on the board of directors for the US Cycling Federation, Connie is active in the promotion and marketing of cycling as a sport and as a recreational activity. I met Connie in Long Beach, California.

Q: *When did you start cycling?*

A: I started when I was 10, so I've been in about 15 years. Actually, I started skating first, but that same summer I started riding, just as something to do. The club that I belonged to had speed skating, bike racing, bike touring, and cross-country skiing. It was a year-round sports club. So, it was natural that most of the people in the club rode either touring or racing bikes. There was a big group of kids my age at the time, 20 of us or so, and probably 15 out of the 20 did both.

Q: Weren't Connie Carpenter and Beth Heiden both from the same area?

A: Most of us were from the Wolverines Sports Club. Sheila Young was from the same club. Sue Novara was also part of that club. Tom Schuler and Scott Berryman were there for a while. Quite a few riders have come from it. Their methods and their system are effective. When we were learning things, we were actually having fun learning them. And they were always there to direct you, whatever area you wanted to go into.

Q: Did the more experienced riders help the younger people or did you have coaches?

A: Both. What you have there is the people that started the club, I don't know how many years ago—mainly Mike Walden and also Claire Young—who truly love cycling and know the sport. They did the sport themselves. And so they have been the core that has kept it going. They're knowledgeable, so they keep producing successful athletes. They take it to a certain level. If you eventually wanted to become an elite cyclist, you had to get more individual attention at some point, so you'd break off. I'm really still following the same philosophy. The basics of the sport are the same. Even when I go out training today, I'll still go over a lot of fundamentals because you can forget those fundamentals.

Q: What are some of those fundamentals?

A: The fundamentals include handling skills and different riding techniques. When I go out onto the track, the first thing I do is play a game called "follow the leader"—just going up and down the track, riding the track at different levels and different speeds, turning different ways. If I were taking a group out for their first time riding the track, I would take them through "follow the leader," not as crazy as I go of course, but, very gradually up and down. That's one of the basics. Another is just the way you position yourself on the bike. The basic things that I learned from day one, I still go out and do every day because you can always improve upon them, and you have to have those down before you can do anything else.

Q: *What made you start racing?*

A: I was fortunate enough at that time to be involved in a club like that, and it was fun. I had a lot of friends, and the club was like a big family. It still is. They generate a real family feeling. And that's what a club is. You should enjoy yourself. I don't know if I'd have gotten involved and stayed in the sport if I'd gotten into a club that wasn't fun. They instilled a lot of my deep-down thoughts about the way I look at cycling.

Connie Paraskevin-Young holds off Melody Wong of the Davis Bike Club in a 1985 Match Sprint Competition.

Q: What has cycling meant to you?

A: I like going fast. I like to compete and, again, I've always liked the people that have been around. I think I came to the sport at a time when a lot of things were opening up. When I was really young, my older sisters didn't have the opportunities that I had. Their school didn't have women's teams. And that seemed really strange to me, because I never saw that. You hear it's a new thing for women to be able to participate so freely, but I always did. So, all through my life as I've come up, it's been very easy for me. I've been lucky to grow up at a time when things were changing so much every year in cycling that I could stay involved.

Ten years ago, women came into cycling just because they had the desire, and they stuck it out. They were great athletes, like Sheila Young. She had the desire and the capabilities, but she wasn't really supported. Now more women are coming into the sport because a lot of them are able to make something of a living out of it, or at least pay their expenses. I don't know if I would have been able to keep it up if I hadn't at least had some kind of financial backing and support.

Q: What changes have you seen in the support for women's cycling programs over the years?

A: One of the positives is that the women's teams are getting more financial support, and there are more races, but that has been one of the things that we've had to fight for. It wasn't long ago that women's cycling wasn't taken seriously. Sue Novara had a father who helped her out a lot; her father was very knowledgeable and coached her. I was lucky, too, because I had my own coach. But that wasn't true for everyone. One of the things I was always fighting for was for the Federation to get a program for women—a place for them to go to reach that next level. My personal concern was that some female cyclists were hitting a certain level and there was no direction for them to go. So they would get discouraged and quit, or just kind of float along at that level and never get to the next level. I kept lobbying for a program for them, even though I had my own coach. I wasn't necessarily going to change coaches and follow the national team coach, but the other women needed it. They were coming to me and asking what they could do.

Q: What else would you like to see change?

A: One thing would be development. I think you really need to get a strong development program together, because we're not reaching the younger women. For a long time the young girls were looking for something and there was nothing. Now there are two women's camps and there's a Junior Women's Worlds. But it's going to take a while to recruit young women.

Q: *Are more women going into track than there were before?*

A: It's the same thing. We're going to have to have more programs, because so many times you have people come up to you and say they want to do it, but they don't know how to get involved. Even elite women riders say they've been training and concentrating on the road and they want to do pursuit this year. But again, there's nowhere for them to go to train for it.

A lot of the women who are coming into cycling were triathletes or runners. They were running or swimming competitively and they rode their bike a bit, maybe for training, and they decided they liked it. They wanted to start racing. They're really good, strong athletes.

Then you have people that have had injuries in another sport and the doctor recommends cycling for therapy, and they end up liking cycling so much that they forget their other sport and stick with cycling. Quite a few people I know did that.

It's interesting, because these women coming from other sports are not too old for cycling. You can compete well in cycling in your 30s. Women have won world championships well in their 30s. They take time off, have a couple of kids, and then come back. Riders don't want to hang it up when they're 21, but many of them have to make a living. One reason why I think we did so well at the '84 Olympics was because riders started getting better financial support so they could stay in the sport longer. If you look at ages, we had a much older team, and they were able to reach their peak. Sheila Young-Ochowicz was over 30 when she won one of her world championships.

I think you get better and better. I don't think you get slow. It's a very good sport for your body. It's very smooth. You're not pounding it on the cement everyday.

Q: *What's your winter training like?*

A: Just weights and time on the bike, what we call slow miles. I use this to get a lot of miles in that will enable me to repeat hard workouts later in the year. In the winter, if I went out on the track and tried to do a hard workout, I probably couldn't repeat too many hard sprints. And when I'm doing workouts or when I'm racing, I'll have to do maybe 10 hard sprints in a day, and it's hard to repeat 10 sprints at the same top level. So having a lot of slow miles, just endurance miles early in the year, enables me to compete.

Q: *How many miles a week would that be?*
  A: I don't really know. I do it by hours. The most would be five hours a day. The majority of the days, I do three hours. In the fall, I do intervals too. I would do a half hour warm-up ride followed by intervals that take maybe an hour, so that even though the day's very short, it's more intense. The next day would be a long ride. So mainly I'm doing just weights, intervals, and miles on the bike. Maybe once a week I'll ride the track, just for fun.

And then in the season, once racing starts, I still put in miles on the road and sprints on the road and intervals. No more five-hour rides; max is about two or three hours with the same philosophy of harder and shorter.

I usually start riding the track in about June. If I started riding the track early in the year I'd be sick of it by the time August comes. I ride it enough to keep in touch with it, but I don't really do too much.

Then, in June, I start riding the track all the time. Gradually all I'm doing on the road is maybe a maximum of two hours, very, very easy every other day. And that is only for recovery from all the hard work on the track every day. It's just as if a runner would stretch for recovery.

Q: *When do you start pushing hard?*
  A: January. Sometimes I'm on the bike for five hours. That's training to me, whether I'm doing it at 40 mph or 20. Then there're still hard workouts intervals. But in January, I start serious training, longer distance stuff. The intervals are longer because they're geared toward being able to ride a criterium.

So, the intensity doesn't change, but what you're actually doing changes. Early in the year, I kind of play on the track and my hard work is done on the road. But, June comes around and all my hard work is done on the track. My recovery work is done on the road.

Q: *When does the season end for you?*
  A: Usually October.

Q: From October to January, what do you do?

A: It depends on the weather. Last year we raced pretty much through October and then tapered down in November and December. The year before, we went to Europe, and we rode the track indoors. That was really good because the tracks there are really steep—they're like a wall. They're also *very* small, 165 meters versus 333. So, everything is speeded up more. All your reactions are speeded up. And that really was good for me; for my bike-handling skills and my perception.

Q: So you don't really lay off during the year?

A: Well, November's pretty easy.

Q: You really just have a month?

A: Yes. Even that is new to me, because I've only had two seasons when I've had November free—last year and this year. Every other year, I was skating, so it was year-round. I don't know what I'm going to do next year.

Q: What advice do you have for a woman who wants to start racing?

A: The first thing I'd say is to join a club, because wherever you're located, the key is to be able to have a group to train with. I think that's really important. I don't care what kind of mileage you go out and do on your own, it's really important to ride in groups. And hopefully there are some knowledgeable people involved with clubs. The second thing would be to go to the Federation and the various camps and clinics.

Q: What would you like to be remembered for?

A: I'd like to make it easier for women to do the kinds of things they do to excel in cycling. I'd just like to make it easier.

RESOURCES

United States Cycling Federation (USCF)
US Olympic Training Center
1750 E. Boulder Street
Colorado Springs, CO 80909
(719) 578-4581

The USCF is the sanctioning body for competitive amateur cycling in the United States. You need a license to compete in USCF events. To obtain a license application, race schedule, or information on development programs, contact the USCF. If you are interested in the track, there is a list of USCF Velodromes in Appendix 7.

Further Information

If you are interested in racing, go to your local bike shop and locate the racing club near you. If you're lucky enough to live in an area that has lots of racing clubs, you can choose the one that best fits your needs in terms of development, sponsorship, team spirit, etc. Eddie Borysewicz's *Bicycle Road Racing*, and Greg LeMond's *Complete Book of Bicycling* are good sources of information on training and racing. Various cycling magazines cover the racing scene and offer information on everything from hot products to training tips and interviews with top racers.

8
Mountain Biking

"One can never consent to creep when one feels an impulse to soar."
—Helen Keller

Mountain biking and off-road cycling have become quite popular in the last 10 years. This kind of cycling had its genesis in a group of northern California bicycle road racers who were fed up with competing against traffic and fellow cyclists and turned to the dirt—to the firebreaks and hiking trails of Marin County, just north of San Francisco. They created a monster of an industry that has bicycle manufacturers scrambling to keep up with prolific technological changes and park officials scrambling to deal with large numbers of cyclists on hiking trails.

The sport is here to stay. Mountain bike sales have increased significantly every year for the past 10 years. And interestingly, 70 percent of the all-terrain bikes are currently being sold to women. Bike shop owners report that many of the people who buy an all-terrain bike do so with the intent of riding it primarily on the street and only occasionally taking it on the dirt. The wider tires and upright bars make for such a comfortable ride that even the most reluctant of newcomers will find something to like about this alternate form of cycling.

Another breed, however, takes to the dirt with the enthusiasm with which nature lovers take to the woods—precisely because this new

195

Photo courtesy of Heidi Hopkins

Jill McIntire (l) and Patty Kline (r) enjoyed a fully supported one-month mountain-bike tour in the Peruvian Andes. Jill says that you don't have to train to enjoy mountain-bike touring. "All I had to carry were my day clothes; the organizers took care of the rest. The tour was fun and not too tough. I didn't train, I just went. I enjoy traveling off-road in other countries. We spent more time in the villages, and experienced the culture first-hand. We saw things we would have missed for sure if we were traveling on the road!"

breed is a combination of athlete and nature lover. While hiking can put them in touch with the great outdoors, a bike can do it faster and better. On a mountain bike, you can cover five times the mileage of a hiker and still be close to nature. As noted mountain bike rider, Rick Denman says, "When I ride on the road, I consider it 'off-dirt' riding!"

Where people ride bikes, they will race and off-road is no exception. The National Off-Road Bicycle Association (NORBA) sponsors an extensive racing program. Next we meet two top NORBA racers.

Jacquie Phelan and her beloved riding partner, Chrome Moly.

Photo by George Nikitin

JACQUIE PHELAN (ALIAS ALICE B. TOECLIPS)
OFF-ROAD MADNESS

"All sanity depends on this: that it should be a delight to feel heat strike the skin, a delight to stand upright, knowing the bones are moving easily under flesh."

—Doris Lessing

Jacquie Phelan is both athlete and nature lover, obsessed with winning and driven to stay in touch with the cosmos through the great outdoors. In addition to winning the 1984 and 1985 NORBA World Championships, Jacquie, until 1986, had never lost a single race—EVER! Before a recent surge in new talent, all races in which Jacquie competed were simply races for second place. Phelan quickly became the touchstone for comparison of all other riders. Talent was judged in the sport by "how far you finished behind Jacquie Phelan."

Phelan has appeared on many television shows, including "PM Magazine," "Sports Beat," and "Evening Magazine." She has also appeared in and written articles for *Rolling Stone* magazine, *Bicycling*, *Cyclist*, *Bicycle Action*, *Women's Sports & Fitness*, *Winning*, *Ultrasport*, and *Outside* magazines.

I talked to Jacquie at her home in Marin County, California, the birthplace of the sport of off-road madness. Jacquie has been there since the beginning. She has not only helped build the sport of mountain biking, she has contributed to the overall image of women as serious athletes in the entire sport of bicycle racing, indeed, in athletics in general.

Q: What do you get out of mountain biking?
A: It lets me be an animal again.

Q: What? Please explain.
A: It lets me tune into the environment—the smell, the physical terrain, the changing seasons. It puts me in tune with the universe. Polluting less and riding more is my little way of being independent.

Q: Why do you like riding on the dirt instead of the road?
A: The cars are the main difference. On the dirt I'm responsible for anything that goes wrong. In traffic there is a huge, uncontrollable variable.

Q: How do you train?
A: In the winter I lift weights and ride cyclocross [a similar sport to mountain bike racing where competitors ride road bikes in extremely muddy, rainy, and inclement weather. It has been around far longer than mountain biking.] I also lead rides and clinics for women.

In the season I measure my training by the number of hours ridden, not just miles. I use the "hard day/easy day" philosophy. When I'm riding I work on technique. I pick a certain trail and practice finesse on my descents and climbs. The first thing that everyone has to do is get to know their bike. This is critical. You have to know how the bike will respond.

Q: How many races do you do a year, and what are they like?

A: I ride maybe 30 to 40 races a year. Whiskey Town, Rockhopper, and Ross are the big ones. The rest I go to depending on who's putting on a good party. Mountain bike races are different than other bicycle races. They are more like "powwows." Sometimes there is a party at the end. Of course, this isn't the main reason we do the races. The reason anyone does races like these is to pit themselves against the mountain. And compared to road races, there are far more entrants in mountain bike races. We get 350 to 400 competitors. That's bigger than anything in the sport except those huge century rides.

It's a love affair with geography, geology, and animal history. And the beautiful part about it is that you don't have to be a jock to try and race. Virtually anybody who buys a bike is capable of mastering it. In a few weeks, she can think to herself: "I'm going to race this thing." In road racing this just isn't done.

Q: What motivates you to keep racing year after year?

A: I'm not so sure. It's hard to stay motivated all the time. Originally I was in racing to win. When I finally lost a race, I lost some of my motivation. Now I strive for excellence and discipline in order to overcome the impulsive and lazy side of me.

Q: What's been the biggest factor in your success?

A: Each win is a reason to keep going. But even in the case of not winning, a particularly fun race or ride is really stimulating.

Q: How many more years do you expect to compete?

A: When I look at Maria Canins I think to myself, "I don't have any excuse to quit earlier than age 37!" I suppose when I have too many injuries or physical breakdowns that I will listen to my body. But I hope it doesn't come to that.

What I'd really like to do is become a believable role model. It sounds funny saying it, but I'd like people to see me as a model of independence. The most lofty goal in the world is to get yourself around by your own power. I did a moonlight ride with a 14-year-old guy last night, and it really changed his life around.

The whole purpose of racing is to have a love affair with nature, not just to be a gladiator for spectators. Criteriums that are only one-half to one mile long and just go around and around are dull. Point-to-point races across a mountain are exciting. It's survival of the fittest. I prefer tour races where you actually cover some ground. You don't really have time to see all the scenery, but you do take some in out of the corner of your eye. You actually go through ecological transects such as woodland, grass, and forest, and it's really neat. We're not out there just to please spectators.

Q: Do the women get equal prize money and equal media exposure?

A: Not by a long shot. It's more like 10 to 1 in favor of the men. There should be equal prize money. If there was more prize money, there would be more women. But ironically, this is good for the sponsors because the smaller the women's field, the greater chance of seeing the sponsor's logo. There isn't equal exposure either. The men get far more coverage. Most of the women in the sport are in it at the hobby level. They just hope to make enough money to pay for the habit.

Q: What do you recommend a woman do to get into the sport?

A: The first thing is to get a bike and a helmet. Then go out for an hour and find your way back home. Do that everyday for a month, and it will give you a good flavor for mountain biking. I also suggest joining NORBA (National Off-Road Bicycle Association).

When you race, don't take anyone's word on the course. You should go out and ride the race course two days before, if possible. You should feel familiar with the bike—that's really pretty critical. One little hint—if you can hop up a curb comfortably, then you have good bike control. In general, if you think you can do it that's all you need.

Q: Could you give a typical training/racing week?

A: • Sunday: Race! One hundred percent effort for approximately two to three hours depending upon the race. Drive home. Get all still and go to bed to rest and recover.

 • Monday: Recover from the weekend. Run errands. Ride approximately five to 10 miles on the bike. Shower and stretch for 30 minutes.

 • Tuesday: Ride two and a half to three hours at 90 percent of capacity. Then stretch for 30 minutes.

 • Wednesday: Ride one hour at 75 percent. Then run errands (on the bike, of course).

 • Thursday: Ride two and one-half to three hours at 80 percent.

 • Friday: Ride two hours at 100 percent.

 • Saturday: Rest and drive to the next race.

 • Sunday: RACE!!

Photo by Don Mertle/Fat Tire Flyer

Cindy Whitehead, 1986 US National Off-Road Association Champion. Whitehead has many talents. She promotes mountain-bike races, and is a top competitor on the Specialized racing team.

TIPS FOR MOUNTAIN BIKE RACING FROM CINDY WHITEHEAD

Cindy Whitehead currently resides in Palm Springs, California. She has been road racing since 1982. In addition to promoting and organizing races, and working with a bicycle-leasing business, the 26-year-old Whitehead has made a name for herself in off-road bicycle racing since 1985.

Whitehead was the 1987 winner of the women's division of the Raleigh Technium World Mountain Bike Championships—Down-hiller, and was the 1987 NORBA California State Champion. She was also the 1986 NORBA National Champion.

Whitehead actively promotes bicycling, particularly off-road bicycling, as a sport and recreation for everyone. She kindly provided the following tips for aspiring mountain-bike racers.

Equipment

The bike, of course, should be a mountain bike and there are many on the market to choose from. But basically the frame geometry (the angles of the tubes on the bike) should be similar to a touring road bike. That is, there should be a 70- to 71-degree angle in the head tube, a 71- to 73-degree angle for the seat tube, and nothing more than 17-inch chainstays. [Author's note: Frame geometry, or the angles of the various tubes to one another, makes a difference in efficiency and comfort. The steeper the tube angles, that is, the closer to 90 degrees, the stiffer and more efficient the frame will be: it will respond much more quickly. Track racing bikes have extremely steep angles and are very sensitive to the input from the rider. However, a stiff frame geometry makes for an uncomfortable ride. Track bikes can afford to be stiff and efficient because they are being ridden on a perfectly smooth track surface. However, when riding on rough roads, or worse, unpaved mountain trails, it is worth the sacrifice in stiffness and efficiency for the tradeoff in comfort and "survivability."]

Tires

Tires are very important in terms of traction. Pick a good tread, such as the Specialized Ground Control or Hardpack, and run tire pressure as low as possible. [Author's note: On the road, the higher the tire pressure the more efficient the ride, but as in frame geometry, you lose comfort. On the dirt, not only does high tire pressure make for a less comfortable ride, it also adds to tire slippage. Low tire pressure is more comfortable and adds to tire traction.] I've been known to have as little as 18 psi (pounds per square inch) in my tires. [Author's note: A typical road tire pressure is over 100 psi!] I also recommend running a little higher pressure on downhills to avoid pinching the inner tube.

Components

Shimano currently makes the best derailleurs and brakes on the market. I have personally tested and prefer the Browning automatic transmission to a front derailleur. They will be available on production bikes, such as Specialized, Diamond Back, and Raleigh, beginning in 1988.

Safety Gear

Always wear a helmet. Since the helmet market is now producing light, cool, and inexpensive gear, there is no longer any excuse not to be wearing a helmet. I also recommend gloves to protect your hands. I once finished a 30-mile race without gloves but my hands were bleeding and sore. It can get pretty rough out there!

Photo courtesy of Don Mertle/Fat Tire Flyer

Cindy Whitehead won the 1986 Sierra 7500 Plumb-line 50-mile mountain-bike race after losing her saddle in the first mile.

Training

I recommend, essentially, a road-racing training program as a good seasonal guideline and a very good conditioning program throughout the off-road racing season. Since off-road riding requires a little more upper body strength, though, I also recommend weight training or swimming. It is also advisable to do some running, since it increases calf strength and aerobic capabilities, and is often required in unrideable sections in races or on the trails. The only other recommendation I have is to keep your off-road bike-handling skills sharp by spending at least 30 percent of your riding time in the dirt. Go for it!

RESOURCES

National Off-Road Bicycle Association (NORBA)
PO Box 1901
Chandler, AZ 85244

NORBA focuses primarily on mountain-bike racing and is the sanctioning body for competitive mountain-bike events.

International Mountain Bicycling Association (IMBA)
PO Box 2007
Saratoga, CA 95070-0007
(408) 741-5254
(619) 387-2757

IMBA is a nonprofit mutual benefit corporation that focuses on all aspects of land access for recreation and touring, education of riders, and formation of local clubs. IMBA's corporate structure provides for voting by the membership.

Women's Mountain Bike and Tea Society (WOMBATS)
Box 757
Fairfax, CA 94930

Jacquie Phelan founded WOMBATS as a fat tire "ladies" networking organization. WOMBATS is a national organization for women interested in all aspects of mountain-bike riding. For $25 you can join WOMBATS and receive a T-shirt and newsletter announcing WOMBAT rides and social events in your area.

Further Information

In addition to the many cycling magazines that include some coverage of mountain biking, there are several magazines that specialize in mountain biking. They are listed in Appendix 3.

9
Endurance

"I can remember walking as a child. It was not customary to say you were fatigued. It was customary to complete the goal of the expedition."

—Katharine Hepburn

Endurance cycling has been around almost as long as the bicycle itself. Several bicycle trips around the world were made in the 1890s and centuries, or 100-mile rides, were also popular at that time. The current resurgence of exercise sees thousands of people coming to run marathons and take part in century rides, and even double centuries. And many of the competitors want more. Ultramarathon events have emerged and participation is growing.

This chapter briefly introduces two of these ultramarathon events and five of the preeminent women competitors.

THE IRONMAN TRIATHLON

The Ironman is probably responsible for the popularity of triathlons and, in large measure, it may be responsible for the ultramarathon craze. Certainly the great TV coverage of the Ironman by ABC's "Wide World of Sports" has provided good exposure for ultramarathon events in general and triathlons in particular.

The Ironman began in 1978 as a test for 12 macho fellows who wanted to see if they could swim 2.2 miles and then ride a bike over

100 miles and then run a marathon, all in less than 24 hours. Now the promoters have to limit the field to 1,500 and the course is regularly completed by grandmothers.

Joanne Ernst, Ironman winner in 1985, describes training for and competing in the Ironman in an interview later in the chapter.

RAAM—THE RACE ACROSS AMERICA

Records for rides across the North American continent have been kept for some time. An individual would gather a few friends and a car to help out and see how long it took to ride across. When John Marino established a new individual record of 13 days, 1 hour, and 20 minutes in 1978, he also established a dream—a race across the country. In 1982, John's dream became a reality and four men set out in the Great American Bike Race from Santa Monica to New York. The race has been renamed RAAM (Race Across AMerica) and has been held each year since then. From 1982 to 1986, it received award-winning coverage from ABC's "Wide World of Sports."

After the first year a qualifying race, the John Marino Open, or JMO, was established. At the first JMO in 1983, Kitty Goursolle surprised a lot of people by qualifying for RAAM along with nine men. She was holding her own in RAAM 1983 when a car wreck deprived her of her support vehicles and forced her to stop in Colorado. (It was Kitty who inspired me to get involved in the JMO and RAAM in 1984.) Since 1985, there has been a separate women's division in RAAM.

RAAM is run as a coast-to-coast time trial. Racers are not allowed to draft other racers or any other riders or vehicles. The clock does not stop during RAAM. There are no rest periods or stages. Once you leave the Pacific Ocean, you are timed until you arrive at the Atlantic Ocean. You may stop and rest, but the clock won't stop and your competitors might not stop either. In addition to the usual test of physical condition, RAAM is a paramount test of will and concentration, which must be maintained over a period of eight to ten days, or more.

As a time trial, RAAM is a test of individual effort. But competitors are accompanied by support crews, which are now mandatory. The crew is crucial in keeping the rider safe and supplied, and sometimes in keeping the rider motivated. So, in a sense, RAAM is very much a team sport.

RAAM is also a test of financial skills. It costs a rider anywhere from $5,000 to $20,000 or more to compete. Finding sponsorship and other ways to offset these expenses is a major factor a prospective competitor must face. We have joked that it is odd that it costs $5 per mile to ride a bike across the country, but in RAAM it is true.

We will look into the world of transcontinental records and racing through the eyes of four women who have done it. Susan Notorangelo is the first lady of transcontinental riding. She has held several transcontinental records, some of which still stand, and she won RAAM in 1985. Cheryl Marek and Estelle Gray established the transcontinental tandem record for women in 1984. Casey Patterson set an example for all of us by winning RAAM in 1987 at age 43.

My story of going from last place in 1984 to winning the women's race in record time in 1986 is told in Chapter 10.

SUSAN NOTORANGELO
TAKING CARE OF BUSINESS

Susan Notorangelo's background is as diverse as she is outspoken. After a couple of years as a registered nurse, Notorangelo received her business degree and worked at a major accounting firm as an auditor.

Notorangelo's competitive cycling career did not begin until 1981. Some of her achievements include the National 24-hour Road Record (401.6 miles) in May 1982, Women's US Transcontinental Record (11 days, 16 hours) in June 1982, First Place in the women's division of the 1985 Race Across AMerica, and Tandem Transcontinental records in 1983 and 1986 with her husband, Lon Haldeman.

Susan has been instrumental in the advancement of women in cycling, most notably by her involvement in the Women's Cycling Network. She is the cofounder and executive director of this four-year-old national organization, which now has 500 members.

At present, Susan is on a leave of absence from competitive cycling, having taken time off to have her child, Rebecca. However, she continues her participation in cycling through speaking engagements and appearances, as well as through the codirectorship of Ultra Week, a series of UMCA races held in Harvard, Illinois.

Susan talked with Michael Shermer in her motor home parked in

Susan Notorangelo, winner of the 1985 Race Across AMerica and holder of Mixed Tandem Transcontinental Record, with her husband, Lon Haldeman. Notorangelo also promotes endurance cycling events and is the founder of the Women's Cycling Network.

Huntington Beach, California, the day before she competed in the 1986 RAAM.

Q: *What is the status of women in cycling in this country today, and what does the future hold?*

A: I think that there is much promise in the sport of cycling for women because there is so much room for growth. I feel more women *are* getting involved. However, a woman needs to be a good business person as well as a cyclist in order to make it in the sport today. Cycling is getting to be big business—and very competitive—and if you don't do well you won't get the financial backing in order to be able to train full time.

You need to have it all together today to be successful. You need personality and drive, as well as athletic background. You have to be able to create a résumé, write a professional letter, and call people, and you have to do all those things. You can't *just* be a good cyclist and compete year after year and make money.

What scares me the most is that there seems to be a lack of large numbers of women getting into the higher levels of competition. There are plenty of women who talk about racing, and they are out riding their bikes, but they don't seem to know *how* to get involved.

Q: How long would it take a woman to get physically and mentally prepared to race competitively? Let's assume that we are starting with a weekend rider who is in decent physical condition and she says, "I want to be the next Susan Notorangelo." How long would it take?

A: I think it takes over a year to get prepared. For the RAAM, for instance, I think it takes the ability to ride a double century in under 12 hours to even begin thinking about doing the race. But it's more than just physical conditioning. You need to be psychologically prepared and you have to be able to handle all the logistics of racing: getting your equipment together, your support crew, and so on. It took me one year to become a competitive cyclist, and that was with no injuries and no problems and good coaching, and I started with a strong body.

Q: Are you into quality or quantity miles?

A: I've got to really enjoy my training. I can't just go out and ride 80 to 100 miles every day and get something out of it. I ride organized rides and races in order to improve my overall performance. Or I will ride with a goal or destination in mind. I might ride to Champaign, for instance, and ride back the same day. [Notorangelo lives in Harvard, Illinois. Champaign is exactly 200 miles due south!] A couple of weeks ago I rode 1,300 miles in one week, but it was all through organized events. I did back-to-back quads (400 miles), then I did 150s day after day. Since then I haven't done much. That's the way I am. I need a plan. Pete Penseyres is a perfect example. He rides to and from work every day. He has a goal. That is so much easier than just going out and riding.

I don't think more is better. The more miles I put on the bike, past a certain level, the more injuries I sustain, like to my feet or rear. I also get really burned out with mega-miles so I try to ride as many fun events as possible.

Q: Do you take days off intentionally to rest?

A: No, not intentionally. It just happens when I travel or have a lot of business to conduct.

Q: What motivates you to achieve?

A: I know if I succeed I can at least break even and keep up the house payments, and I don't have to go back to that nine-to-five routine. I think right now that is what spurs me on to greater accomplishments. Lon and I have turned cycling into a secure profession, and we feel secure as long as we are winning. When you are winning you have more leverage to use with sponsors. I think it is truly the desire not to go back to the other world.

Q: It beats working for a living?

A: Well, I wouldn't exactly say it's not working. There are many nights I'm up until 11 or 12 o'clock writing letters or driving home from a talk 300 miles away. But it sure beats the accounting job I had!

Q: There has been a trend in the United States in the last 20 years for women to be more participatory than they ever were in the past. More women are making a living at sports. What do you think the reason for this is?

A: I think it is a change in the population. It is the baby-boomer generation coming up. I believe I read that in my age group there are two women for every man. That means there are twice as many women to compete in athletics as there were in the past, in proportion to men. I'm 32 and a product of the requirements for equal time for sports for women in high school. They had to have women's teams in tennis and golf and other sports, as well as men's teams, and this gave women the impetus to get involved.

The women who are following me up the ranks now are even more athletically inclined and have had more cultural support in their upbringing than I did, so I expect that we will see even more participation. I was 21 when I started competing seriously in sports, but it wasn't until I was 28 that I realized sports could be such a large part of my life.

Q: Is it just population, or are there other factors?

A: No, it's many things. Business, for instance. McDonald's realizes that half the people who eat their hamburgers are women, so they are getting involved with women's sports. McDonald's is my primary sponsor. And the television networks realize that since major corporations, like McDonald's, buy commercial time, they need to cover women as much as they cover men.

Q: But the majority of women in the weight rooms of America are not doing it for television coverage or for the money. Why are they working out?

A: I know when I first got into working out and training, I did it because I wanted to have a nice body, look good, and be attractive to men. I don't know that this is why all women work out, but it was my reason for first getting started.

Q: In cycling you are a role model for women. How does that feel?

A: I get a few people who come up to me and say really nice things. I admit it really is a boost. But sometimes I feel it is pressure. It's more pressure to stay on top because "they" don't want you to lose. Lon's fans always come up to him and ask him if he's better now. They don't mean it negatively, but they expect their heroes to win all the time. It's a lot of pressure, and I think I'll be ready for retirement soon. I don't know how Connie Carpenter did it for as long as she did.

Q: Did you have any heroes?

A: No, I didn't know of any woman athletes and I wasn't very interested in sports growing up.

Q: Where did you get the desire to achieve and get ahead in life? Did you get it from your parents?

A: It may have come from my parents, particularly my dad. I remember getting yelled at when I did something wrong. So whenever I did something, I tried my hardest to do it right.

In college, I carried a 4.0 for seven straight semesters. In nursing school, I graduated in the top 10. It's not a normal way of life, and I guess I got that from my parents. But I still had fun. You can't be too serious all the time.

Book learning is so different than cycling, though. I enjoy riding my bike so much. It just isn't like having to sit down and study for hours on end until your eyes are bloodshot and you can hardly see.

Q: *Are your parents achievers?*
A: Yes, they both are achievers. They both went to college, and all my brothers and sisters went to college, so this was a way of life for my family.

Q: *Should women train differently than men do for cycling?*
A: I think everyone needs to train according to their own individual needs. Everyone is different. I think it is more individual than it is male-female.

There are factors to consider with women. For instance, the monthly reproductive cycle makes certain training days more difficult than others, and this has to be taken into consideration. If you schedule a training program to train a certain way on all Mondays, and another way on all Tuesdays, a woman isn't going to respond the same every week because of her monthly cycle. Personally, I can't train as hard right before my period. But afterward I feel real charged up and ready to go out for a good workout.

A man's training program will not take this into consideration. In fact, I know that Lon doesn't take this into consideration when we train together, and he doesn't understand it.

Q: *Is there still sex discrimination in sports?*
A: Oh, positively, absolutely, it is still there and I can give you a prime example. After last year's Race Across AMerica, the final press release was concerned 99 percent with men and the same will happen this year. I definitely feel that there is still discrimination.

Q: *But at least there is equal prize money. Does that make you feel better?*
A: Yes, but I can beat 70 percent of the men out there. Last year, I came in fourth place overall. Only three men beat me. Equal prize money is no bonus. Twenty-three men started and only four finished, while all three women finished. That's quite a difference. Of course, I realize that's not exactly a fair comparison, but we do work hard and the money should be there. The money should be there in *all* sports.

In the Tour de France, the women ride 40 percent of the distance the men ride. Do they get 40 percent of the money? And take the Coors

Classic, for instance. I could never ride that race. It feels like the women's event is there for entertainment, to gather the crowds for the men's finish.

Q: *What can be done about the problem of sex discrimination and the double standard? What progress can be made?*

A: I think the progress needs to come from the race offices of these events. When they put out press releases, they should be equal for the men and women. The official RAAM T-shirt has the men's record on it but not the women's. My record is just as important as the men's. That T-shirt represents sex discrimination. We represent 50 percent of the population and 50 percent of the market and they've discriminated against us.

Q: *Cycling is still a man's world, then?*

A: Oh, definitely. But it makes me feel better to remember that when Hannah North was doing all those Coors races, she told me that she *knew* she would never see the day when there would be a woman's road race in the Olympics—not in her lifetime. And now there is, and in 1988 there will be track racing.

Q: *So there is hope.*

A: Yes, there is hope.

ESTELLE GRAY AND CHERYL MAREK
TOURISTS

Estelle Gray has been a "tourist" (by her own definition) since 1974. She began riding in long distance events in 1980—but claims that she never has "competed."

Yet, this native of Seattle, Washington, does hold some records of her own. Gray's 1983 Seattle to Portland Women's Tandem Record (200 miles in 9 hours, 7 minutes) still stands, as does her 1985 Tandem Transcontinental Record (with partner Cheryl Marek).

Estelle has been the general manager of R & E Cycles in Seattle for a number of years, in addition to being a cycling instructor.

Her other interests include kayaking, soccer, and mountain biking, and she is an experienced bicycle mechanic. In fact, Estelle was the chief mechanic for Cheryl Marek in the 1987 Race Across AMerica. "If Estelle wanted to do the RAAM I'd try to talk her out of it," said

Photo courtesy of In Tandem

Cheryl Marek and Estelle Gray, Women's Tandem Transcontinental record holders (10 days, 22 hours, 48 minutes). Cheryl Marek finished second in RAAM '87 and was named "Rookie of the Year."

Angel Rodriguez, owner of R & E Cycles. "She's far too valuable to the business."

Cheryl Marek was born in Dearborn, Michigan, on September 17, 1955. She has attended Michigan State University and the University of Washington and is finishing her accounting degree while working as a carpenter/bricklayer.

Cheryl has been cycling for 14 years. She regularly commutes to work. Cheryl told me she took her car to work the first day, and has ridden to work every day since, for years through rain, sleet, heat, and snow. Cheryl has done many bike tours. In July 1984, Cheryl and Estelle Gray established a Women's Transcontinental Tandem record of 10 days, 22 hours, 48 minutes. On the basis of her accomplishment she was invited to race RAAM '87 and finished second in a time of 12 days, 5 hours, 41 minutes, and was named "Rookie of the Year" (awarded for outstanding performance by a first-time RAAM competitor). Cheryl plans to compete in RAAM '88 with the hope of winning.

Cheryl is very much an outdoors woman and enjoys hiking and cross-country skiing. Cheryl shares her home with two long-term pets: Zeus, a 15-year-old parakeet, and Loner, a cat she's had for eight years. Loner came with the house! Cheryl is also an avid science-fiction reader, her favorite author is Marion Zimmer Bradley.

Q: How did you get started in cycling, Estelle?

A: Gray: I started cycling in 1973. The first thing I did was go on a six-week self-sufficient bicycle tour. I had never toured before—I didn't even own a bike—when a friend asked me to go to Nova Scotia. We had a screw driver, a crescent wrench, WD40, and a patch kit with us—no tire irons.

After that, I never stopped. I toured a lot, with one other person or alone. No real "bikies."

In 1976, I had a three-day weekend and I went away, with a friend again, totally loaded with junk on our bikes and we went too far. We were supposed to be gone one day, and we ended up doing two 100-mile days, which meant we had to do a 200-mile day on the last day. So, I did a double century, fully loaded, in '76, not having a clue that that is a big deal.

I didn't know anything about bikes until I started working in a bike shop. When people talked about centuries and double centuries, I didn't know that it was a big deal, because I'd been doing it for ages. I just did it for fun, and then my awareness changed a bit.

Q: What kind of equipment and clothes did you take on that first tour?

A: Gray: I bought a Peugeot U08 with steel wheels for $129 and borrowed a pair of canvas touring saddlebags. I brought some dress-up clothes so I could look nice when I got off the bike—an extra pair of shoes or two, a nice little sweater, blue jeans. We rode in cut-offs and sneakers. I didn't have gloves. I didn't have a helmet. I wouldn't have even known what that stuff was for if I'd seen it.

We climbed 6,000-foot passes over the John Cabot Trail in Nova Scotia. It was just fun. We got very lucky.

Q: How did you get into cycling, Cheryl?

Marek: My story's a little different. I have had a bike ever since I can remember, and I used to go on Sunday rides with my next-door neighbor. Debby and I used to ride five or ten miles to stores to go shopping. We used to pack a little lunch and take it with us. This is probably when I was 10 or 12. Our parents used to worry about us, but we just took off anyway.

Then in the last two years of high school, I started commuting. I continued to ride after school, but I don't have any idea of the distances because I'd just hop on my bike and go. I commuted in college, and I commuted to work when I got a job. Then I started going on short two- and three-day tours. That led to a week tour, and then two-week tours, and then to training for Seattle to Portland, which is a 200-mile race.

Q: What year was that?

Marek: I started training for my first one, I think, in '81. My brother-in-law gave me his used pair of polyester biking shorts—my first pair.

My background, like Estelle's, is all commuter and tourist.

Q: Is your biking based on an ecological philosophy?

Marek: I definitely do it for the exercise. If I'm not riding my bike or running, I feel as if I'm not complete. Exercise is such a part of my life that I have to be doing it. I wish everyone was on a bicycle. I've been at my job for two years now, and I have not ever driven my car to my job. It's so close, and it's so much easier, and I get rid of so much stress. I don't understand why other people don't see those kind of benefits. And, yes, I definitely don't think my car needs to be on the road during those times. Ecologically, I think bicycles are a definite must.

Q: Has your trip across country been the biggest event for both of you?

Both: Yes.

Q: How did you get the idea to do your tandem ride?

Gray: I met Cheryl on a tug-boat trip. Some friends had rented a tugboat and we were going touring on some islands. We'd get off with the bikes and ride.

Marek: I was on my single, by the way.

Gray: Right. And I was on a tandem with another friend. One day Cheryl asked if I wanted to go for a tandem ride. So, while everybody rested, we got out the tandem. There was this incredible hill when we hadn't gone even 200 yards yet. I told her I like to stand on the tandem, but it's kind of tricky with two people. She asked what I meant. I looked back, and, sure enough, she was standing behind me. And we powered over the hill. We've ridden a lot since then.

Q: How did you get the idea to go across the country?

Marek: After that first tandem ride, we started riding with a group of four to six women in Seattle who were riding a lot together. Between them, they had a couple of tandems, so we decided to do tandeming and to train for the Seattle to Portland on a tandem. We were already doing long-distance on tandem. When John Marino and Michael Shermer came to Seattle for a slide-show/talk, they were talking about the Great American Bike Race. We looked at each other and said, "Let's do it on tandem." We decided to think about it overnight and see if we still felt the same way. Neither of us slept all night, and the next morning we both agreed we'd really go across country on a tandem.

Q: What was it like raising the money?

Marek: We hired P.R. people and they went to work for us. We were competing with Olympic cyclists for money at that time because it was an Olympic year. We were unknowns. People had never heard of what we were doing, plus we were women. So, we didn't get very much money.

Q: How did you finance the trip?

Gray: Bank loans.

Marek: We got a lot of community support. They gave us lots of little things.

Gray: Lots of $50 donations.

Q: What was your cost?

Gray: It depends on how you define it. We both quit our jobs, and we did three-day training rides. There's a lot of gas involved, using two vehicles for three days. Feeding everybody is expensive.

Marek: Our expenses came to $40,000.

Gray: That includes the six months beforehand and the ride. We were going to spend whatever it took.

Marek: So, we spent a lot of money.

Gray: Of course, we were spending for two because everything is doubled.

Q: *What about sponsorship?*

Marek: We got very good media coverage.

Gray: The part that I'm angry about is that our P.R. firm had a major company very, very interested. They liked our P.R. package, but they wanted to see another picture besides the one we had sent, which was an upper-body picture of us wearing nice silk blouses. They wanted to see what we looked like in competition. So we sent a beautiful picture of us on the tandem. Our legs were incredibly defined. It's the best picture I've ever seen of either of us. And they looked at it and said we were a little too husky for their image. It was the stereotype. We want foo-foo women for our ads, not strong-looking athletes, and we just radiate strength in that picture. The word they used is "husky." And it was just our legs that they didn't like, because the rest of us looks fine in that picture. That incident really upset me.

Q: *Do you think that women have to be good athletes and look good too?*

Gray: They don't want you to look like an athlete. They want you to *not* look like an athlete.

Marek: Also we don't come across as dumb women, which, a lot of the times, some people want.

Q: *How did you know how fast you wanted to go? Did you meet your expectations?*

Marek: We were using Lon and Sue's time (Lon Haldeman and Sue Notorangelo set the Tandem Transcontinental record in 1983, and again in 1986) as a guideline for us, because we didn't know what women could do on a tandem. The motivating force was that we just really wanted to do it—I know we both agreed on this point—to inspire more women. Our real motivating force was to do our very best. We're both pretty disciplined people because that's the only way you can train for one of these and actually do it. Also, we had an excellent crew who threw out all these motivations at us. You really want to please the crew.

Gray: I also wanted to prove that an average person could do something exceptional, you could explore your potential and probably find that you can do more than you thought you could. I've never been in a bike race. I don't ever want to be in a bike race. I came from being a tourist, from enjoying being on a bike for a long time, and I wanted to prove to myself that I could do something exceptional.

I work in a bike shop and two women in their late fifties or sixties bought a tandem from me. One of them came in one day and said they rode nine miles on it and were going to try for 15 next weekend. I thought about her all week, hoping that they'd do their 15. When she came in, she said, "We did 15 miles—oh, my butt hurts so much, but it was so much fun. Next time, we're going to do 20." She said their goal was to do 50 miles in a day by the end of the summer. Every time I'd see her I'd get really excited. Then one day she came in and was embarrassed to talk to me. When I asked her why, she said she had found out that I was Estelle Gray, who rode my bike all the way across the country in 10-plus days. But that's the point. Fifteen miles to that woman is like 500 to me. What's the difference? I just want women to feel good about what they're doing. And, I was embarrassed that she felt so bad.

That was why we did it: to show people that if you pick up something and work hard at it, you can do it.

Also, when you have $40,000 in loans out, it's pretty hard to think about turning back.

Marek: Actually, I think the hardest part of the whole ride was getting to the starting line. Once we got to the starting line, what we didn't get or whatever else we were expecting wasn't there, and we just had to rely on ourselves.

Gray: We had no trouble getting equipment though. There was a sports company called Sports Mind that gave us a lot of mental training.

Q: What kind of mental training did you do?

Gray: We did some visualization. We did some biofeedback.

Marek: Stress management. They'd make sure we were going to get along together. We had a lot of motivation. And they linked us up with companies that tested our blood sugar, measured our body fat, did blood analysis for us, and got us into a gym. We did a lot of good prep work. We felt as if we were training well. We were eating well. We had all the support we needed except the money. That was the only part that was ever really a strain on us.

Q: How close did you get to Lon and Sue's record?

Marek: We got within two hours. We were trying to beat Lon and Sue's record, because we thought it was attainable. We were also the first women to go across. But when we got back to Seattle, all anyone could think about was that we didn't break the record. Real negative stuff. Sometimes people still say that it's too bad we missed the record. Well, yeah, we missed it by two hours.

Gray: We really were unknowns—even to each other. We put together an all-woman crew, and we got a lot of flak about that beforehand too. We had nine good people who just happened to be women.

Q: Did you pick all women for any special reason?

Marek: Yes, we did. First, we wanted to do it so women's companies would support us. We thought it might be more appealing to potential sponsors to offer a whole new thing—all women. We were really hoping to get a women's product to sponsor us.

Other than that, I'm definitely more comfortable with women. You know that when you're on the ride, whoever's with you in that crew sees you. I mean, they see every part of your body. They know everything about you. I'm more comfortable with women in that position. I have to do what works for me.

Q: Did you ever have times when you didn't get along?

Gray: We had one fight. It was in Missouri somewhere. I snapped. Cheryl snapped back. I snapped back at her. And we rode in silence for about five minutes. The crew went away, and we rode silently. Then I reached back and put my hand on Cheryl's and apologized. She apologized, too, we got the crew, and that was the only time.

Q: How do you make decisions like when to change clothes or eat?

Marek: That's one of the problems of being on a tandem.

Gray: We did really well the first three days in coordinating everything. And the crew was really good about helping us.

Marek: We found out later what tricks they used. If we'd want something from the motor home, they'd CB the motor home and tell them not to come anywhere near our sight. And they'd say, "Well, we don't know where it is! We can't find it! It's not in range of our CB."

Gray: They'd say, "You want your jackets? You can get off and get your jackets when we get to the motor home." Because they knew that we were making up excuses. All we really wanted was to get off the bike.

Marek: The hard thing about it was you both had to be really motivated and into it. You had to trust each other too.

Gray: Cheryl and I both trained with different attitudes. I will listen to anybody, and if it makes a bit of sense, I will try it. Cheryl's much more critical. She has to really be convinced before she tries something. We had to work this out too.

We were getting a lot of conflicting advice. It was starting to mix us up, so we called a meeting one day with all the trainers, the men who were helping us. We said, "Let's hear everybody's advice, and then we're going to take it home and process it." What came out of the meeting was the advice that we *girls* couldn't cross the country in 10-plus days; we should think about a 14-day crossing.

Marek: Or you'd better think about doing it next year.

Gray: Or next year. What was going through their minds was: "We men can't do this; how can you women do it?" We had to take that home and mull that one over for a long time. These were the people who had been behind us the whole time, backing us and trusting us. But when all their male egos got together, all of a sudden the guys who had been saying, "Sure, shoot for 9, shoot for 10," said, "You'd better try 14."

Marek: That was a motivating force for us.

Gray: But it hurt.

Marek: It really did.

Q: What have you done since the trip?

Marek: I definitely had to find a job. I've spent the last two and a half years paying off my debts. And I had more expenses than Estelle, so I still owe $2,000. That's why, up until this point, I haven't been able to think about any serious competition.

I have been riding, though. I want to keep in good enough shape so that I can pick up and do 100 miles at any time. I figure that as long as I can do that, then I can start training for anything.

Gray: I hate being in debt. I hate it! So, I ate oatmeal for a year, for dinner and breakfast. And I paid off my debt the first year. You can't believe how frugally I lived.

Now I want to play. Last winter [1986], I did an off-road bicycle trip to Costa Rica. Last year I bought a kayak. This year, I'm taking a kayak and bicycle trip to Costa Rica. I love cycling. One of my goals is to be the little old gray-haired lady behind the counter at the bike shop, and somebody will come in and ask what toe clips are, and I'm going to laugh and say, "Back in the 1970s, they were these funny things that went around your foot to hold it in the pedal." I hope to be seventy and working in the bike store still.

As for my cycling goals, I want to be in good enough shape so that whenever anything comes up, I can train quickly enough to do it.

Q: Has the trip changed of your life?

Marek: It definitely has for me. I think I have much more self-confidence. I feel much better about myself.

Gray: It's interesting how afterwards was different for both of us. I went back to the bike world and every day, when I went into work, people at the store would talk about the trip, ask me tons of questions. I got very sick of it very quickly. Cheryl did all the legwork, getting us recognized, getting an article in the *Guiness Book of World Records* about us. They printed a beautiful picture, the one with our "husky" legs. The enthusiasm stayed with Cheryl a lot longer because she doesn't exist daily in the bike world.

Marek: The other thing that I did was that I stayed on the East Coast for three weeks before I came home, and then as soon as I got back to the West Coast, I went on a 2,000-mile tour on my single bike. It was really thrilling. So it was two months before I even got back to Seattle. I was really willing to acknowledge the ride, be happy about it, be excited about it. Estelle got a lot of the flak about not breaking the record. There was a lot of negative stuff about that.

Q: How can women be recognized for their achievements?

Marek: The only thing that we can do is be motivating forces for other women. We can make it easier for other women. Because of you and Susan for example, it's easier for me to get sponsors for the Race Across AMerica.

Gray: Everybody helps each other. Susan Notorangelo told us how to get across the country in good time. She gave us advice—it wasn't, "I know something and I'm not going to share it." In my daily life, I try to help too. When women come into the bike store, I ask if they know how to change a tire. If they don't know how, I show them. That might be sexist; when guys come in, I don't always think to ask them. But I'm very careful. When a woman comes in who's new, I'll teach her how to change a tire and anything else she needs to know about cycling.

Photo courtesy of Dave Nelson/PIW

First-place Casey Patterson crossing the finish line at the 1987 Race Across AMerica (11 days, 21 hours).

CASEY PATTERSON
IT'S NEVER TOO LATE TO START

Casey Patterson was born in Hollywood, California, in 1944. She is the mother of three children: Kye Sharp, 24; Mary, 11; and Charlie, 9. Kye was born shortly after Casey graduated from high school. College was interrupted as she went to work. For the next 10 years after the birth of Kye, Casey held a variety of jobs. She worked as an accountant and administrator in a law office. Casey moved to the eastern Sierra Nevada mountains near Mono Lake and worked as a librarian in a high school library. Off and on she has waitressed. Casey says she's a "damn good waitress. It's like swimming—once you learn how you never forget."

Casey took up cycling when her son Kye set up a mountain bike for her. She was 36 at the time. Two years later Casey entered her first mountain-bike race. In 1983, after competing in mountain-bike races for a few years, Casey placed second in the NORBA-sponsored 1983 Off-Road Nationals. Casey founded Wilderness Bicycle Tours, the first fully supported mountain-bike tour in the United States.

Always seeking new challenges, Casey took up road riding. She has ridden many centuries and double centuries, placing first in the '86 and '87 Hemet Double Century. Casey won the 1986 John Marino Open (West) and qualified for the Race Across AMerica. She entered the 1986 RAAM, but was forced to withdraw in Bald Knob, Arkansas, with knee problems. Casey trained hard and came back to win the 1987 RAAM on the San Francisco to Washington, D.C., course in 11 days, 21 hours, and 15 minutes.

Casey likes a lifestyle focused on cycling-related activities, although the essential part is that "I don't know what I'll do in five years." When she is not training for transcontinental races, Casey likes to read, especially about politics. Casey periodically writes articles for cycling magazines and currently resides in Topanga, California.

I talked with Casey in the fall of 1987 after she had won the women's division in the 1987 Race Across AMerica by fighting off a challenge by Cheryl Marek in Illinois.

Q: How did you get into bicycling? And how does someone who started riding when she was 36 decide to undertake something like the Race Across AMerica?

A: I rode a bike as a child a lot more than my friends did. So I used my bike for transportation and covered quite a bit of ground and really enjoyed it.

That was when I was 10 to 12 years old. But then I got into high school and quit riding a bike. I was 36 when my son Kye, who was 17 at the time, persuaded me to try mountain biking. He was a mountain biker at a time when you couldn't just go out and buy a mountain bike; you had to build your own. He persuaded me to give it a try. We lived in the Sierras, and I really missed getting back into the country. My little children were out of diapers, so I guess they were about 3 or 4 years old. Mary is now 10, and Charlie is 9.

Anyway, Kye persuaded me to try it. We went out and traveled around the L.A. area getting the parts, and he built the bike for me. I took it out the next day and rode in the Topanga State Park in the mountains where I live. Just like the ads say, in 30 minutes, I was hooked. It not only brought back a lot of memories of riding a bike as a child, but also there was the independence—being able to get into the hills in 20 minutes and look down on this urban sprawl and be absolutely alone. It really appealed to me. I got very much into mountain biking, started a mountain-bike touring company, did a little racing. But I got diminishing returns: I used to win because I was the most experienced rider, but then more and more women got into it and it wasn't that easy.

As far as getting into RAAM, it was seeing Elaine Mariolle on TV. It's true! I was contracted by Lon Haldeman to cater his first Rapi-Tour in the summer of '85. I knew that I was going to be feeding 25 people as they crossed the country on bicycles in two weeks.

Q: That's about 200 miles a day.

A: It's practically a RAAM pace, 14½ days. It happened that the telecast of the '84 Race Across AMerica was on television one Sunday. I'd been out riding a century with a bunch of friends, and they all decided to watch the show on TV afterwards. I was particularly interested because I knew I had to feed these long-distance bike riders. I never thought I would like any of them. To get into something like that was just too weird and too intense, and I thought these people would be real strange. I just wanted to know what they ate. So I watched the show and I was captured by it. Particularly by you. It really is true. The joy that was apparent in what you were doing, the challenge of it, your personal appeal just fascinated me.

I didn't start riding those long distances right away. I did cater the RapiTour and met some wonderful people who will be lifelong friends, I'm sure. It was at the end of that year, 1985, that I considered at least trying the JMO (the John Marino Open, a qualifying event for RAAM). I wasn't thinking of RAAM, but I wanted to race the JMO.

Q: You won that JMO, didn't you?

A: I won big-time. That was my first race, the first time I'd ever raced on a road bike. Certainly my first big win.

It was then, only then, at the end of April 1986, that I even began to think about doing the RAAM. I had two months to put it together, from initial concept to sponsorship and everything. I really scrambled. I had some real good luck getting the cash that I needed, and I found a wonderful crew chief, John Lehrer. He helped me enormously, getting equipment and then getting it all to the starting line.

Q: So, you showed up at the line for RAAM in '86. I remember seeing you for the first time, a petite woman with her kids.

A: Yes, I was ahead of Elaine Mariolle for five minutes. My kids are still impressed that I was ahead of you that year, but that was the last I saw of any of you. My knees started to go at about 1,000 miles. They started to hurt, both of them. By 1,500 miles, it was really excruciating. I knew at the halfway point that I wasn't going to make it all the way. My crew had some kind of a little halfway rah-rah ceremony. I wouldn't even pull in to the time station because I was crying too hard. I knew that was it; I wasn't going to make it. I made it another 250 miles to Bald Knob, Arkansas. That was it.

Q: Do you think some of it was the fact that you just didn't have the miles in your legs? You'd only been riding since January.

A: I didn't have enough base. And I had done some stupid things. I changed equipment just a couple weeks before the race. I made some changes in my cranks. I got the bike itself only three or four weeks before the race. You can't make changes that close to the race! It was lack of experience.

Q: So you dropped out and you didn't finish it the first year for physical reasons. When you went back to do it a second time was there any lingering doubt about whether you could really go the distance? How did you deal with that?

A: I knew the first time that I could make it across the country. I never gave any air time at all to the possibility that I wouldn't finish. It seemed inconceivable. So I was reeling when I realized I was in trouble. I hadn't even discussed it with my crew or anything; I just never considered that I wouldn't finish. It was a total shock.

The second time, I felt confident that I would finish, but I had given some thought to the possibility of having to retire. I didn't have the certainty that I had the first time.

It's funny. Everybody has doubts, even people who have gone across the country and successfully gone the distance. The race is so long and so many things can happen. One of the big questions—the exciting draws—of RAAM is the uncertainty. On the one hand, you can be really prepared and confident that you can go the distance. On the other hand, there's everything that can happen despite the best-laid plans. Something can happen and it's all over.

You'd be a fool to be certain that you can make it, and I certainly was in '86. It was foolish, almost an arrogance, to be so certain that I could do it. But one learns. You learn an awful lot in that race.

Q: How did you resolve the feelings of not making it the first time?

A: I think I probably only resolved them when I finished this year [1987]. I didn't dwell on it because I started looking ahead to the following year right away. I was just in there planning. I could feel all along how much better prepared I was in '87. I was looking forward, looking ahead all the time.

But just being there in '86 and seeing you finish, seeing Pete [Penseyres, who came in first in the men's division] finish, made me very happy that I went ahead and drove that other 1,200 miles to the finish line. I'm glad that we did that; I'm glad I saw all that. It was painful to watch. There were a couple of women this year who dropped out who also drove quite a long way to the finish, and I saw them when I finished. I could see in their eyes the same kind of pain and hunger that you must have seen in mine.

Q: What I also saw in your eyes was a certain amount of determination. What did you do between '86 and '87? When you made a commitment to go ahead and do it again, what did you feel?

A: I didn't know until November of '86 that I'd be able to do it again. I had another RapiTour to cater. Preparing and doing that just took up the whole time from the end of June until November 1. On that day, I took off and joined Bonnie Wong on a road tour in Baja. We were going to do two weeks of cycling on the road, averaging around 60 miles per day, with a high day of about 100. I was her guest, just down there to have fun. My main concern was what was going to happen when I started putting miles on. Had I wrecked my knees? I had no idea. I didn't know whether I was going to be able to do it or to race again.

My knees were great! A couple of times I rode a whole day ahead of those guys just so I could get more miles in. I felt wonderful knowing that my knees would be all right, that at least it was feasible to try, took a load off my mind. Then it just became a matter of beginning the training and using the experiences and the things I'd learned the year before to prepare myself. I handled my training very differently. I had two attitude adjustments, but first I'm going to tell you about the one that came second; that was realizing that I needed help and allowing people to help me.

In the beginning of March, I set up a training program for myself that was similar to Pete Penseyres's: doing all-night rides every week for eight weeks before the race. Every all-night ride required somebody to support me. In the past, I'd always been real independent, which is a common trait among RAAM riders, but I knew that I wasn't going to make it without a lot of help from my friends. I had to ask. I had a party at my house, served them all mad-dog chili, and made a little speech. When I got started, a couple guys brought out their check-books thinking I was going to ask for money, but it was nowhere near that easy! I had to ask them for their time. Everybody there signed up for these support rides! We had a wonderful time. Later we watched the tape of your race and another RAAM tape that I had and got everybody all steamed up on the project. But just to make that admission to myself that Casey "I'll do it myself" Patterson needs help, and to ask, and to get the immediate rewards of everybody saying yes made the difference.

But before that, I went out in February to Death Valley by myself in my VW camper. I spent 10 days by myself to lay on some miles and to get focused on the training that was ahead. It worked beautifully. I cooked my meals in this car, and I had a crate of books, which I read, and a tent which I set up. I had three bicycles. I spent those 10 days alone riding in Death Valley, eating healthy food, and thinking about the race. During that time, I planned my entire training schedule and did a lot of planning about the logistics of the race. I really got focused on it, centered on it, which was the most important thing.

I came back at the end of that period feeling very good about what I'd accomplished, but worried about whether I would really have the discipline to do all these training schedules that I'd set up for myself.

Q: Why did you worry about that?
A: Saying you're going to do something and then doing it has been a constant struggle in my life. I realize in retrospect that I tend to

follow through, but as it's happening, there's no certainty. There was a period of years in my life when going to work every day was a 50–50 proposition. I look back on it and realize that I did it; I went to work every day. But I had the same internal debate every morning about whether I'd go or not. I'm just used to operating that way. So I knew that I'd have those internal debates.

My second important attitude adjustment was accepting the "training the dog" concept: don't expect big breakthroughs; there are no shortcuts to it. You pointed out to me that you have to go out there and "train the dog." You have to go out there and train over and over again without any big rewards or dramatic breakthroughs. I think of it now as training that mindless part of me that would rather lay in the sun and scratch. I just had to get out there and ride the bike. I had to ride fast; I had to climb; I had to do long rides; I had to do sprints. It's the only way to get ready. I never failed to meet my goal for a given training adventure. Usually it was a time and distance function. If I did the distance and had time left, I would do more distance.

Q: I did it differently. When I was training, I had the distances and my incentive was that if I could do them faster, I got to get off the bike. So I would always try to knock out x hundred miles faster, because then I could get off and have more free time. It just so happened that for my birthday in '86 I had a training ride of 300 miles or something like that scheduled, and the end was going to be my birthday celebration. I intended to have a break on that day, so I just cranked it out as fast as I could so I could have a fun day.

A: I needed help. The all-night rides were really excruciating at first. I couldn't believe how hard the first one was. It's like having babies; you don't have any real visceral memory of what it feels like. To ride all night just seemed incredibly difficult when I first started doing it this year. I'd done it a lot last year, but I had forgotten. In one of the earlier rides, we had horrendous conditions. I trained through snow and through sleet and through freezing temperatures. I trained through a wind storm that threatened to blow me over at times. During that storm, there were many times when I would have to put a foot down and someone on my crew would get out and hold me so I wouldn't get blown across the road. But we didn't stop, because we had a commitment to ride so many miles and so much time. It certainly eliminated any fear of wind that I might have had in the race! But the wind made it a very, very difficult ride for me. When we finished the time we were seven miles short on the distance.

Coincidentally, just as we finished the time we got into an area on the highway that was under construction where we really couldn't proceed any farther without a lot of difficulty. So I said "What a coincidence; let's just quit now." My friend, Jonathan wouldn't let me quit. So I did the next seven miles I'd committed myself to do. He really had to push me to do it, but we did it, just by pacing back and forth on a mile-and-a-half stretch of the highway. But each goal accomplished propels you to the next one. That's what was so important about it. It's like a sling-shot; it just ratchets you right up into the next level.

Q: When I won in '86, a major difference from the previous years was an attitude change, a sense of confidence. I talk to a lot of bike clubs and lots of women have asked, "How do you develop that sense of confidence?" That's a really good question. For me, seeing positive results of the training propels you to the next step. But then there's something else that happens too; you start to visualize yourself as a real contender. Part of that has to do with your physical ability. Part of that has to do with the way you see yourself. Have you found that to be true?

A: There was a crucial moment for me in the race this year when Cheryl Marek was really biting at my heels. She was less than 90 minutes away from me in Illinois. That was way too close for my comfort. In fact, when I woke up in the morning after my sleep and found that she was maybe an hour and 15 minutes back, I was ready to give it to her. After leading for so many days, I thought it was just some wild conceit for me to imagine that I could win that race and that Cheryl was moving in to take what was hers to begin with. Jonathan told me, "That may be true, but it's your duty to give it all you've got. If you're going to be passed now, you're going to be passed kicking and screaming. You owe it to yourself and to your crew and to your family and to all those people who came out cheering you along as you crossed the country." That was in my mind that day. We put on the disk wheel, and I just hunkered down. For five hours I didn't get off the bike, I scarcely changed my position. In that period I got blisters on my thumb, the only injury I got in the race. I went a lot faster than I had been going before, and by the end of that day, I was five or six hours up on her. I didn't do it to win the race because I'd already figured I wasn't going to win this race, that it was hopeless. But when I started off that morning, I found that strength. It wasn't as high-minded as winning the race. It was a real simple, almost dog-training, concept of giving it all I've got. It is not my background, not my nature ordinarily, to give it all I've got, just as it's not my nature to get it in on time. But I am more uncomfortable with the knowledge of holding back, of not giving it all I've got, and losing. There's no satisfaction there for me. My goals for next year, for instance, are to improve my time substantially. I have an idea in mind of how much faster I want to go, and it's pretty definite.

Q: Do you want to talk about that?

A: Well, I'd rather not, but I know what I want to do and I know exactly how I'm going to do it. I'm not concerned about winning. It's a big liberation. It's nice because I already won the RAAM, so I don't have to worry about winning it again. I'm concerned about achieving the goal of REALLY giving it all I've got.

For a lot of people, women especially, winning, the trophy, the accolades, certainly are nice, but they're not the only thing. Winning can be, like you said, giving it all you've got, being the best you can be and knowing that you've put in your best effort. It doesn't matter whether it's the Race Across AMerica or a century ride or a 25-mile time trial or just going to work on time.

Anytime you attempt RAAM, anytime you get to the starting line, you've already achieved something pretty extraordinary in terms of goal-setting. Anybody who gets to that starting line has given it darn near all they've got just to get there. I'm not saying I was a dilettante or anything like that in RAAM '87. I gave it very nearly all I have, but I long for that experience of giving it everything, absolutely everything.

Q: Do you think that you can manage to do that in '88? And do you think you'll need to go across the country again after that?

A: So many RAAM riders have sworn they'll never do it again but they get hooked! But if I feel that I've done my best, I don't think I'll feel the need to go back after '88. It's the fact that I know I can do better that haunts me.

It haunts me less than I was haunted last year because I did finish this year and I did win and I'm very proud of that. I'm proud of my crew. I'm really pleased with that accomplishment. I don't mean to imply for a second that I'm putting it down or denigrating it at all. We did an amazing thing. I had some very good help, good people, and I wouldn't trade that experience for anything. I just want to go faster!

Q: Do you wonder what inspired you to do the Race Across A Merica and play out this struggle with yourself across the American highways?

A: Oh, you bet! I do most of my second-guessing on these long training rides. It's putting a huge amount of productive effort into a time that just goes into the black hole of space. The time that I spend training I'm not doing anything for anybody. I'm putting all of my physical and much of my mental effort into nothing, really, nothing that I could show for it. I worry about that. I think I'll want to do something after this obsession subsides, to use whatever visibility I've gained in the broader community to some good end to kind of pay back all that nonproductive time.

Q: What about your kids?

A: They are very supportive. They're excited about what I'm doing. They're much more involved now because they are a bit older. Their father has been real helpful. They're coming through it OK. There was a time early in the school year when their father and I were concerned about their progress in school and it caused me to wonder what would happen if one of them were having real troubles in school. What if just a few more hours a week with Mom, of quality time with Mom, would make a difference? Would I bag the whole thing for that? You bet I would. There's no doubt. Right now, we're spending a lot of time together, but once I get started training the time becomes short. But I don't think they're suffering for it.

Q: Don't you think you're a good role model because they can see how hard you work, and they can see the rewards that you get?

A: We're talking about the younger ones now. The older one was my mechanic on the race, so he has a much better understanding and direct involvement in my racing. Mary and Charlie are much different people. Mary is totally social and involved with her friends. I don't think what I do really has an impact on her emotionally. She's proud of me and she likes to get sweatshirts from faraway places, but she's not emotionally involved. Charlie is very much emotionally involved in all of it, and it's a real love-hate attraction-repelling kind of a thing for him. In the first place, he is at an age when it's so important to be like everybody else.

Q: So they want to be like everybody else. Do they want mom to be like everybody else?

A: Yes. Charlie's teacher has asked me to come talk to the class. I told Charlie that. He said, "Oh God, I would die!" I asked if it would embarrass him if I came to the class, and he said it would. I'm glad I asked; I was going to come in my cycling clothes and bring my bike and everything. He insists he would have just died. Later on, that very same day, we were talking to a new friend of his that just came to the school this year. I can't say Charlie was introducing us because for some reason kids don't know how to introduce anybody. But I heard Charlie say, "You know the Race Across AMerica? My mom won that race."

Q: You've talked about starting late and accomplishing something remarkable, managing to do it with a family, with kids. Is there anything you'd like to say to women in general about the rewards of being in sports and living an active life?

A: There are a thousand things I'd like to say. What this sport has done for me, the changes it's made in my life, have been remarkable. I am having a good time. My life is full of surprises. It's not just this year because of the race. From the very beginning, when I first started riding a mountain bike, the characteristic of cycling that was so wonderful for me was all the new doors that opened up.

Q: Can you be more specific?

A: Friendships are one thing—the people that I've met. And it's been a new way to get somewhere. You don't need to get a friend to follow you to the dealer when your car needs servicing. You can just take your bike and get home yourself. That in itself eliminates one of life's little problems.

Another positive result has been becoming physically fit. I'm not talking about becoming a racer or having a dynamite figure, but of the rewards you get from being capable of doing an hour's worth of vigorous exercise every day. That will change your life. Having that kind of physical well-being allows you to look at life in a completely different way. Women get stuck with so much drudgery. Whether we're career women or whether we stay home with the kids, we're still the ones who do a lot of life's repetitive chores. I think it gets us down after a while. Physical well-being isn't part of our program as a rule. To have that is a treasure. What I'd like to tell women is "You CAN have it!" Just get out there and ride your bike. Women tend to operate in groups. I don't think we're trained to do things independently. So if you decide to take up a new sport or to make yourself more effective or competitive, you think of forming a group of like-minded women to go out and ride together. My advice is to do all that if you can, but more importantly, to get yourself a bike that fits properly, so you're comfortable on the bike, which is really easy to do these days, and just keep it by the door. When you have time, ride it. Just do it! The rewards are immediate.

Q: That's one thing that's nice about cycling: there is a certain amount of instant gratification. Also, sports is a way of getting self-confidence so you can go out and face a lot of the other tough situations.

A: That's really true. It isn't just the physical improvement, as you say, it's an emotional thing and a self-confidence that comes along with it. What we do, if you could take any little section of it, is within everybody's reach. We just tie all those sections together in RAAM. I'd love to see it if women who are interested in developing in this way can just keep themselves from being intimidated, get the bike by the door, and ride it.

JOANNE ERNST
TRIATHLETE

Joanne Ernst was born in Calgary, Alberta, Canada, and lives now in Palo Alto, California. She received a B.A. in economics with honors from Stanford University. Ernst was accepted to Harvard Business School but declined admission to pursue a career as a triathlete. She has been a full-time triathlete since 1984.

Ernst began running competitively in 1974. She started cycling for triathlon training in 1983, only two years before winning one of the most grueling sports competitions in the world.

Twenty-nine-year-old Ernst was the winner of the Women's Division of the 1985 Bud Light Ironman Triathlon World Championship, and came in third in the 1986 competition. Ernst is a top competitor who has enjoyed commercial success. *Triathlon* magazine named her Female Triathlete of the Year in 1985.

Photo courtesy of Jeff Reinking

Joanne Ernst, 1985 Ironman winner, is a top competitor and enjoys commercial success.

Q: As a triathlete, does everything come down to one race?

A: In our sport, Ironman is THE race, in terms of broad media exposure. *Triathlete* magazine covers tons of little triathlons, but really, as far as getting major endorsements, it's all based on what happens in Ironman. It's like the Olympics.

Q: What do you eat for an endurance event like the Ironman?

A: My biggest nemesis in racing in Ironman is getting enough calories. I'm really bad at it. I don't know why; I just think that I don't need it somehow, that I'm there to race and this other stuff is not that important. Of course, I've learned the hard way that it's really important.

In 1984, I tried to eat figs and lemon drops and then bananas. A lot of triathletes eat figs because they're really highly concentrated in calories. But it was over 100 degrees that year on the bike, and these figs congealed into my back pocket. I will never eat another fig as long as I live. I think I ate three of them and then I didn't eat for the rest of the race. Of course, it was incredibly difficult to finish the bikerace and then a full marathon on no calories, which was what I did. Not eating obviously makes you a lot slower, and it hurts a lot more when you're that depleted.

The next year, I decided I would take licorice and fortune cookies. I had to take something I would eat. When I'm not competing I'm careful to eat a lot of carbohydrates and not as much fat. But if I want a hamburger or ice cream once in a while, I go eat it. I feel it's less stressful for me than to be on a really strict diet. The other thing is that normally I burn off enough calories. The fortune cookies and licorice worked pretty well in 1985, but it certainly wasn't optimal.

So, in 1986, I wanted to drink my calories. I found that, like you, when it gets really hot, I lost my appetite completely. I used Exceed's high carbohydrate liquid, which has 900 calories a quart, before the Ironman. I drank a quart a day for four days, and that helped a lot. It was hot and I got nervous before the race and my appetite. In the past, I would go into the race already depleted. Right before the race, I drank two cans of the nutritional beverage, which is about 350 calories a can, with a little bit of fat, carbohydrate, and protein in it. It's a balanced thing. That was good for me because normally on the morning of a race I'm nervous enough that I don't really want to eat. This way, I got 750 calories, and it was liquid, which is another plus. When you're going to be out for a long period of time, you don't want to be having to stop to go to the bathroom. On the bike, I was drinking almost entirely the Exceed fluid replacement, which has glucose polymers in it that empty out of your stomach as fast as water. In the Ironman you want to avoid dehydration at all costs or you'll be really suffering. I also ate one and a half bananas and two granola bars before the race, because I thought that I should have a little bit of solid food in my system.

I highly recommend that people use what they are going to have on race day ahead of time. In Ironman, you either have to either carry your food, or you have to rely on what's out on the course, usually peanut butter and jelly sandwiches, cookies, orange slices, and bananas. Then they have liquids: water, Coke, and Exceed.

Q: *So all you get is what's out there?*
   A: That's right. Particularly with any of those replacement drinks, people may find they get sick to their stomachs if they're not used to it, so it's really important to use it in practice beforehand.

I thought getting liquid calories worked really well, but the mistake I made was to quit taking calories when I started running. I got fatigued, and I stopped thinking straight. I should have been drinking every single mile. For the first seven miles I ran OK, but for the next six, I *really* went downhill. So when I got to the next aid station, I stopped and ate two small sandwiches and six cookies and drank a glass of Coke, and then I started running again. That stuff was sloshing around, but I felt so much better!

Q: *That's why I like the liquid diet, it hits your bloodstream really fast and maintains a stable blood-sugar level. I don't like the peaks and troughs.*
   A: I'd rather have it even.

Q: *I'm certain that a lot of the emotional rollercoaster that endurance athletes experience is biochemical.*
   A: The interesting thing is that someone else has to give you something to boost your system when you get into a low emotional state while you're competing. You're not generally aware that you're low on calories. You think, "God, I just want to stop."

Q: *When I talk to people about endurance sports, the temptation to quit is a big thing.*
   A: Frequently, you get to the point where mentally you want to quit, but you really never quit. In Ironman this year, I got passed. Part of the problem was the chemical thing; I was definitely low on calories. But then there was the mental thing with dealing with getting passed. I thought, "Well, I'm really hungry. I could stop right now, and I could go home and take a shower and have dinner. I'm so hungry, I just want to do that. I can do that and I probably wouldn't even be mad at myself." But then I started running again, and I decided, "No way am I going to quit out here." I dropped out of two shorter races, but they were for things that were really beyond my

control. In one, my goggles broke in the surf, and I didn't want to swim in the ocean without my goggles. I could have, but I didn't really want to do that. Then in one race, I had diarrhea, so I decided to drop out. You can also finish a race, but you'll have quit mentally—quit pushing and quit trying. If I know I really quit out there, I can't be happy about finishing the race. People don't understand that. That's actually one of the reasons I think that I go back. You're curious about whether you can go farther before you break or if you can go the whole way without breaking.

Q: What's "breaking" for you? When does it usually happen?

A: It always happens to me—and I think for most triathletes—on the run. It comes last, and that's when I'm really tired. That also happens to be my weakest event. Cycling's my strongest event, so I almost never give up on the bike, but on the run, I start getting really tired. I've had chronic injury problems, so a lot of the times I'll be running in a lot of pain anyway. And usually, with the Ironman, I've been out there for God knows how long, and it's 95-plus degrees and really, really humid. They're just miserable conditions. Everyone thinks Hawaii is going to be great, but the course there is the kind that humbles anybody. It doesn't matter whether you're going to finish in 17 hours or whether you're going for sub-10. Nobody really knows what it's like until they've been out there. With something like RAAM, obviously, it's the same way. Nobody really knows what it's going to be like until they try.

Q: Endurance events, even marathons, give athletes an opportunity for more self-reflection, the chance to ask why they're doing it. What do you think about during a race?

A: A lot of top marathoners say the race doesn't really start for them until about 20 miles. If you were racing from the gun, what would happen is that you would fall apart before you get to the finish line. That's more or less true, depending on how good you are. The way I approach Ironman is that the swim and the bike are just things that I have to do to get to start the race. That way, I'm a lot more calm through the race. In a short-course event, I'm a lot more nervous going into it because I know that I'm going to be out there such a short time, only two hours, that any little thing could blow the race. But in a race like Ironman, things can go wrong and you can still win, or you can still place. Two years ago, Grant Boswell got a flat tire, and he still finished third. But in a short course, you're liable to quit if something goes wrong.

Q: How many triathlons do you do a year?

A: I don't race that many compared to a lot of competitors. Last year I only did six; just one of those was Ironman length. The rest were about two hours. Sometimes I'll do a half-hour event. The year previous to that, I did 10 triathlons, total. That was plenty for me. Some of the top men do 25. Triathlon season generally runs from March through October because water temperature is important, and unless you travel to Australia or New Zealand it's hard to race in the winter. So they're racing almost every single weekend during the season. I think it's crazy, but everybody has their own way of doing things.

Races are an emotional experience for me so I can't do that many. I don't go there just to pick up a paycheck the way a lot of people do. For me, it matters a lot, and I want to be in top form. Otherwise I don't have any business being there. So, I prefer to race hard and take the time to get in shape and then race hard again.

Q: Have you always been an athlete?

A: Yes. My mother was very athletic, and she taught swimming when I was growing up. I started skiing when I was five, and I did some ski racing in high school. I started running competitively when I was 15. When I came to Stanford, I ran cross-country on track. We went through the transition while I was going to school there from a club sport in track into varsity programs. Brooks Johnson came in to coach at that time, and he and I didn't get along well, so I dropped out of all my running my junior year.

My first triathlon was in 1983. I was still working full time, and I placed tenth at the Bonne Bell women's triathlon. I'd always wanted to know what I could do if I just focused on athletics, so I decided to take a chance and skip school and do that instead. So in February 1983 I started swimming, in March I bought a bike, and my first triathlon was in May.

The swimming was hard because I hadn't done it competitively, but when I first started cycling I absolutely hated it. I just couldn't stand it.

Q: What didn't you like?

A: To be honest, the real reason I didn't like it was because I didn't think I was good at it, and I'm the kind of person who doesn't like to do things unless I'm good at them. It took me a while to convince myself that I could be good at riding my bike. Now it's my favorite event, and I almost always beat everyone.

Q: How do you train for triathlons?

A: There're a couple things about my training. One is that I'm a quality versus quantity trainer. I'm very different than a lot of the triathletes who feel that mega-mileage is the only way to go. This year, for about 14 weeks before the Ironman, I averaged 190 miles a week on the bike. A lot of people think that's very little riding, but I had the fastest women's bike time by about six minutes. And the other women probably rode more miles than I did.

Actually, I ended up finishing in 47th place overall, and I out-cycled a lot of the men.

My training is definitely high quality. I do a lot of hill climbing, basically because we have almost nothing flat here to ride. I have to go up. And I like hill climbing. I'm really good at it, and you have a tendency to do things that you're good at because it makes you feel good.

The things that I like to do on a regular basis are time trials. Usually I have hill time trials and I also have a couple of flat ones that I do—anything from about 5 miles to 20 miles. Probably the shorter ones are more valuable for you because you really push. With anything longer than 10 miles, you start having lapses in concentration and stuff like that.

One of the keys to getting ready for the triathlon is specificity of training. As far as I'm concerned, riding 70 miles a day, seven days a week is not going to help my Ironman performances. What helps my Ironman performance is that as the race gets closer I start doing hard 100- to 150-mile rides. That means I do them race pace. My husband waits at the aid station for me so I don't have to stop. In early-season rides, I'd be stopping at a store and filling up my water bottles and putting drink mix in the bottles, so I was taking a lot of time out. It's better to be able to pick something up and keep on going down the road. That simulates your race situation. I've had a lot of success with that training method, and therefore I haven't felt any need to pick up my mileage.

Q: *Let's turn to some of the more physiological aspects of being a woman athlete. Does your period affect training or competition?*

A: I do have problems with my period because I get really severe cramps. Once my period started on race day, which for me is a complete disaster. That day, I have really severe cramps that get worse with exercise. It almost never happens for me on my bike; I'll have cramp problems during the swim or the run. There's just something about those sports that brings them on. Even a week before my period's going to start, I get really bad cramps while I'm running. I have to stop and sit down, sometimes for three to five minutes before the cramps'll go away. And then I'll run and I can run fine with no cramps. It's a real problem, and I worry about it. The day after my period starts isn't a real big problem in terms of cramps, but then you get other problems. You're going to sit on the bike for 112 miles with a tampon in. You've got to cut off the string so it's not uncomfortable. Sometimes, I'd pay a million dollars to be Scott Tinley and not have to worry about whether your period's going to start on race day. But, I've done 31 triathlons, and it's only screwed up my race once. I'm nervous enough about it that it comes early or late. But you have to worry about all these things.

I get really irritated with the press, which always takes the point of view that women who are elite athletes, who are really fit, don't have their periods, which I think is only sometimes true. It depends a lot on the woman. It depends on when she started training. It depends on what sport she's involved in. I have 6½ percent body fat, and I still have my period very regularly, and I get cramps.

Q: *You regularly have 6½ percent body fat?*

A: That's what I was measured at before I started training full-time for the triathlon. But when you get down to really low body-fat percentages, underwater body-fat weighing is not that accurate. It can vary by a lot when you get down in the low range.

Q: *Do you train alone?*

A: I like to train alone because I find that I can do what I want to. If I feel lousy I can ride easy, and if I'm feeling good I can really push it. There have been cases where I have gone riding with other people and they couldn't keep up or I couldn't keep up with them which is an uncomfortable situation. I feel I concentrate a lot better if I train alone.

Q: Do you write it all down?

A: I do. But I don't focus on my mileage. I think it's a mistake. If I feel lousy and take a day off, the week's mileage is going to be low. But the thing that I found is if I take that day off, the next day I'm going to come back and have a great day. Then I feel really good about my training.

Q: Do you do interval training?

A: This year is really the first year I did any intervals. We had a one-mile interval mapped out on a relatively flat road. I'd time myself down one mile and then turn around and ride back really easy, maybe five to eight times. I didn't like it very much. I don't know why. I'm not sure it was helping my riding that much either although, theoretically, it should have been. I find that weekly time trials work a lot better for me.

Q: Do you ever get hassled when you're riding your bike or training alone?

A: I do worry about it sometimes, particularly, on some of the isolated mountain roads that we have here, but I've been really lucky so far. I have to get in the training, and it's very hard to mesh my schedule with anybody else's. Generally, I'll let Jim know where I'm going to go so if I'm gone much longer than normal, he'll know where to start looking. I have standard loops. So if I say, I'm going to ride the beach loop, he'll know where that is.

Actually I think I've had fewer problems on the bike than when I'm on a run. I think a lot of people have trouble identifying whether you're male or female when you're on a bike, which is a plus, whereas in running, it's pretty clear to most people.

After the first time I was on television for a triathlon, I started getting a few phone calls. One particular person called and claimed to be a photographer for *Outside* magazine and wanted to know where I trained so he could take some photos. Before I checked with the magazine, I told him where I swam, because there are a lot of people there, so I didn't figure there was any problem with that. When we checked with the magazine, it turned out that they had never heard of this person. You have to be really careful, because a person can set himself up on your route and plan to attack you. The more public you become the more opportunities there are.

Q: You have enjoyed commercial success as a triathlete. Was it difficult to achieve? Do you have any suggestions for aspiring women triathletes?

A: It has been hard, actually, because a lot of people in sports promotion take it for granted that women cost less. Women's performances are somehow less important; therefore they cost less. I'm lucky enough to have my husband Jim do all my negotiating for me. He's worked really hard at it. Let's just take Nike, for example. I work with Nike. In the past they have given their women athletes, no matter what sport, significantly less than their men. The triathlon was no exception. They were paying women one-third to one-half of what they were paying the top men. So we made a proposal to Nike that just blew them away. We told them we wouldn't settle for less than what they pay their top men. The thing is, the better you perform and the more exposure you get, the more leverage you get. I have a rule that I don't work with companies if they're not willing to accept those terms. After I won Ironman in 1985, I got a lot more exposure than a lot of the men do for Nike, because I work very hard at that. I take it seriously. It's my job. A lot of other athletes still don't make the connection between exposure and what they get paid from a company. They think that what they do on race day is all that matters, and that's not really true. We've found that unless you're talking a fair amount of money, a lot of companies don't want to bother. So you have to up your aspirations.

The other thing that works is to get the right people on your side. With Nike, we have done a very good job of keeping Phil Nike, who's the CEO, informed of what I'm doing for them. That's really important because when he comes down to the triathlete area he'll ask about me by name. And then, the people who run the triathlon program know that means I'm important.

There are a lot of things you have to do. It's a lot of hard work. People think you've got a great job; you're a full-time athlete and all you've got to do is train. They don't realize two things: one is, that your whole livelihood depends on what happens in one race. That's a lot of stress that many people just aren't strong enough to deal with. Two, you spend an incredible amount of time trying to find sponsors and trying to keep sponsors happy. Normally, it's very hard to find an agent you can trust, unless you're lucky enough to be married to or living with somebody who can do these things.

We have been very frustrated with the financial inequities for women in sports, and the 1986 Ironman is a very good case to bring up. The prize money in the beginning was set up to be unequal. It was equal for the top three men and the top three women, but they did not pay equally for 4th through 10th places. In fact, it was approximately a $1,000 difference per place. I feel that was completely wrong. Their justification was that women are less competitive. It really kills me to hear that because it's something that people say without even thinking or doing analysis. It turns out that the women were as competitive or, in some cases, more competitive, in terms of depth of field, than the men.

We fought that battle very hard because I wanted to try and make the money equal. I didn't accomplish that, but I felt that we made persuasive arguments. It's an educational process. It takes time. I just want to make the sport better, not only for everybody else, but also for myself.

Q: What about media coverage? Do you feel it's fair?

A: Oh, I don't know. I watch the ABC coverage of the Ironman and I see that the men's race is two thirds of the coverage. It's really irritating because in some cases in the Ironman, the women's races have been more exciting. In 1985, the top two women were separated by a minute and a half while Scott Tinley won the men's division by 25 minutes.

Q: Do you find that equality is the real issue as far as women are concerned?

A: I definitely feel like a second-class citizen in cycling. In triathlons, because it is a young sport, we have fewer of those problems because women have been at it as long as men. It's not like cycling or marathon running where women are trying to break in after men have been doing it for 100 years. With women doing RAAM the fact that they think 50 miles is too much for a woman to handle is just laughable.

However, I meet a lot of men who do take me seriously. We met a guy at the Chicago Marathon who said he and his friends always like to buy the products I endorse. He said if it's good enough for Joanne

Ernst, it's good enough for him. That makes me feel good because it's the kind of thing I like to get across to a sponsor. I'm not just a spokesperson for women in sports and a good role model for women, I'm a good role model, period. Men respect my accomplishments.

Q: *What do you think have been the most important factors in your success?*

A: I think there're a couple things. My marriage helps a lot. That support has been really important. From a financial standpoint, it provided the flexibility to be able to quit working and start training full-time when, in the beginning, I wasn't making any money at it at all. In fact, I was losing money. It took a long time before I could just break even. And so, from that point of view it was really important.

But also, Jim goes to all my races with me and we're a team in almost anything we do. Whether it's sports or business or whatever, we do things together. We support one another, and it's really important. I know that if I fail, I'm going to come home and Jim is still going to love me.

Another factor that's contributed to my success is that I rely on my intuition a lot. I don't sit down and read a book and find out how athlete A does it and figure that's how I have to do it too. I try things. If they work, I keep doing them. If they don't, I stop and look for something else. It's a creative process. There's something more than physical talent to being a major champion. There's intuition or whatever that spark is—the ability to be creative and figure out your own way—that separates the people who make it and the people who are there sweating and working hard but frustrated because they're not making that leap.

Another important thing is to concentrate on what you do well. What I like to do is ride hard, so I concentrate on that. It's not my job to figure out whether the bike is in working condition. I have a mechanic. He does everything for me. I know almost nothing about how to take care of my bike. I keep it clean and all that, but I don't ever work on it. The guy gives it to me, I get on it and I ride hard and I get off and I run hard. I'm not bothered with anything else.

Q: *Have you ever had any role models or heroes? And do you have any now?*

A: The athletes that come to mind are mostly runners because I've been a runner since I was 15. Frank Shorter was probably one of the first athletes I really respected. And Edwin Moses was another, because he's so beautiful when he runs.

It's interesting that I don't really have any female heroes. There are female athletes I really respect, like Martina Navratilova—what a talent! But the athletes that come to my mind are male.

The thing that's really important to me, not just in terms of other athletes, is that someone isn't just a one-dimensional person. Probably a lot of little boys look at things like who's got the best stats and that kind of stuff, but what kind of person an athlete is off the playing field is really, really important to me.

Q: *Do you ever think about having kids?*

A: People ask me that a lot. Jim and I are not real interested in starting a family right away. I don't see having kids for at least another five years and maybe never. People ask me that a lot, and I'm sure they never ask Scott Tinley that. Of course, it doesn't affect his life in the same way.

Day	Cycling	Running	Swimming
Sunday	Long		
Monday		Track	Intervals
Tuesday	Time trial: flat	Easy	
Wednesday	Steady, mid-distance	Fast	
Thursday		Long	Intervals
Friday	Time trial: hill		Intervals
Saturday	Easy, short	Easy	Long

JOANNE ERNST'S
SAMPLE TRAINING SCHEDULE

WEEKLY TOTALS

Swim 14,000 yards
Bike 200 miles
Run 35–40 miles

DESCRIPTION

Swim: The majority of my swim training is "intervals" with the Los Altos Masters Swim Team, 3,500–4,500 yards per session. I take one day to work on endurance, doing longer multiple repeats (e.g., 3 times 1,000 yards) or one long swim in open water if there is a local open-water swim event.

Bike: My cycling training involves lots of hill climbing because the terrain near my home is almost entirely hilly. I generally include one long ride per week of 80–120 miles and will ride it with as few brief stops as absolutely necessary to simulate race conditions. Occasionally, my husband will act as an aid station during these long rides so that I need not stop. I also include: 1 hill time trial (20–50 minutes) and 1 flat time trial (5–20 miles) weekly. My other rides will be steady 20–50 milers. Generally, my training is done alone. In winter, I replace time trials with intervals and time trials on the wind trainer.

Run: I usually include one longer run of 13–25 miles (the longer ones are part of pre-Ironman training) and one day on the track for 4 miles of intervals (e.g., 16 times 440 yds., 8 times 880, 4 times 1 mile). I also do some easy runs and some time trials on the road with a good mix of flat and hilly running. I enjoy running on trails and include trail runs regularly in my training. I try to do all of my longest runs on the dirt.

I do take an off-season, usually winter, when I let my mileage drop in one or more of the sports and/or train without the clock.

Generally, I do only two sports per day, perhaps doing all three on one day once per week.

RESOURCES

International Randonneurs
Old Engine House #2
727 N. Salina St.
Syracuse, NY 13208
(315) 471-2101

The International Randonneurs sanction the qualifying races for the 750-mile Paris-Brest-Paris endurance race held in France every four years. Although the 200km, 300km, 400km, and 600km races are scheduled around the United States annually, you must qualify the same year as Paris-Brest-Paris to compete in the event. Handsome medals are awarded to those who complete the qualifying races within the alloted time. The 100th anniversary of the Paris-Brest-Paris event is 1991.

Triathlon Federation USA
PO Box 1963
Davis, CA 95617
(916) 757-2831

This is the national sanctioning body for competitive triathlon events.

Ultra-Marathon Cycling Association
4790 Irvine Blvd. #105-111
Irvine, CA 92720
(714) 544-1701
John Marino, Director

This membership organization has a monthly newsletter and is the sanctioning body for the Race Across AMerica, regional RAAM qualifying races, and long-distance cycling record attempts. The UMCA sponsors a National Points Challenge for ultramarathon events and produces a manual covering various aspects of ultramarathon cycling.

Women's Cycling Network
PO Box 73
Harvard, IL 60033

WCN is a national membership organization that promotes women's participation in cycling. WCN publishes a quarterly newsletter and a directory of hospitality homes for cycling tourists and holds conferences and seminars around the country. Susan Notorangelo was one of the founders and is the executive director.

Further Information

Michael Shermer's *Sport Cycling* and *Cycling: Endurance and Speed* are published by Contemporary Books. Triathlon training books by Sally Edwards, Scott Tinley, and Mark Allen are all published by Contemporary Books.

10
Three RAAMs

"The purpose of life is to live it, to taste experience to the utmost, to reach out eagerly and without fear for newer and richer experience."
—Eleanor Roosevelt

RAAM '84: ON A WING AND A PRAYER

I'll never forget the start of the 1984 RAAM. I cried in the hotel room as I ate some oatmeal and put on my purple and pink Vigorelli cycling attire. Then, as I was trying to make my way onto the pier, a man tried to stop me saying, "Only the racers are allowed onto the pier." "I am one of the racers," I told him, nervously trying to find a place in the line-up for the start. I was a somewhat unlikely competitor. In fact, I didn't really come to compete. I had only been riding a bike for a little over a year at the time! My aspirations were more humble—I just wanted to see if I could make it across the country.

Getting into Cycling

When I purchased my bicycle in April of 1983, I had no thought of racing across the country—I didn't even know such events existed. I had been lifting weights, but I wanted to do something outdoors and thought I might take up triathlons. I mentioned my new bike to a friend at work, Linda Skinner. She was a cyclist and she invited me to go on a ride with her club, the Grizzly Peak Cyclists. As a result, I did my first 100-mile ride in May, and I loved it. I started doing all the

251

RAAM 1984

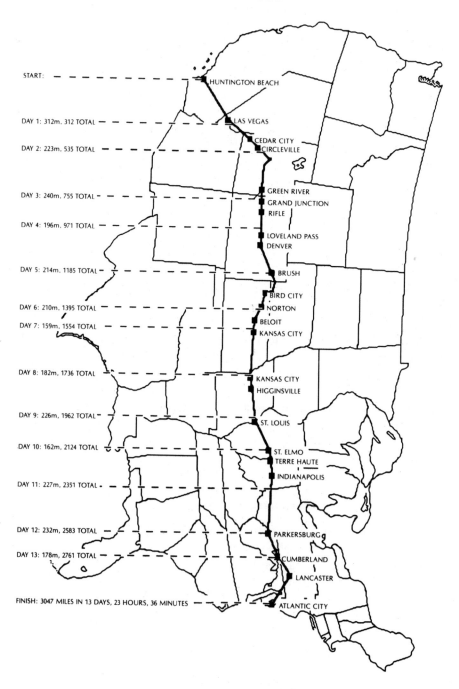

START: — — — — — HUNTINGTON BEACH

DAY 1: 312m. 312 TOTAL — — — — LAS VEGAS

DAY 2: 223m. 535 TOTAL — — — CEDAR CITY
CIRCLEVILLE

DAY 3: 240m. 755 TOTAL — — — GREEN RIVER
GRAND JUNCTION
RIFLE

DAY 4: 196m. 971 TOTAL — — — LOVELAND PASS
DENVER

DAY 5: 214m. 1185 TOTAL — — — BRUSH

DAY 6: 210m. 1395 TOTAL — — — BIRD CITY
NORTON

DAY 7: 159m. 1554 TOTAL — — — BELOIT
KANSAS CITY

DAY 8: 182m. 1736 TOTAL — — — KANSAS CITY
HIGGINSVILLE

DAY 9: 226m. 1962 TOTAL — — ST. LOUIS

DAY 10: 162m. 2124 TOTAL — — ST. ELMO
TERRE HAUTE

INDIANAPOLIS

DAY 11: 227m. 2351 TOTAL

DAY 12: 232m. 2583 TOTAL — — — PARKERSBURG

DAY 13: 178m. 2761 TOTAL — — — CUMBERLAND
LANCASTER

FINISH: 3047 MILES IN 13 DAYS, 23 HOURS, 36 MINUTES — — — ATLANTIC CITY

RAAM 1984
DAILY MILEAGE AND LOCATION

Day	Miles per day	Total Miles	Approximate Location
1	312	312	Beyond Las Vegas, Nev.
2	223	535	Near Circleville, Utah
3	240	775	Thompson, Utah, almost to Colo.
4	196	971	Beyond Avon, Colo.
5	214	1,185	Beyond Brush, Colo.
6	210	1,395	Beyond Norton, Kans.
7	159	1,554	Nearing Kansas City, Kans.
8	182	1,736	Kansas City, Mo.
9	226	1,962	Warrenton, Mo.
10	162	2,124	St. Elmo, Il.
11	227	2,351	Indiana-Ohio border
12	232	2,583	Beyond Parkersburg, W.Va.
13	178	2,761	Beyond Cumberland, Md.
14	286	3,047	Atlantic City, N.J.

long rides I could find, including the 200-mile Davis Double Century. At the Davis Double, I met Vance Vaughan, a long-time cyclist who has subsequently helped me on all my long-distance adventures.

Another friend, Patty Rose, noticed my enthusiasm for distance riding and gave me a magazine article about the first John Marino Open. I was immediately intrigued. The JMO is a qualifying race for the Race Across AMerica. It was held for the first time in 1983, and a local woman, Kitty Goursolle from Sacramento, had ridden it and qualified for RAAM. I looked Kitty up in the phone book and called her. Kitty was about to have a "last gasp" party before she and her crew took off to do RAAM. She invited me to her house and we did some riding together. She took me to the Markleeville Death Ride, a 150-mile ride over five passes in the Sierra Nevadas, which she was doing as part of her preparation. I was introduced to the ultramarathon racing crowd! I immediately began planning to ride the JMO in 1984.

Photo courtesy of Marina Fusco-Nims

I placed second in the 1984 John Marino Open: 792 miles in 73 hours and 30 minutes and only 35 seconds behind Shelby Hayden-Clifton. However, Susan Notorangelo rode unofficially and lapped both of us on a 100-mile course! I'm satisfied anyway. I've got a ticket to ride RAAM 1984!

Qualifying for RAAM

The 1984 JMO was 792 miles. The rules were that you had to finish in less than 80 hours to be official. That was my goal, to be official. I had been preparing, but my longest previous ride was 300 miles. I didn't know if I could ride 792 miles in a week, let alone in a little over three days! The fact that the JMO was the qualifier for RAAM was not a serious part of my thinking.

Eighty riders, including six women, started the race on May 19, 1984. I had a crew to help: Vance, Lee Trampleasure, and my dad. There were lots of problems, but after about 400 miles, things were leveling out and I was doing OK. In fact, I was doing better than OK—I was the second-place woman. Ahead of me was a woman named Shelby Hayden-Clifton. For the last 400 miles, Shelby and I were locked in a real duel. I was ahead of her briefly one night, but she passed me back and built up a two-hour lead with 100 miles to go. That last hundred miles was a big thrill. Shelby was tiring and I chased her with everything I had. I closed the gap but couldn't quite catch her and finished 35 seconds behind in a time of 73 hours, 30 minutes. I not only made the cutoff for an official finish, I had qualified to ride RAAM!

Pat Hines finished just behind me and also qualified. Sue Notorangelo had also ridden the course, unofficially. I had had my first

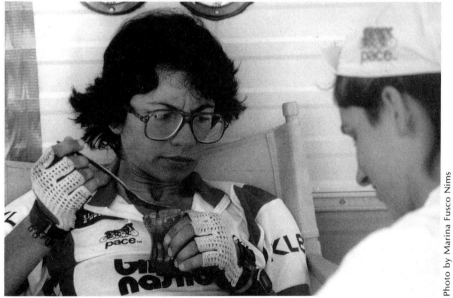

Kitty Goursolle stops for a break in the California desert during RAAM 1983. Kitty was the first woman to compete in the RAAM.

Photo by Marina Fusco Nims

glimpse of the holder of the transcontinental record for women when she had passed me the previous night. Sue had gained an entire 100-mile lap on Shelby and me, and finished more than eight hours ahead of us. Sue had been invited to compete in RAAM because she was the record holder. She rode the JMO just for practice!

Vance and I immediately decided to give RAAM a shot. It was only three months away. It was a mad scramble to assemble a seven-person crew, a small RV and a chase van, three bicycles, and a small mountain of miscellaneous supplies. Oh, yes, and train too. But somehow, we did it.

Photo by Marina Fusco Nims

Vance and I enjoy a few quiet moments at Huntington Beach Pier before the start of RAAM 1984.

The Start of RAAM '84

So there I was, on the pier at Huntington Beach, California, on the morning of August 19. My knees were knocking on the top tube. The Race Across AMerica had grown from the four-man Great American Bicycle Race in 1982 to 23 riders—19 men and 4 women. All my reigning heros—Lon Haldeman, Susan Notorangelo, Pete Penseyres, Michael Secrest, and Michael Shermer—were introduced to the roar of the crowds. Pat Hines and my nemesis Shelby rounded out the women's field. The television cameras were rolling, last-minute interviews were being conducted, and the crowds were cheering best wishes to their favorite racers and a few of the unknowns like me. On the one hand, I wished we could get started and on the other, I savored every last moment before the overwhelming task began. At 9 A.M. PDT, amidst thousands of spectators, the mayor of Huntington Beach fired the gun, and we set out for Atlantic City, New Jersey, 3,047 miles away.

We rode from the pier onto the city streets. The pace was controlled for the first 45 miles, and we rode at a comfortable speed of 15–16 miles per hour. The parade section of the race gave the competitors a chance to visit with each other and provided the press opportunities for group shots. The ABC trucks and helicopter were filming as the excitement grew. I rode next to Susan and asked her if it helped having crossed the country before. She told me no, because she just knew how much it was going to hurt! That comment went right by me as did a few other bits of advice Sue imparted to me that morning. I was just thrilled to be there! I clearly didn't know what was ahead or what to expect. In some ways the ignorance was bliss. Had I known how hard a journey actually lay ahead, I might not have accepted the challenge.

Phase 1—Racing

After the 45 miles of paced riding, the race officially began. The race director waved the flag and everyone took off in a blur of color. Going into the race, I knew that I wasn't prepared to be competitive. I didn't have the base miles and training background to ride the race, let alone be considered a strong contender. I just wanted to make it across America. I had come for the adventure and the thrill. And to learn. Any thoughts of serious competition were focused on the 1985 race.

My plan was rather vague. I hoped to complete the course in 11 days. This target was born more out of necessity than any realistic appraisal of abilities. The RAAM promoters had decided that only those who finished within 36 hours of the winner would be official finishers. There was no separate women's division. We expected the winner to finish in about 9½ days, so I needed to complete the race in 11 days for an official finish. Eleven days translates into an average of 275 miles per day, which we used to gauge our progress.

We proceeded out of the LA/Riverside area along I-15 toward Las Vegas and beyond. It was hot, but overcast, as I started the 26-mile climb out of the LA Basin. I was in last place as we expected, but it upset me nonetheless. No one likes to be in last place! I was convinced that I was going very slowly. The crew had trouble convincing me that I was climbing and doing OK. This was to be a recurring theme on the long graded climbs where the pitch isn't obvious; many times I felt I was on level or downhill terrain and became depressed because I was going too slow.

After dark, a huge rainstorm struck. I had no useful raingear and

Photo by Marina Fusco Nims

Shelby Hayden-Clifton, winner of the 1984 Spenco 500 and the 1984 John Marino Open, rides through one of the many thunderstorms we encountered during RAAM 1984.

was soaked and a bit cold on the descents. I was disappointed that I couldn't descend as quickly as I had expected because of the rain and slippery conditions. The previous year had been very hot, and I expected similar weather. But, as sports commentator Jim Lampley says, you have to expect the unexpected in an event like the RAAM. You must prepare for all possible conditions.

At dawn on Monday, I was in Las Vegas, Nevada. I had heard a lot about the glamor and the glitter, but it looked like a stale party to me. To liven up the situation, my sister Jan called sprints from casino to casino. It was a relief to get back out in the desert. Twenty-four hours after starting RAAM, I had ridden 312 miles without sleep. This was my best distance ever for 24 hours. I was pleased about the mileage but not by how far I was behind the leaders. I was hours behind Secrest, and hours behind Shelby or Sue. I was still in last place but I started to catch other riders.

It was hot as I made my way through the desert north of Las Vegas. The scenery was sparse and dry. If if wasn't for the Stevie Wonder and James Taylor tapes, it would have been a long afternoon. I made a pit stop in a casino in Mesquite, Nevada. It must have looked incongruous for a sweaty cyclist balancing on cleated shoes to be wandering through the mirrors and glitter looking for a bathroom. A few miles up the road at the Nevada-Arizona border, the crew was planning one in a series of state border celebrations. This memorable occasion complete with banging pots and pans and a toilet paper "finish line" was captured by ABC.

By early afternoon I found myself in the Virgin River gorge, one of the most spectacular canyon lands I had ever seen. It was awe-inspiring to climb through the picturesque rock canyons ribboned with color and to watch the rusty river coursing through. It was a steady uphill for miles, but I settled into a rhythm and enjoyed the climb. Vance recalls the event in his journal:

> I expected some great times and this is one. Elaine is tired. She is climbing well, but the climb is relentless. From the chase car, you watch the figure on the bike in front of you and think this hill has to end. But time and time again, a turn reveals a new vista of uphill work. At one such point, I see Elaine slump, take one hand off the bar and shake it in resignation. I fear she will get off but she continues. About halfway up, she hits a rhythm and really starts to move. It's inspiring, it makes a lump in your throat.

I stopped for my first sleep break at the Arizona-Utah border in the early afternoon on Monday 406.5 miles into the race. Lee Tramplea- sure massaged my legs and Earle Young worked on the bikes. Lisa Bassett coped with the pile of wet and dirty cycling clothing—we had used almost everything we had in a vain attempt to stay dry and warm in the rain the previous night. Our tiny motor home was hot and crowded and invaded by flies that made it impossible for me to

Photo by Marina Fusco Nims

I took my first real break just past the Virgin River Gorge in Arizona. After riding all night in the rain, my feet were swollen, blistered, and hurting. My crew took good care of me.

sleep, tired though I was. We learned an important RAAM lesson: never sleep during the day! It's always better to ride when it's light out because it's simply easier to stay awake. The nights are so long that it's better to take advantage of the daylight hours for riding.

My first actual sleep was in Cedar City, Utah, where we camped in some random parking lot in the wee hours of Tuesday morning. I woke up an hour or two before dawn and enjoyed riding through the Utah countryside. The race course took us off main highways for the first time. The motorists were very friendly and lifted everyone's spirits. The morning was crisp and one of those days when you truly love to ride. To cheer me up for a stiff climb to 7,900-plus feet, Lee and my brother Matthew gathered wildflowers from alongside the road and put them in a water bottle for me to carry on my bike. ABC

My crew gave me flowers to cheer me up after a long climb in Utah. Flowers in a water bottle became my trademark.

Crew photo

captured this picture as we rolled into Circleville, Utah, a few hours later. Matthew continued to gather fresh flowers all the way across country. They became the trademark many people associated with me long afterward. In places where it was dry and there were no flowers, he'd gather unique weeds and grasses. The flowers weren't aerodynamic, but they sure boosted my spirits when times got tough.

At noon on Tuesday, I had covered 535 miles since starting the race two days before. In the last 24 hours, I had managed to cover 223 miles in spite of two long stops. We were only 1 hour behind the 11-day schedule, and we were catching riders here and there, usually as they were dropping out of the race. Such was the story when I caught up with John Marino early Tuesday afternoon in Circleville, Utah. He had serious knee problems and was forced to abandon the race. ABC was there filming the occasion. John Marino organized the Great American Bike Race, and has since served as the chief RAAM race promoter and director. I had started to develop serious chafing from riding in the rain, and John donated his water-saddle. A few minutes later ABC rolled up and asked me if I was experiencing any physical difficulties, like problems with my knees or rear. With a grimace on my face, I explained to Diana Nyad that I was taking necessary precautions so I wouldn't have to drop out due to physical problems. But within the hour it became almost unbearable to sit on the saddle. I tried creams and saddle pads and adjusted my riding position, but nothing seemed to help. At 600 miles, I had barely

Photo by Marina Fusco Nims

Pat Hines powers her way along I-70 in Utah. Pat has competed in many triathlons, including Ironman and is an accomplished marathon swimmer.

started the race! However, there was no way I was going to drop out because my butt hurt. It was going to take a major catastrophe to get me to quit.

Late Tuesday afternoon, I caught up with Pat Hines, who was stopped by the side of the road. I stopped for a minute, exchanged a few pleasantries with her, and then continued to ride into gathering rain. Pat had decided to sleep through the storm. I thought that I could easily make some time on her. But the weather took a turn for the worse, and I found myself in a hideous downpour that included hail. Inch-deep water on the road rendered my brakes useless. Visibility was practically zero, but I just aimed the bike down the long grade and hoped for the best. I thank God I didn't have to corner with rain washing over my rims.

Tuesday night, I encountered my first fatigue-induced hallucinations. Most of the time hallucinations cause you to slow down, but if you get really scared the adrenaline rush can wake you up, giving you another hour or so of riding time. This happened as we approached the Green River; I was attacked by what I called the "Lee monster." It was a clear evening, a change from the rain I had ridden through all day. I could see stars as I continued to roll over the long grades through the Utah canyon lands. Large rock formations started to take on the appearance of animals and other assorted creatures. Lee Trampleasure had been pushing all day, trying to get me to stay on the bike. He had the right idea, but it wasn't always easy to take his advice. As I was riding, I would occasionally look to my right at the rocks. I saw a large, hunched-over cat-like figure, that must have been 40–60 feet high. It had Lee's face. I was prepared to ignore it when it turned and gave me a menacing look. I screamed and swerved toward the doubled yellow line. This created chaos in the chase vehicle. Liz yelled at Lee and Matthew to get me off the bike. Lee, who had been napping, struggled out of unconsciousness and stepped out of the bus, which was still rolling. He bit the dust but fortunately wasn't hurt. He managed to get up and run over and put his arm around me to see if I was OK. I told him about the Lee monster and we laughed together. Lee knew he had been pushing me pretty hard, so he understood where it came from.

Wednesday morning was crisp and clear. The canyon lands of Utah were behind me. The terrain was changing. I was on a high plain or plateau with black-eyed Susans and small red rocks all around. It was open land and relatively flat for as far as I could see. There was a nice tailwind and I rolled along at a good clip listening to a recording of "Fup" and anticipating the Rocky Mountains and the climb to Loveland Pass that lay ahead.

At noon, I had covered 240 miles during the previous 24 hours for a total 775 miles. I was falling farther behind the 11-day schedule. Saddle sores continued to be a problem, but my feet, which had developed a few raw spots riding in the rain, were getting better. I was now going beyond my longest previous ride at the JMO. Every mile from this point on would be new territory.

With all the excitement the first few days, most of the crew hadn't slept and it was starting to catch up with them. Earle, Matt, and Vance went grocery shopping in Grand Junction and managed to leave the market without one of the bags. The RV was very small, the plumbing had quit, and there was no air conditioner. Motel rooms would be the only way any of us could get adequate rest.

I started to get a little cranky myself. I appreciated the crew's care and attention, but I was starting to feel self-conscious. It was embarrassing that I was so far behind the leaders—over a day by this time. I couldn't hide the fact that it was uncomfortable sitting on the saddle. My squirming was obvious. It was clearly more my problem than

Photo by Janice Mariolle

My crew (left to right): Liz Vaughan, unidentified helpers, Lee Trampleasure, and Lisa Basset deal with another motor home breakdown. In three RAAMs, it's the cars, not the riders, that have the most problems.

theirs. I'm very independent and it was difficult relying so intimately on the crew. I missed my privacy, particularly when it came to potty stops. When the motor home plumbing quit, so did my facilities. We had a porta-potty, but I misunderstood how it was to be used. I thought the crew was going to set it on the side of the road and I wasn't about to be a public spectacle. Vance decided to demonstrate the intended use. Rolling along I-70 with the bus's sliding door open, Vance sat on the porta-potty as Lisa pulled the bus up alongside of me. At exactly that moment, we passed a car parked by the side of the freeway. I hope they enjoyed the demonstration. Needless to say, I laughed so hard I nearly fell off my bike.

Due to some miscues at the start, we did not have the correct phone number to communicate with the RAAM officials! We were too busy or too tired to figure this out and were unable to get information about the other riders. As we passed through Debeque, Colorado, Wednesday evening, we got rare information about our position from another crew. We scarcely had the energy to deal with the information

Wasted and resting near Rifle, Colorado. At this point, it was starting to sink in just how long a race it really was.

Photo by Janice Mariolle

at the time. We were already an ominous 23 hours behind race leader Michael Secrest, but we were ahead of Pat Hines and we were within shooting distance of Sue (seven hours) and Shelby (five hours). Six racers had already dropped out.

A serious morale crisis broke out at Rifle, Colorado, 882 miles into the race. I was quite fatigued and disappointed by how quickly we had fallen behind the leaders. It began to sink in for the first time just how long a race RAAM really was. Until now, we had been racing. We had caught some other riders and we were ahead of Pat Hines. But now, without our noticing it, RAAM had just slipped into its second phase.

Phase II: Fried

Everyone was tired; nobody had slept enough. The novelty and excitement of the first few days had worn off, and we still had over 2,000 miles to go! There was dissension in the ranks. Some of the crew had come prepared to press on through whatever obstacles arose, but others were unprepared to cope with me when I lost the will to ride. I don't blame them. We pulled off the road and decided to mellow out a bit. We didn't see how we could make the 36-hour cutoff holding this pace. We decided that just making it would be a miracle. If more rest was the key, that's what we'd do.

Lee gave me a tape his brother Calvin had made for me. Calvin

Trampleasure is a strong racer who made an attempt on the transcontinental record in 1982, just before the Great American Bike Race. The tape contained songs and motivational messages that Calvin thought I could use. Lee was instructed to give it to me when the going got rough. Now was the time. For the rest of the trip, I listened to this tape many times, sometimes for five or six hours in a row, as a sort of meditation.

This was our first truly substandard day. We lost some time arguing, more on a bike trail where I got lost in the dark, and then we spent six hours at the sleep stop. At noon Thursday, we had covered only 196.5 miles for the day. On the positive side, we had united as a crew and renewed our commitment to go the complete distance and make it to Atlantic City.

After the six-hour sleep, things were a bit more comfortable as I started the climb to Vail Pass. Earle customized the Spenco saddle pad by cutting out the front area that had caused problems by bunching up. Vance and Earle were in the chase vehicle, and we enjoyed a beautiful morning. The grade to Vail was steep, but the scenery took my mind off the climb. When I stopped for a late morning break at

Photo by Janice Mariolle

A quick break at the top of Loveland Pass, Colorado, the highest point on the course at just under 12,000 feet.

the scenic overlook near Vail Pass, we ate some trout that had been donated by a gentleman who had helped fix the RV the night before. While we were eating, ABC showed up, and Jim Lampley, Diana Nyad, a cameraman, a soundman, and director Joel Feld were invited into the motorhome for a visit. Quite a crowd to fit into such a small RV. They asked how it was going, and I told them that RAAM is sheer lunacy. The excitement was intoxicating and I dissolved into giggles. The ABC crew must have been thinking, "This kid doesn't know what she's gotten herself into!"

Loveland Pass, 1,000 miles into the race, was a benchmark for me. At almost 12,000 feet, it was the highest point on the course. It had been highlighted on ABC's 1983 RAAM coverage, and I was looking forward to it. Believe it or not, I enjoy climbing, and the elevation never bothers me. That afternoon, there was a string of tourists I was able to catch riding up the pass. It felt good to catch other cyclists! When we neared the summit, Lee and Matthew played the theme music from *Rocky* and I felt like a hero. It was inspiring. At the top we stopped for a few minutes, took pictures, and enjoyed the moment. Then it was off down the mountain into gathering darkness and rain, through the sprawl of Denver, and out into the plains.

I had expected to make good time through Nebraska and Kansas. After all, they are flat. Unfortunately, flatlands also tend to be windy lands, and the wind seems to be in your face more often than not.

At a quick stop at the Nebraska-Kansas border Friday evening, I watched an electrical storm building ahead. Eventually I set off into the gloom. After many hours of bucking a head wind, I was forced to quit just before Bird City, Kansas. It was dark, I was surrounded by clouds and lightning, and I was being blown all over the road. The storm was huge, with lightning for miles and miles in all directions. The veins of lightning were truly spectacular, but dangerous. I envisioned myself as a human lightning rod. The skinny, wet sew-up tires were hardly enough to ground me. This was the kind of storm that's wonderful to watch, but no fun to ride in. We bivouacked in the RV again, and Jan, Lisa, Liz, and Matt had the good sense to find a nearby motel room.

Oh, the wind in Kansas! I expected to see Dorothy, Toto, and the Wicked Witch of the West fly past at any time. Although the rain from the night before had cleared up, the stiff wind out of the south

Photo by Janice Mariolle

I took a short break in Nebraska and watched the storm clouds gather all around me.

remained. It was usually a crosswind, not as bad as a head wind, but bad enough. The crew sometimes fed me my meals bite by bite—I was afraid to let go of the bars to eat. When the course turned south, I felt as if I was riding against a wall of wind. Lee forced me to stop and put the hill-climbing cluster back on my bike. I used gears in Kansas that were unnecessary climbing Loveland Pass! Crawling into a stiff head wind hour after hour was heartbreaking. The wind ate at my spirit—especially when we heard reports that the lead men, who passed through days before ahead of the storm track, enjoyed a tail wind! It was a thoroughly miserable and discouraging time.

Vance has a penchant for schedules and benchmarks, which makes him a great crew chief. He was pushing me to cross the halfway mark in less than seven days. It was questionable whether I'd even make that target at the rate I was going. About 5-10 miles west of Beloit, Kansas, I stopped for the night. I couldn't make it to the motel just up the road so the crew loaded me into van and drove me to the motel. This procedure is legal as long as the rider is brought back to the same point before starting again, but I disliked it because it wasted valuable riding time. In this particular case, it was to be a real disaster. After my sleep break, I was shuttled back to where I had stopped the night before. It was drizzling and I started riding still half asleep. A few miles down the road, I reached the motel where I had slept and the temptation was just too great! I turned in and headed for

Photo by Marina Fusco Nims

Susan Notorangelo riding with Steve Krueger through windy Kansas. Neither one would finish the race.

Photo by Marina Fusco Nims

Shelby Hayden-Clifton battles head winds in the Midwest. Clifton and Hines arrived in Atlantic City at the same time, finishing the race in a sprint.

bed. Lee and Lisa looked baffled and slightly bummed out as I announced that it was over, that I was going to quit, and that I never wanted to ride a bike again as long as I lived! I fell into bed wearing all my clothes, including rain gear, shoes, gloves, and helmet. I felt disappointed with myself for stopping, but sleep was just too seductive. No one tried to argue with me, and no one woke me up. I was out cold for an hour or two or six.

When I woke up, I was still emotionally drained—but I knew I couldn't quit. We'd come too far to turn back now. I tried to sneak out the door undetected and head for the highway. It was again important to me to make the trip a good one even if our place in the pack wasn't so hot. Just saying the words "I quit" scared me so much that I found myself back on the bike and pedaling east.

I resolved to "start over" and try to make the second half of the RAAM better than the first. I wanted to make it to Atlantic City. If the crew would give me one last chance, I'd never quit again. It's hard to accept yourself when you're not doing a great job. It's hard to handle the fact that you're not fast enough, that you're not holding up well physically, that you aren't always nice. In the short run, quitting is easy because you don't have to deal with these realities. In the long run, though, I think there would always be that question "I wonder if we could have made it?" For the better part of an hour these thoughts were going through my head. Calvin told me before the race that I'd learn what my limits were if I didn't know them already. He also said that I'd say and do things I'd never expect. For the first time, his words started to hold some meaning.

It's ironic; after I had been on the road again for a few miles, ABC rolled by and told me how great I looked. I almost died! Diana Nyad asked me if I was proud of myself, even if I was in last place. I told her, "If last place is the best I can do this year, then that's fine." Even as I was answering her question I knew that I could do better in the future. This would be the last time I'd see Diana, Joel, Julie, and the others with ABC in this race. I was so far back that they had to wait half a day for me. Now they needed to push ahead to cover Susan's withdrawal from the race, and Pete Penseyres's challenge to perennial champion Lon Haldeman.

The combination of slow speed into the wind and horrendous ground time made for the worst mileage of the trip. We only managed to cover 159 miles in a 24-hour period. The same wind at my back would have made 250 miles an easy ride. But we did make it halfway in seven days. From Vance's journal, noon Sunday:

Passed halfway in a little less than 7 days. The proposed 11 day crossing is but a peculiar memory. To the extent that anyone has the energy or courage to think about it, we are trying to keep it under 14 days.

Despite my best intentions, I continued to flounder through Kansas. Certainly these middle days and miles were the most difficult. I was wasted from days of effort and the end was still so far off that it wasn't real. After deciding that I needed more rest, I sent the chase crew up the road so that I could "ride alone" for awhile and be free of their surveillance. It was then that I made the most stupid mistake in my three years of riding RAAM. I pulled off on the shoulder of the road, lay down in the tall grass, and went to sleep. The chase crew couldn't see me and spent the next hour driving around frantically trying to find me, worried sick and thinking the worst. When they finally located me, Vance was furious and justifiably so. My precious purple bike got thrown on the roadside as we "discussed" my transgression. Vance and I looked at each other in horror.

Days 7 and 8 in Kansas had been by far the hardest days of the race. Both were short of 200 miles. As we crossed out of Kansas and into Missouri, the crew played the songs "Surrender Dorothy" and "Es-

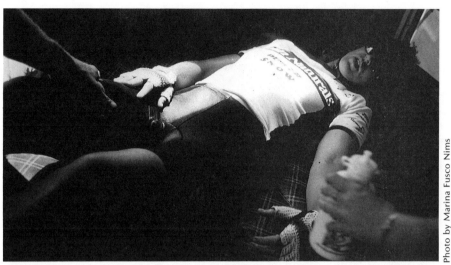

Photo by Marina Fusco Nims

Pat Hines rests in her motor home after a fall.

cape from Kansas." I was relieved to leave the flatlands and get into the rolling hills of Missouri. I liked the trees and the big bugs, and bullfrogs croaking in the night air. We stopped in a park in Higginsville, Missouri, Monday afternoon and caught a scent of Pat Hines when a reporter told us that she had slept there the night before.

"The race doesn't start until you reach the Mississippi."
—Pete Penseyres, winner, RAAM 1984

Pete Penseyres was approaching the finish in Atlantic City Tuesday afternoon. I was in the outskirts of the St. Louis metropolitan area, not yet across the Mississippi. Would I ever get there, I wondered? I had seen the city-limit sign earlier, but getting through St. Louis took the better part of the day. The city was hot, muggy, trafficky, and just generally unpleasant. At one point, I was riding on a frontage road paralleling the highway. A woman pulled off the highway, got out of her car, rushed to the chain-link fence, and shouted "Hang in there honey!" as I rolled by. This woman, like so many other upbeat people along the way, really gave me a boost. But it had worn off by the time I got into downtown St. Louis, and I was thoroughly depressed. I was starting to think that I'd never make it to the big river, and I was sobbing as I rode through the traffic. Then I had this eerie feeling

Susan Notorangelo explains to Diana Nyad her reasons for dropping out of the race in St. Louis. Notorangelo saw no reason to finish the race if she was outside the 36-hour limit for official finishers.

that something was too close or that someone was looking at me. I took a quick glance over my shoulder and there was an ABC sound boom leveled at my face. It was a local ABC crew assigned to cover me crossing the river. I was startled and embarrassed. I pulled myself together and, inspired by the woman earlier in the day, made a little speech thanking people like her for supporting the event and helping me out. It was an upbeat speech and was used to close ABC's TV coverage that year. But if you watched carefully, you could see tear-streaks in the grime on my face.

Phase III: Leveling Out

I did finally get across the river at 8:00 P.M. on Tuesday. Two thousand miles down, only 1,000 to go! Again, we had moved into another mode of operation. We survived the crisis where everybody was tired and bickering and we established a pretty workable routine. We were leveling out. We kept track of daily RAAM mileage (noon to noon), and the mileage between the daily sleep stops. I was off the bike too much and wasn't close to the 275-mile daily target, but it did seem like we would make it across the country. Vance described the daily routine in his notes:

It's working roughly this way. Normally, sometime around midnight, the RV goes ahead to get a motel. When Elaine turns up, we get her off, showered and patched up as necessary, then Lee massages her legs as she dozes off. I set a timer to give her 3 hours in bed counting the massage and then I get some sleep. Somebody does "burnout"—stays up just in case nobody gets up, watches the bikes and gear, just in case. I get up and start the burnout person doing some breakfast and other chores. I wake the chase crew and start getting Elaine up. Elaine and the chase folks eat something and hit the road. We typically get on the road an hour or so before sunrise. Although Elaine (and the chase crew!) tend to be a little rocky in the dark, riding through the dawn seems to be a real worthwhile boost.

Mornings are good to me. If I chase, I enjoy the dawn and the countryside and Elaine's good morning mood. It is a reflective time and I get good thinking done. Sometimes I make notes or strategize if I am not driving. If I don't chase, sometimes I go back to sleep for a while, but then I get up and hit a restaurant for breakfast and tend to my notes, etc. Try to update the recording.

The non-chase crew sleeps in and then attacks chores: laundry, shopping, cleanup. They generally set off after Elaine in the late morning and catch around noon. The morning chase is relieved. After Elaine has put in at least 100 miles since arising, and typically not until mid-afternoon, she gets a break if she wants it. We find a spot, she stretches out, gets a little rub, a little rest, and a little food. Roughly an hour off the bike.

The RV folks try to come up with the hot evening meal. Sometimes we buy pizza. Sometimes Elaine will get off the bike in the evening or after dark to eat, spending 15 or so minutes off the bike. By that time, we will be checking the route sheet for our target motel for the night. Invariably, the motel locations fall into two categories: too close and too far away. We typically solve this problem by making Elaine ride farther than would have been best under ideal circumstances. Sometimes we ferry her to the motel from some other checkpoint and ferry her back in the morning. Both tactics cost time, but the ferrying business is a real loser. Not only does it cost time, but it really breaks the rhythm of the ride.

Photo by Janice Mariolle

Kye Waltermire comes out to ride with me near Terre Haute, Indiana. Kye became interested in RAAM after riding with us in 1984 and went on to race in 1985 and 1986.

Lee Trampleasure offers some encouragement and support in the hills of West Virginia.

Photo by Janice Mariolle

Rolling through Illinois, Indiana, and Ohio was routine. In Indiana, an older gentleman flagged me down and asked me to autograph his application for his first century ride. I wrote him a short note of encouragement, remounted my trusty steed, and rode off through the cornfields. This was the first time anyone had asked me for an autograph. I couldn't figure out why he'd want mine, but I certainly wasn't going to complain. The thought of this gentleman, sitting on the trunk of his big car waiting for my autograph, still makes me smile!

Near Terre Haute, a rider joined me for a few minutes and told me how good I looked compared to the other racers who had ridden by. He asked me lots of questions about RAAM. This was Kye Waltermire, who would qualify and compete in 1985. He also told me that Terre Haute's big claim to fame was that gangsters from Indianapolis hid out there when the heat was on in Indianapolis.

In Ohio, a couple of really disreputable-looking characters in a beat-up truck followed us for awhile and asked a bunch of questions. We thought they might mug us, but they gave us a dollar for gas!

Friday afternoon, I crossed the Ohio River into West Virginia. Because of the climbing, riding through West Virginia was difficult, but I thoroughly enjoyed the plush, green richness of the Appalachians. It was bittersweet countryside. How could such poverty be interspersed in such gorgeous landscape? I saw some rundown mobile homes parked off the narrow state highway. They looked abandoned. Then as I passed, I saw a small child looking out through a broken window partially covered with cardboard. My heart sank.

These are old hills, wild hills, mysterious hills. I was intrigued, and I would like to go back someday. West Virginia passed quickly for me. Maybe because the end was near, or maybe just because of the beauty of the mountains, I was starting to feel spunky again. At the top of Roundhouse, I asked in the gas station if they had seen Pat Hines's entourage. "Yesterday afternoon," they said. Without doing the math in my head and realizing that there was no way I'd catch her in 375 miles, I got enthusiastic about "competing" again. Even if I couldn't finish officially, there was one goal I could still make and that was to finish the trip in less than 14 days. I planned to ride the last night straight through.

That last night was Saturday night on Labor Day weekend. We were concerned about drunks on the road. Indeed, I was offered a beer by four young men in a car, but I never had a real problem with drunk drivers. I did encounter a different apparition in the Amish country of Pennsylvania. I caught a slow-moving vehicle on a country road that turned out to be a horse and buggy. I said "Hello" into the darkness, but nobody replied. I don't think they meant to be unfriendly, but it scared me a little.

What Race?

Philadelphia—a mere 100 miles to go. All of us could see that the end was near. As we rolled along the flat expressway nearing Atlantic City, the destination signs took on a dreamlike quality. In Atlantic City, the course hit the boardwalk where the chase car couldn't follow. Vance got out of the car and ran along, helping me make my way through the Labor Day beach crowd. I didn't know where I was going and I rode into some open-air casino looking for a pier like the

I'm all smiles when the end is near—20 miles to Atlantic City!

Photo by Janice Mariolle

The Atlantic City Fire Fighters gave us a warm welcome and invited us to hang out on their fire truck.

Photo by Janice Mariolle

Crew photo

My fantastic crew. Top, left to right: Earle Young, me, Matthew Mariolle. Bottom, left to right: Lisa Basset, Vance Vaughan, Janice Mariolle.

Photo courtesy of the Atlantic City Fire Fighters

When we arrived, the Atlantic City Fire Fighters were on the boardwalk holding a fund-raiser for muscular dystrophy. The fireman asked me if I'd volunteer for the dunk tank. Sure, I was game! My crew was the first in line to dunk me. Even though this wasn't an "official" finish, the celebration was terrific!

one in Huntington Beach, California. We asked a janitor if this was where the bike race ended. He said, "What race?"

In a way, that summed it up for me. The officials had left, there was no trace of a finish line, no confetti, no cameras. There had been no consistent structure to my race, partly due to organizational and communication problems, partly because I was so far back.

But there was a celebration on the boardwalk—the Atlantic City fire fighters were raising funds for muscular dystrophy. They were real nice folks and let us hang out on their fire engine, gave us cold drinks, and talked with us. It was a good celebration. They asked if I'd volunteer for their dunk tank. I was game, but really—ride 3,000 miles and wind up in a dunk tank? Of course my crew lined up to dunk me first!

I was already home in Berkeley when I found out that Amy Smolens and Julie Anderson of ABC Sports had returned to Atlantic City to catch my finish. They expected me to sleep more the last night and ended up missing us at the pier. But they did talk with the fire fighters, who told of this woman who had just crossed the country on a bicycle. The fire fighters donated some film. We weren't forgotten after all.

RAAM '84 Results:

OFFICIAL

1st: Pete Penseyres	9:13:13
2nd: Michael Secrest	10:02:03
3rd: Jim Elliot	10:07:49
4th: Michael Shermer	10:16:30

UNOFFICIAL
(more than 36 hours back)

Rick Bozeat	11:22:39
1st: Shelby Hayden-Clifton	12:20:57
1st (tie): Pat Hines	12:20:57
3rd: Elaine Mariolle	13:23:36

With no separate division for the women none of us made the controversial cut at the Mississippi River. Under the "36-hour drop rule," anybody who was more than 36 hours behind the leader at the Mississippi River was dropped from the race. Susan dropped out when it was clear that she would be unofficial and she drove forward to join her husband, Lon, who was also racing. Pat and Shelby continued unofficially. Pat caught up with Shelby as they approached Atlantic City. They sprinted on the Boardwalk where John Marino created a spontaneous finish line and declared a tie.

RAAM '84 Postscript

Fourteen days isn't 11, but I did finish and I was pleased. I had come to learn, and I certainly did that! I felt better at the end than I had felt throughout much of the race, and I already knew I would be back the next year, with improvements in several areas:

Logistics. At the finish, we guessed that we could improve my time by a day simply by having a better motor home, straightening out our sleep procedures, and making other adjustments to our routine. No training necessary!

Training. No big mystery here. I rode through a series of problems with my feet, my butt, my knees—you name it. I was in better shape at the finish than at the start. I just needed more endurance training.

Time off the bike. We tried to do it the way the "real racers" do: not sleep the first night, sleep only two hours per night after that, minimize other time off the bike. But we had been off the bike more than five hours a day, and that is way too much. The problem was clear. The solution was not.

RAAM '85: THE TOUGHEST RACE

The start of RAAM '85 on Sunday, July 21, was exciting, but it didn't hold the same unbridled high I had experienced the year before. The excitement was tempered with a sober understanding: I knew what I was getting myself into. The naiveté and enthusiasm that turned a rough ride into a great adventure in 1984 would not be motivation enough this time. I had already ridden across country, so just making it wasn't good enough. I came to race.

Preparation

Going in, I set the following goals for myself:

1. Complete the course in 11 days, riding under Susan Notorangelo's 11 day, 16 hour record.
2. Finish within the 48-hour cutoff as an "Official Man."
3. Win the women's division in the process.

I had trained for the mileage and the pace. I had done a lot of distance rides. In RAAM '84 I averaged 220 miles per day. To make the 11-day goal, I'd have to average 285 miles per day. Earlier in May, I practiced the 280-mile per day schedule by setting a women's record from Seattle to San Diego—1,300 miles in under five days.

Our logistics were better too. We took 11 crew members and three vehicles—a motor home, chase car, and a small errand car. Everyone was assigned a job (masseuse, cook, mechanic, and so on), and we scheduled shifts and planned rest time. We spent more money on a larger motor home to make sure the crew was well rested and cared for.

Photo by Vance Vaughan

I could never have made it to the starting line without the encouragement and generous support from friends. "Le Clan Ordinaire": Back, left to right: Arthur Dembling, Tony Manno, Leslie Julian, Cindy Benes. Front: Bucci, me, and Paul Camardo. Bucci and friends held a large yard sale a few months before the race to raise money for midnight snacks. Le Clan also made some of their homemade pizzas for the crew.

RAAM 1985
DAILY MILEAGE AND LOCATION

Day	Miles per day	Total Miles	Approximate Location
1	353	353	Yarnell, Ariz.
2	282	635	Nearing N. Mex. border
3	321	956	Nearing Tucumcari, N. Mex.
4	293	1,249	Beyond Sayre, Okla.
5	306	1,555	Fort Smith, Ariz.
6	294	1,849	Memphis, Tenn.
7	255	2,104	Just past Nashville, Tenn.
8	248	2,352	Just past Knoxville, Tenn.
9	242	2,594	Nearing Roanoke, Va.
10	246	2,840	Front Royal, Va.
11	280	3,120	Atlantic City, N.J.

RAAM 1985

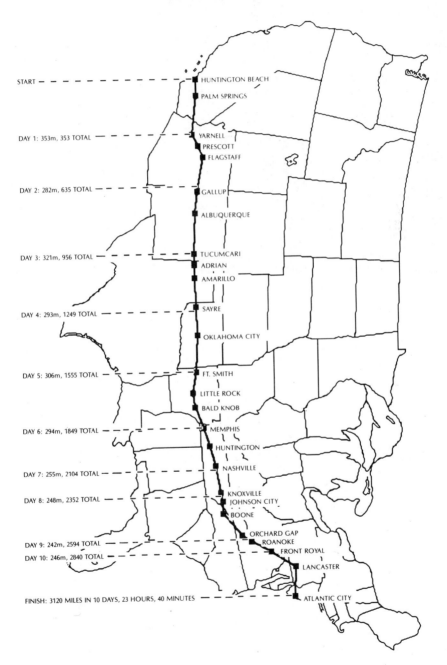

START

HUNTINGTON BEACH

PALM SPRINGS

DAY 1: 353m, 353 TOTAL

YARNELL
PRESCOTT
FLAGSTAFF

DAY 2: 282m, 635 TOTAL

GALLUP

ALBUQUERQUE

DAY 3: 321m, 956 TOTAL

TUCUMCARI
ADRIAN
AMARILLO

DAY 4: 293m, 1249 TOTAL

SAYRE

OKLAHOMA CITY

DAY 5: 306m, 1555 TOTAL

FT. SMITH

LITTLE ROCK

BALD KNOB

DAY 6: 294m, 1849 TOTAL

MEMPHIS

HUNTINGTON

DAY 7: 255m, 2104 TOTAL

NASHVILLE

DAY 8: 248m, 2352 TOTAL

KNOXVILLE
JOHNSON CITY
BOONE

ORCHARD GAP
ROANOKE

DAY 9: 242m, 2594 TOTAL

FRONT ROYAL

DAY 10: 246m, 2840 TOTAL

LANCASTER

FINISH: 3120 MILES IN 10 DAYS, 23 HOURS, 40 MINUTES

ATLANTIC CITY

Personal photo

My crew for the 1985 Seattle to San Diego record ride (4 days, 22 hours, 1 minute). Top, left to right: Bob Fabry, Frank Herr, Vance Vaughan, me, Helen Anrig. Bottom: Gilly Furnivall, Nancy Mariolle, Davis TeSelle.

Photo by Janice Mariolle

The crew takes care of last-minute preparations.

Photo by Janice Mariolle

Susan Notorangelo and I sport our Jones sunglasses in the parking lot before the start of the race.

Scott Terriberry, Gilly Furnivall and Janice Mariolle relax in the Huntington Beach parking lot. The message NO EXIT spray-painted on the wall behind them was prophetic.

Crew photo

The Competition

There were 25 riders in 1985, including two other women and myself. I had seen the competition before. Susan Notorangelo was the transcontinental record holder. She had dropped out in 1984 and had something to prove. Shelby Hayden-Clifton had beaten me in both of our previous encounters in the JMO and RAAM in 1984. Although I trained hard, I had lingering doubts about my ability to keep pace with Shelby and Susan. I was faster and better organized, but I assumed they would be too. Was I fast enough? I had also injured my right knee in the Seattle to San Diego ride only 10 weeks before RAAM '85. Would my injury recur?

The night before the race I visited with Susan. It was a friendly but guarded conversation about race strategy. It was clear that she wanted to win. At the prerace meeting, Susan and I admired the winner's trophy. Susan said she wanted me to have it if she didn't win. Susan and I are good friends, and we'd trained together for three weeks in Texas and St. Louis. The rivalry between Susan and Shelby, on the other hand, was intense. I guess it grew out of bitter battles during the wee hours of the night on rural highways in RAAM '84. I was not part of the rivalry and not considered much of a threat. I got along with both of them. It was clear that both Susan and Shelby thought the race was between the two of them. Standing there with Susan, with her fierce competitive energy, I also wondered if maybe that wasn't so.

The Start of RAAM '85

The race began on the same pier in Huntington Beach as the '84 race. There was the same excitement as we rode out along city streets and bike paths accompanied by ABC and thousands of local cyclists. The pace was controlled for this first stretch and we visited. When the racing began in earnest, something else happened that was all too

Photo by Janice Mariolle

The start of RAAM '85 at Huntington Beach Pier, California. From right to left: Jonathan Boyer (RAAM '85 winner), Michael Coles (RAAM sponsor), Shelby Hayden-Clifton, and Michael Shermer.

familiar: I quickly dropped to last place! It was hot and I was depressed. That afternoon, about 100 miles from the start, I got off my bike on a long climb and told Vance that I was going to quit. He talked me out of it and I continued, but it was a shaky start. That first day I dehydrated to the point where I quit sweating and urinating. The crew was worried and really worked to get me out of the red zone. One time I got into the motor home and was rubbed with ice!

When the sun set and the heat moderated, my outlook improved, and I rode through the night without sleep. I was still in a questionable mood the next morning, but as I started to catch other riders, my mood improved. At the end of 24 hours, I had covered 353 miles. I was trailing Shelby and Susan, but at least this time I was ahead of a lot of the men. Michael Secrest and Jonathan Boyer were tied for the lead five hours ahead, averaging almost 20 miles per hour. As expected, Shelby led the women, riding in sixth place overall and averaging 17 miles per hour. I finished the day in 16th place. I was ahead of my schedule, but three hours behind Shelby and two hours behind Sue.

The next day was similar. I suffered through the heat of the day, hanging two to three hours behind Sue and Shelby. Shelby's strategy was to ride fast and take lots of breaks. Sue, on the other hand, rode more slowly, but she stubbornly stayed on the bike most of the night. I

Photo by Marina Fusco Nims

Holding a speed tuck in Prescott Valley, Arizona.

wasn't losing ground, but then I wasn't gaining on either of them either.

Near Flagstaff, Arizona, Shelby slept, Sue took the lead from her, and I began to catch them. My sleep break that second night was two hours, and it worked very well. By the time we were approaching Albuquerque on the evening of Day 3, I was within an hour of both Sue and Shelby. Janet Tamaro and Dave Epperson, a writer and photographer covering the race, interviewed me and told me that the two were right up the road, that I looked good, and that I should catch them soon. I was encouraged, and started to push a bit harder, expecting to see them at any moment. A little farther up the road, ABC cruised up to shoot me in action. I knew I was close then. But a half hour is hard to make up, especially when no one is getting off their bikes. After awhile, I started to get demoralized because my big effort hadn't put me in contact with the competition. It took a day or more for the lead to build, so why did I think I'd make up all the time in one afternoon? Fatigued by my effort, I started the 50-mile climb out of Albuquerque on Highway 40 at nightfall on Tuesday. It was cold and rained off and on that night. I had a continuing, tantalizing thought: "Shelby is just up the road and everybody says she looks bad."

Partway up the climb, at 3 A.M. on Wednesday, I slept for the second time. (Note: the racers always used "RAAM time," which was EDT. Times given here are EDT unless otherwise stated.) It was another good sleep stop. I was back on the bike in two hours and I even got a shower! I was rejuvenated and resumed the chase. At noon Wednesday, the end of 72 hours, the gap had widened again. Sue was two and a half hours ahead of me, and Shelby was only 35 minutes behind her. Evidently, Sue and Shelby decided not to sleep or slept very little. After coming so close the day before, seeing that gap open again was truly demoralizing. In two years of competition, I had never seen them once the gun went off. I had been afraid that maybe I wasn't fast enough, and sure enough my worst fears were coming true. I was just plain intimidated by both of them. I spent some time off the bike sulking. What do you do when you come to race and you're not even in the competition? It's not like most sporting events that are over in a few hours and you can forget it. This was Day 4. I still had over 2,000 miles left to travel and more than six days to live with the problem.

It didn't help when ABC pulled up and Diana Nyad asked a few

Photo by Janice Mariolle

A rolling visit with the ABC crew in eastern New Mexico.

Photo by Lee Trampleasure

Fatigue and stress is expressed in laughter or tears, and sometimes a combination of both.

questions. Besides the usual "How do you feel?" and "What are you going to do?" she asked me what kept me going since I was not in the competition. "Would I quit?" Ouch! Diana hit a raw nerve. I gave some sporting reply about doing my best and breaking my own record. I tried not to let on how bad I felt psychologically. I was taking no comfort from the fact that we were 76 miles ahead of schedule or that I had moved up to 13th place overall. Sometimes the TV folks are a real boost, but sometimes, particularly when you feel the most vulnerable, it's a gamble to get into any penetrating discussions. I was taking a lot of cues from the outside. I remember asking Vance and others on the crew if they thought I could do it. If you're a serious competitor, you don't need to ask those kinds of questions.

A Race Within a Race

Wednesday afternoon, I passed the 1,000-mile mark near Tucumcari, New Mexico, and enjoyed the celebration whooped up by my crew. I was riding steadily and was ahead of my schedule. But I didn't really have a grasp on where I was in the race. The Abilene Century Riders were staffing one of the time stations and they had a computer. They gave me a printout with a map showing the position of every race participant. Secrest and Boyer were way off in front. Lon Haldeman was missing; he had been maintaining third place but had withdrawn in Amarillo, Texas, with the flu. Mike Shermer inherited third place—in front of the main pack but not really in contention for the overall lead. Then came a pack of 10 or 11 riders. I was at the tail end, and Shelby and Sue were at the front. Fifteen or more riders were off the back, behind me. For the first time in two years, I felt like I was really part of a race. I could visualize the event and besides riding as hard as I could, I started to think of strategy. The race is so long that you can get lost in the bigness. Even if I couldn't catch Sue and Shelby, I could certainly work on catching some of the guys in our pack.

For the next several days, as we rode down off the high desert in New Mexico, through Oklahoma, Texas, and Arkansas, all the way to Tennessee, my attention was focused on racing with my little pack of comrades. I exchanged places with Steve Krueger many times. I had won a sprint with Steve way back at the Continental Divide in Arizona, and here we were leapfrogging each other through a huge rainstorm approaching Amarillo, Texas. I rode in the rain; Steve slept. In Amarillo, I ran into the Penseyres team. Pete Penseyres, who had won the '84 race, was not riding, but he was crewing for his brother Jim. Jim had also slept through the rain and was riding strong. I wondered if I had made the wrong decision to ride through this storm. Everyone else looked so good. My plan was to ride under all conditions unless it was absolutely impossible. I thought in the long run my persistence would pay off—maybe not in this particular storm, but it might in the next. After Jim and I rode together for our allotted 15 minutes, he pulled away into the darkness. It was fun being in "the Penseyres sphere of influence." Pete is one of my heroes, and I love his whole family. JoAnn (Pete's wife) and Penny (Jim and Pete's mom) would cheerfully wave and say hello every time I saw them.

Liz and Vance Vaughan prepare a 1,000-mile celebration complete with a ribbon of toilet paper.

It was fun riding in the Penseyres "sphere of influence" for a few days. The whole family was always friendly and upbeat, even at 2 A.M.

Photo by Janice Mariolle

The crew relaxes in our motor home, dubbed "Mother-Ship." Left to right: Liz Vaughan, Frank Herr, Matthew Mariolle, Scott Terriberry, and Ben Fabry.

As I watched Jim pull away into the night, the chase crew (Jan Mariolle and Lee Trampleasure) and I began to make up songs to pass the time. My favorite was:

> This Lane is Your Lane, this Lane is My Lane
> from California to Atlantic City
> from Tucumcari to the Blue Ridge Parkway
> This Lane was made for you and me. . . .

Through Oklahoma, Steve Krueger, Rob Templin, Jim Penseyres, and I continued to exchange places frequently. This ongoing competition was exciting. In RAAM it takes days to drop someone. It's not like a regular road race where you can attack and sprint for a few hundred meters and then throttle back to a fast cruise to the finish in a few more miles. In RAAM, you don't always notice that someone is slipping back. Maybe it takes them a little longer to pass you after a sleep break. Pretty soon, they're an hour back, and by the end of the race, they could be 11 or 12 hours back. Each person has their own "rate of decay." Some people may ride faster and then just blow up after a few days. For others, it's the steady-grind approach. My plan was to work my way steadily through the pack. I had already made contact with all but Kye Waltermire, Susan, and Shelby.

On Thursday night, about 1,400 miles and four and a half days into the race, the first major crack in my routine occurred. I was not supposed to sleep until about 3 A.M., but at 11:25 P.M. I summoned the motor home for a potty stop. When I got in there, I told them I didn't need to go to the bathroom, I was just too tired to go on. I fell facedown on the bed fully clothed and was asleep in an instant. I slept badly, due to guilt. After an hour, I got up and continued riding. A few hours later, I was asleep again.

At noon on Friday we passed the halfway point in Fort Smith, Arkansas. My crew had another celebration complete with signs. I remember one sign in particular that my little brother Matthew had made. It read, "Halfway! It's all downhill from here!" In terms of

A quick break in a Safeway parking lot in Fort Smith, Arkansas, just past the halfway mark. Matthew's sign "Halfway! It's all downhill from here!" had a certain ironic truth.

Crew photo

The lack of sleep was starting to catch up with me. Vance helped me get started again after my 1½-hour sleep break.

terrain, much of the climbing lay ahead on the Blue Ridge Parkway in North Carolina and Virginia, but in terms of my overall condition, there was a certain ironic truth to Matt's message. I was 1,560 miles into the race in 5 days, 22 minutes. I was in eighth place overall. I was averaging over 308 miles per day and was 159 miles ahead of my 11-day schedule. But I was still falling further behind Shelby (5 hours) and Sue (3 hours).

The lack of sleep was starting to catch up with me. Friday night, I had to go to sleep at 11 P.M., which is much too early. Sleeping early means that when you wake up there are many hours of darkness to struggle through. Back on the bike after two hours, I literally fell asleep on the bike on a rural Arkansas highway. I swerved, and my sister Jan demanded that I be taken off the road. When Vance came up to see how I was, I had no idea where I was or what had happened. I believed I was back in the California desert. When Vance told me I'd been on my bike for nearly a week, I was surprised. They let me go back to sleep.

Saturday morning, we were cranking out the last few miles of

Arkansas, approaching the Mississippi River and Memphis, Tennessee. We were rolling through open, flat agricultural country, and I was still exchanging places with Steve Krueger and Rob Templin. Steve pulled off at a check point to nap and I never saw him again. Rob wasn't that simple. He would pass me going really fast, and I'd jump to catch him and get tired. Then a few hundred meters down the road he'd slow way down. After a few of these attempts to catch him, I pulled off the road, got off my bike, and started crying. It was very foolish of me, but I was having huge mood swings by this time and was not thinking rationally. After one in a series of pep talks from my crew, I got back on the bike and vowed to just ride steady for the next few hours. A short way up the road, Rob pulled off. He got back on when I passed and pulled ahead once or twice. I let him go and just kept a steady pace. Within a few minutes, he pulled off again. I never saw him or any of the group we had been trading places with during the previous four days, until Atlantic City.

This Race Ended at the Mississippi River

At 11:39 A.M. on Saturday, I crossed the Mississippi River. Secrest had crossed it in the lead over a day before with Boyer 40 minutes behind. Everyone else was fading at various rates. Mike Shermer was still in third. Shelby remained in fourth (8 hours ahead of me), Sue in fifth (3 hours ahead of me). How could it be? I rode 1,849 miles, averaging over 308 miles per day. I was 129 miles ahead of my record-breaking schedule. Yet I was losing ground on Shelby. We would spend the next 1,300 miles hoping that Shelby and Sue would crack. But what about me? From Vance's trip log:

> Elaine is in new territory. We have put her back on the bike semiconscious several times. Someone runs along side to see if she can actually ride and (if so), the chase car tries to talk her into full participation. I got two hours sleep last night in one stretch. I vaguely recall one other block about that long. But I really don't know how much sleep I'm getting.

I continued riding, but without the competition from my comrades, it got very abstract and I didn't focus well.

Days 7–9 were spent in the rolling hills of Tennessee, which was my

Photo by Lee Trampleasure

As I slept, Scott Terriberry made sure my bike was in good working order while members of the crew looked on.

favorite state. I loved the expansive green, grassy hills, the dense woods. Tennessee was like a roller coaster—up and down. My moods mirrored the up and downs of the mountains.

In Memphis, before the hill climbs, I was caught at a stoplight in front of the Elvis Presley estate and took the opportunity to see what I could see, which turned out to be little except the huge wrought-iron gate and the stone wall. I was curious about the rest. At least the crew did a little exploring and stopped in the souvenir shops across the street. They picked up an assortment of Elvis paraphernalia—collector spoons, pennants, plastic dolls—and decorated the motor home. Of course, I didn't even notice these choice items until the ride home! I didn't spend much time in the motor home, and when I did, I was usually sleeping.

We had another flurry of excitement in Memphis. The chase car blew a fan belt, and the errand car was pressed in to chase. In the confusion, Jan, Lee, and Matt were left standing on somebody's lawn. They were rescued by the race officials we knew as "RAAM 4" and delivered to us. I took my first daytime sleep at about 4:30 P.M. A few

Photo by Janice Mariolle

Photo courtesy of RAAM

During a crew change, Janice and Matthew Mariolle are left stranded on someone's front lawn in Memphis, Tennessee. They were picked up by RAAM race officials and returned to the motor home a few hours later.

Riding through dawn always gives me great pleasure. It's a real boost!

Photo by Janice Mariolle

Cruising past Elvis's house in Memphis. Later, some of the crew "abandoned" me to check out the gift shops.

miles outside Memphis, a RAAM fan at a time station had an "I love Elaine" sign. This encouragement came at just the right time. I tried to pick up the pace a little—I at least wanted to look good.

In one day, we rode from Elvis's home in Memphis, Tennessee, to the home of country music in Nashville. The leaders passed through Nashville well over a day before me. Boyer had taken the lead from Secrest, who was two and a half hours back. Shermer was in third and Shelby was fourth, almost a day behind. Sue trailed Shelby by two and a half hours. I was in seventh place, trailing Shelby by six hours.

Photo taken by crew

Another celebration at the North Carolina border, complete with purple Burger King crowns the crew acquired and wore most of the way.

In Texas, I had wished for hills, any kind of hills. In eastern Tennessee, I got my wish. I liked the hills, but I was having a peculiar problem. At night, I could climb pretty well. But once on the downhill, I would fall asleep. I had to be taken off my bike and put to bed once because of this problem. I wanted to continue, but my crew wouldn't allow it because it wasn't safe.

The Blue Ridge Parkway through North Carolina and Virginia is beautiful. I would like to ride it sometime when I haven't just ridden eight straight days to get there! It is a lovely park but it is all hills. It is where Secrest blinked in his duel with Boyer. Secrest spent a lot of time on the ground because of the fog, conceding first place. And it is where something very unexpected happened to Shelby—Sue passed her! Shelby is a much better climber than Sue, so nobody would have predicted that. Nobody, perhaps, but Sue. Shelby had worn down, and Sue's enormous, competitive will to win propelled her past Shelby, hills or no hills.

Wasted in Roanoke, Virginia. Lee Trampleasure and Gilly Furnivall massage my feet and legs as I catch a short nap in the shade.

Photo by Janice Mariolle

Photo by Janice Mariolle

Kye Waltermire and I rode together one morning on the Blue Ridge Parkway. After we shared breakfast, he went on ahead.

I had a different kind of experience on the parkway. I passed Kye Waltermire, who was sleeping, and found myself in sixth place. That didn't last for long. Kye caught me on Tuesday morning. I traded him some french toast for some of his waffles as we rode along eating breakfast. It was good to see him, but I let him ride off and drop me. That competitive spirit just hadn't clicked. I was still trying to break 11 days, but I wasn't able to focus on the other riders.

After we pulled into a time station in Pennsylvania, a kind woman stopped to give me a hug.

Susan Notorangelo, winner of RAAM 1985, presents me with a bouquet of flowers on behalf of the Golden Nugget Casino in Atlantic City.

Shelby and I congratulate each other after a long hard race.

Wednesday we were off the parkway, closing in on Atlantic City, 300 miles away. It seemed strange to be on regular highways with regular traffic. I took one last sleep break at 2:45 A.M. When I got up at 5 A.M. I had to ride 105 miles in seven hours. People ride centuries much faster than that all the time, but I was wasted and it was hilly. I rode furiously and finished at 11:40 A.M., with 20 minutes to spare.

ABC escorted me onto the boardwalk and there was a finish line. It was quite a change from '84. Susan and Shelby were there to greet me. Susan gave me a big bunch of flowers and lent me her room so I could shower before going to a press conference that was starting just as I arrived.

RAAM '85 Results:

OFFICIAL

1st: Jonathan Boyer	9:02:06
2nd: Michael Secrest	9:06:08
3rd: Michael Shermer	10:07:57
4th: Kye Waltermire	10:21:13
1st: Sue Notorangelo-Haldeman	10:14:25
2nd: Shelby Hayden-Clifton	10:20:33
3rd: Elaine Mariolle	10:23:40

UNOFFICIAL
(more than 48 hours back)

Steve Krueger	11:11:11
Rob Kish	11:12:19
Michael Trail	11:14:22
Rob Templin	11:22:37
Jim Penseyres	11:22:37
Rob Gillis	12:04:52
Tally Chapman	12:22:14
Dwight Callaway	14:01:47

RAAM '85 Postscript

A lot had changed in one year. The RAAM organizers set up a series of time stations across the country in 1985. Many of them were staffed day and night by volunteers from the League of American Wheelmen.

We were required to check in as we passed the time stations and this information was available to all the racers. This made it easy to keep track of the competition. Coming across one of those time stations in the middle of the night, with some lights and people to cheer you on, was a real rush. It felt more like a bike race than a solo adventure.

After 1984, the RAAM organizers decided to have separate divisions for the men and women, each with their respective 48-hour drop rule. Ironically, in 1985 the three women surprised everyone by placing fourth, fifth, and seventh overall, and we were all within 48 hours of the winning man. The women went from the back of the pack to a respectable standing overall. We had arrived.

Unfortunately, there was a sad edge to the 1985 race for all of us. Wayne Phillips from Canada was racing without a support crew. He was hit in the darkness near Tucumcari, New Mexico, by a driver who left him lying on the side of the road. Wayne was left paralyzed and the driver was never found. Because of this tragedy, the RAAM officials now require support crews for each competitor and enforce strict rules about safe night riding.

I had a minor problem of my own: numb hands. Anyone who does distance cycling has probably experienced numbness in various parts of her body. I had complained about my hands early on and we had changed back to my old reliable gloves and forgotten about it. I wasn't too worried when I couldn't close my fist in Atlantic City, but I was plenty worried when I still couldn't use my hands a week later. A neurologist predicted a partical recovery after about four months and advised me never to ride very far again.

RAAM '85 left me ambivalent. My crew had been wonderful. The organization had worked well and I never knew about several car problems that they solved during the race. I took three days off my time from the previous year and I finished as an "official man." I was pleased about that. But I was discouraged to be the last-place woman.

RAAM '86: FIRST AT LAST

After RAAM '85, I had decided to take a break and not race in 1986. Susan Notorangelo brought me back to Huntington Beach in 1986. She had announced her retirement after winning RAAM '85, but then changed her mind and decided to race just once more. That settled it for me. I had something to prove in RAAM and I wanted to do it

RAAM 1986
DAILY MILEAGE AND LOCATION

Day	Miles per day	Total Miles	Approximate Location
1	383	383	Beyond Yarnell, Ariz.
2	326	709	Gallup, N. Mex.
3	349	1,058	Near Adrian, Tex.
4	313	1,371	Tuttle, Okla. (near Oklahoma City)
5	295	1,666	Morrilton, Ark. (near Little Rock)
6	314	1,980	Huntingdon, Tenn.
7	291	2,271	Maryville, Tenn. (near Knoxville)
8	281	2,552	Orchard Gap, Va.
9	232	2,784	Elkton, Va.
10	293	3,077	Nearing Atlantic City, N.J.
11	30	3,107	Atlantic City, N.J.

when the champ was there. Since Susan had declared that this would definitely be her last year, if I wanted to race with her it was now or never. The year before, I had come to race. This year, I came to win.

Preparation

Preparation for this race had to be perfect. In the past I had followed the training regimens of other successful RAAM riders, usually previous winners. Although many of their suggestions were helpful, it was time to focus on my own strengths and weaknesses, and develop my own style. I had successfully crossed the country in 1984 and 1985, and I knew I had the determination and endurance to go the distance. Over the years RAAM had become much more than an exercise in sleep deprivation. Anyone who is competitive can ride at least 20 hours a day. It comes down to who rides fastest, and who can handle the pressure. I focused on speed training instead of endurance training.

In some ways, the physical training is easy compared to solving the abstract psychological puzzle about how to be competitive. In speed training, performance is measured objectively through a function of time and distance. You simply go out there and do the work. I did interval and sprint work, and used a heart rate monitor to gauge my fitness level. I also joined the daily training rides with the Berkeley

RAAM 1986

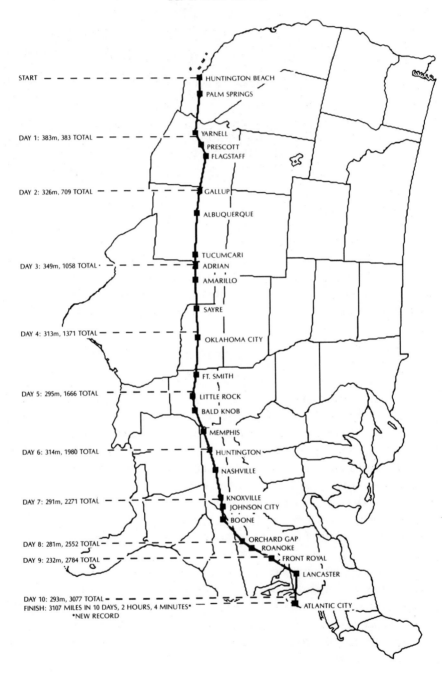

START — — — — — — — — — — — ■ HUNTINGTON BEACH
                              ■ PALM SPRINGS

DAY 1: 383m, 383 TOTAL — — — ■ YARNELL
                              ■ PRESCOTT
                              ■ FLAGSTAFF

DAY 2: 326m, 709 TOTAL — — — ■ GALLUP
                              ■ ALBUQUERQUE

DAY 3: 349m, 1058 TOTAL · — — ■ TUCUMCARI
                              ■ ADRIAN
                              ■ AMARILLO

                              ■ SAYRE

DAY 4: 313m, 1371 TOTAL — — — ■ OKLAHOMA CITY

                              ■ FT. SMITH
DAY 5: 295m, 1666 TOTAL — — — ■ LITTLE ROCK
                              ■ BALD KNOB

                              ■ MEMPHIS
DAY 6: 314m, 1980 TOTAL — — — ■ HUNTINGTON
                              ■ NASHVILLE

DAY 7: 291m, 2271 TOTAL — — — ■ KNOXVILLE
                              ■ JOHNSON CITY
                              ■ BOONE

DAY 8: 281m, 2552 TOTAL — — — ■ ORCHARD GAP
                              ■ ROANOKE
DAY 9: 232m, 2784 TOTAL — — — ■ FRONT ROYAL
                              ■ LANCASTER

DAY 10: 293m, 3077 TOTAL — — — ■ ATLANTIC CITY
FINISH: 3107 MILES IN 10 DAYS, 2 HOURS, 4 MINUTES*
          *NEW RECORD

The start of RAAM 1986, July 6th at Huntington Beach Inn.

Photo by Carol Shanks

Bicycle Club, a local racing club. These group rides were very productive. I was pushed harder and I rode faster. I attended a race camp, and got some formal coaching through a grant from the Women's Sports Foundation. The speed training indirectly helped my attitude and helped build confidence. I entered a few local races for competition and experience. I was winning all the endurance events I entered and placed in several road races as well.

One thing I didn't do was overnight rides. I didn't do so much as one 24-hour ride between RAAM '85 and RAAM '86. That wasn't really the way I planned it, and I wouldn't recommend it in general, especially for a first-time RAAM rider. I banked on my solid endurance background but knew that this decision to emphasize speed over endurance training was a calculated gamble. I was definitely riding faster. I just hoped I could sustain the effort for 3,100 miles.

I also made significant nutritional and technological changes. I

Photo by Todd Buchanan

Lon Haldeman and Susan Notorangelo. Lon won RAAM twice (1982, 1983) and Susan once in 1985. Susan held the Women's Transcontinental Record prior to RAAM 1986. Together Susan and Lon hold the Mixed Tandem Transcontinental Record.

have always eaten good food, but many times during **RAAM** I was hot or tired and had difficulty eating. Jonathan Boyer impressed me with his liquid diet in 1985. I called him up and he was very helpful. He explained what he had done and put me in touch with **UNIPRO**, and they helped me out too. I experimented with their Carboplex on long training rides and found that it worked well. It provided a steady energy level, eliminating the peaks and troughs. It's easier to stay hydrated on a liquid diet because you're already consuming lots of water. This was particularly important in 1986 because the temperatures were rarely below 90 degrees and were often well over 100 degrees in the desert areas. I planned to consume 85 to 90 percent of my meals in liquid form.

Photo by Carol Shanks

Casey Patterson and I visit prior to the start of the race. This was Casey's first RAAM. She would eventually drop out in Arkansas due to knee problems. She came back strong and won the RAAM 1987.

Photo by Carol Shanks

Shelby and Eric Clifton. Shelby tied for first with Pat Hines in RAAM 1984 and placed second to Susan Notorangelo in RAAM 1985. Eric placed second in the JMO West (John Marino Open) and qualified to race in RAAM. He rode the paced portion of the race and then crewed for Shelby.

As the winter months progressed, I started to develop a fightback attitude. The training program was showing positive results, we were assembling another great crew, and sponsors were getting behind our effort. By early spring, I started having "RAAM dreams." A few times each week I'd dream about various situations that could occur during the Race Across AMerica. Most of the time they involved strategy. If I were behind, how would I make up the time? If I were passed how would I rally back? If I were in the lead how would I handle the pressure? In all of these situations, I would work through the rough spots to resolve the simulated race in my favor. By the time the actual event came along, I had strong strategies worked out. Going into the race I felt confident that I could handle the pressure and stress of competition. I remember dreams in which Sue, Shelby, and I were within minutes of each other until the finish line. It's funny, sometimes I remember the finish in those dreams better than the actual finish.

Our team had come to Huntington Beach very well prepared. The chase car was set up and even the motor-home lettering was done before we left Berkeley. With the exception of some last-minute gluing of tires and a little grocery shopping, we had much more time to rest and relax before the race. The experience of two previous trips was paying off. I remember telling Jim Lampley in a prerace interview that I was no longer intimidated by Sue and Shelby. For the first time I believed that I, too, was a contender in the race. The night before the race, I walked on the beach to relieve prerace jitters. I watched the roll of the ocean and thought of the continuous circles I'd spin until I reached Atlantic City.

The Start of RAAM '86

A field of 20 men and 6 women assembled in Huntington Beach on Sunday, July 6, 1986. Pete Penseyres and Michael Secrest promised a duel at the front of the men's race, with many new faces hoping to break into the action. In the women's field, Susan Notorangelo was back to defend her title, and Shelby Hayden-Clifton and I had something to prove. There were three aspiring rookie women: Casey Patterson, Deb Haas, and Karen Winterhalter. I had met Deb and Karen at the JMO in 1984. Casey was a new face. She was a petite woman with three kids, one a teenager bigger than she. Although we

Casey Patterson says good-bye to her children, Mary and Charlie, at the start of RAAM 1986.

Photo by Todd Buchanan

were to follow the same route as the previous year, the start had been moved a few blocks into town to the 2-Wheel Transit Authority bike shop. While city streets were easier for the officials to control and gave the thousands of spectators a better view of the competitors, I missed the drama of starting right on the pier.

The starting routine, following the bike paths and streets during the parade at the beginning of the race, was now very familiar. But when the competition started, something new happened. John Marino dropped the flag, and I sprinted away from the pack, side by side with Shelby. It was a bit silly considering how far we had to go, but it served notice that I had come to race. As things settled down to a more reasonable level, Shelby pulled away, and I was passed by a lot of the men on the first long climb.

It was hot and heat always bothers me. In Berkeley, where I live, 75 degrees is a hot day. In Palm Springs during July, it's rarely below 100. I try to train in heat, but it's just not my natural element, and I had problems that first day as always. Sue and I traded places a couple times. Once, as she passed me, she scolded my crew: "What's wrong with Elaine? Get her going!" Later that evening, Casey Patterson caught me. As the day faded and the heat moderated, I started to hit

Photo by Carol Shanks

Susan and I ex-
changed places many
times during the
night. I passed her for
the last time out of
Congress, Arizona, as
we began the climb
to Yarnell.

my stride. Susan and I traded places a couple times during the night,
never more than a few minutes apart. Shelby was opening a lead. We
all rode through the first night without sleep.

Dawn Monday found Sue and me together in the Arizona desert. I
passed her one more time outside Congress just before the long climb
into Yarnell. Climbing is not Sue's forte, and I started to build a lead.
At the end of 24 hours I had ridden 386 miles. After all that work, I
was only eight minutes ahead of Sue, and Shelby was almost an hour
ahead of me. She must have ridden about 400 miles that day! Casey
was about an hour behind. Deb and Karen couldn't match the pace
and were four or more hours back. I was in 11th place overall. Pete
Penseyres and Michael Secrest were battling it out for the lead in the
men's race, almost four hours ahead.

Day 2 was spent climbing the Arizona canyon lands to the New
Mexico plateau. I was staying about an hour behind Shelby, through
the Prescott Valley up to the bohemian town of Jerome. The bone-
jarring descent down pitted, winding streets was punishing on
muscles that were already sore and fatigued. It was beautiful high
desert country though, and the view made up for the rocky ride.

By late afternoon I reached the picture-rock canyons of Sedona. As I
began the serpentine climb up Oak Creek Canyon, I knew I was in
for a visual treat. Each switchback showed off the canyon from a
slightly different angle, or under a different light. In 1986 we had the
advantage of having ridden the same course the previous year. Knowing the terrain and what to expect helped immeasurably in planning

strategy. It was surprising how much I remembered. Sometimes I'd even tell the crew where to turn. Usually it was the little things like a unique road sign or an unusual barn that had caught my eye the year before and stuck in my mind. Darkness fell as I made the final staircase climb to Flagstaff. Shelby, Sue, and I rode on into our second night.

Shelby slept first. Around midnight on Monday, just past Two Guns, Arizona, I passed Shelby's vehicles parked on the side of the road. I didn't know for sure that she was in there sleeping until I reached the next time station and found she hadn't been through yet. I was leading the women's race for the first time ever and I didn't even know it! The ABC crew appeared out of the darkness to talk to me. They were piled into a large van and looked a bit crowded and tired, but upbeat as usual. Diana Nyad asked me what my strategy would be. Would I go without sleep and try to build a lead? I told her I would stick to my original plan and ride to the next time station and then take my full two-hour sleep break. I was careful not to get too excited, too soon. There was still a long way to go.

I continued riding until 4:45 A.M. Tuesday, when I went to sleep for the first time a few miles short of the New Mexico border. My plan was for a two-hour sleep stop. I expected Shelby to pass me back at some point during my sleep break. Trading places at sleep breaks is really common on RAAM. If Shelby had slept for two hours, she should have passed by about 5:45. But it was almost 6:30 when Shelby came by and my crew had already started to get me up. Any concern we may have had about my ability to ride with only two hours sleep was postponed. When I hit the road, I was only eight minutes behind Shelby and I was READY.

I caught up with Shelby before dawn on Tuesday. I was tense and excited. I have great respect for Shelby's athletic prowess, and I had anticipated this moment for years. When I rode up next to her I could tell her emotions were at extreme opposites of the spectrum. I was delighted and high with enthusiasm. Shelby was caught. I wished I could see behind those bee-face Oakley riding goggles. We rode together for a few minutes unable to drop each other. I was so excited I didn't say anything, and that's unusual for me! Shelby spoke first.

"Nice morning isn't it?" Somehow that's not what I expected to hear. "Yes, yes! Nice morning," I replied. This was THE race, THE moment. I half expected fireworks. Here we were out in the morning

Photo by Marina Fusco Nims

I caught up with Shelby just outside of Gallup, New Mexico. We rode within minutes of each other for the next 200 miles.

desert, locked in a duel that could potentially last a week, with both crews cheering on both riders.

The two of us rode together into Gallup, New Mexico. Later that morning we passed Kye Waltermire, and caught up with Rob Templin. For 200 miles, Shelby and I rode minutes apart leapfrogging our way across the New Mexico plateau. We passed through time station 17 in Grants, New Mexico, at 747 miles, only three minutes apart. As I pulled away into the head wind on the east side of the Continental Divide I never guessed it would be for good. I thought Shelby would rally back—she always did. But I felt confident. I had passed her once while she was riding and I knew I could do it again. My batteries were charged and I was turned on.

By the time I was approaching Albuquerque, I had fought for a 26-minute lead over Shelby. The head wind earlier in the day turned into a wailing tail wind, making speeds over 20 mph comfortable. Vance asked me to guess who was in fifth place overall. I really had no idea. When he said it was me, I was totally surprised and thrilled. Pete Penseyres was screaming across the country at an unbelievable pace, with Michael Secrest in hot pursuit. Lon Haldeman and Matt Beerer trailed in third and fourth place. Although I was in no danger of catching Pete, I was pleased to be leading the women's race and doing so well overall.

The crew celebrates the repairing of our broken-down motor home. When they finally caught up with me they were surprised to find that I had taken the lead.

Photo by Todd Buchanan

Building a Lead

Once we crossed the Rio Grande and started to negotiate our way through town, it was obvious which way to go. Up. Albuquerque is laid out on a slope. On the east side of town near the car lots, I got back onto I-40 and started the long freeway grade up into the mountains. My 26-minute lead was nice, but not enough to let me relax. Shelby had slept early the night before, and Sue wouldn't like this climb. I figured a strong effort this night might give me a little breathing room.

Eight miles into the climb, the desert air became humid and the sky clouded over with thunderheads. Within half an hour the temperature dropped, the wind picked up, and pea-sized hailstones pelted down. I put on a rainjacket and my clear Blades to protect my eyes, but I had to stop, as the hail kept pinging on my kneecaps and stinging my face. My Mom was in the chase car and she said, "I was wondering when you'd stop! All the other cars have pulled off the road and we're the only ones still crazy enough to keep rolling!" I dove into the small Mazda with Mom and John Tofield and raided their lunch basket as I quickly pulled on more rain gear.

The storm didn't last long, and soon the sky cleared, leaving dark broken clouds with the faintest trace of early stars poking through. I asked Mom and John to keep checking the rearview mirror, half expecting Shelby to roll up to our back door at any time. What I didn't know was that Shelby was caught in rain a few miles back down the road. After nightfall, ABC rolled up—all smiles under a cover of umbrellas—for an interview.

Photo by Carol Shanks

I was slowed a bit by a hailstorm in the mountains above Albuquerque, New Mexico.

I rode long into the night. As I made the long gradual descent out of the mountains, I could see the Tucumcari city lights flickering in the distance. They looked close, but were actually 25 or 30 miles away. I was uneasy riding toward Tucumcari that night. I thought of fellow competitor Wayne Phillips, left paralyzed by an unresolved hit-and-run accident near here the year before. I took my second sleep closing in on Tucumcari, 965 miles into the race. I was over three hours ahead of Sue and Shelby. My crew rewarded my hard work by giving me an extra 30 minutes of sleep. When I hit the road again after this extravagant indulgence, there was a little "pack" of five riders spread out from 1:40 to 2:18 behind me: Kye Waltermire, Shelby, Georges Helaouet, Sue, and Rob Templin.

I wanted to know how Shelby and Susan were doing, so I dispatched Lee Trampleasure and Mom to drive back down the road and "spy" on the competition. RAAM officials had a long list of rules detailing the proper spying techniques. We thought we'd have fun

Lee Trampleasure and Mom, wearing our official "spy attire," position themselves discreetly behind an upside-down newspaper and wait for Shelby and Sue to ride by.

with this. Before we left Berkeley, David Shanks picked up our team's official spy attire at the local toy store. It consisted of Groucho Marx glasses with a big nose attached. Lee and Mom positioned themselves on I-40 out in the middle of nowhere and waited. They'd stand by the road wearing the glasses as Sue or Shelby approached and pretend to read a newspaper. They'd lower the paper as the rider passed, exposing their disguised faces and getting a good laugh. In the middle of this mission, a local sheriff happened by and asked them what they were doing out there and suggested they move along!

It was a relief to come down from the mountains and switch to some flat riding. The next couple of days would be spent spinning across the desert flatlands of eastern New Mexico, Texas, and Oklahoma. I enjoyed another favorable tail wind all morning, and worked with it to build the lead I had opened up during the night. I had gotten into one of those voids in the race. I was staying ahead of the people chasing me, but unable to catch the lead men ahead. Once I

Photo by Carol Shanks

Photo courtesy of Dave Nelson/PIW

Strategist Vance Vaughan kept track of the competition and helped me stay on a record-breaking schedule.

Bindy Beck, a veteran member of Lon Haldeman's crew and an accomplished cyclist herself, did a wonderful job of keeping me fed throughout the race. Bindy knew what I needed even before I asked for it.

got past Shelby in New Mexico, I would encounter another racer only once in the last 2,000 miles of the race.

Contact with other racers can really keep you charged up. During this long spell, my crew did a magnificent job of keeping me fueled, entertained, and motivated. Vance was in charge of strategy, and he kept track of all the other racers with split times and position charts. He also kept me on a record-breaking schedule. Bindy, Lee, Carol, and David were the core chase crew. They made sure I was well fed, watered, and happy. Bob Fabry's ingenious communication system provided two-way contact between rider and crew. It came in most handy during the wee hours of the morning when it's particularly difficult to stay awake. We told stories, discussed philosophy, and sang songs to pass the time. My brother Matthew was spunky as usual and always had a few tall tales to tell. Pups (that's what I call my father) was commander of the "Mother Ship" (motor home) and Mom made sure the crew was well fed. Ed Gould dealt with a myriad of mechanical difficulties and made sure all the vehicles proceeded down the road. John Tofield made sure all my bicycles were ready to roll, and

Sparky caught lots of these activities on film for future viewing.

Later during the afternoon of Day 4, the winds shifted and began to blow from the south, producing very strong and consistent cross-winds. I was down on the drops and worked hard long past sunset. These conditions favored Sue, who is a real powerhouse. She passed Shelby to become the second-place woman, seventh overall. Wind still depresses me, unless, of course, it's at my back. Listening to messages that friends had left for me on my phone answering machine at home helped to cheer me up. A few times each day, Vance would call the machine and transfer the messages to a tape; then I listened to the tape on my "Rideperson."

I arrived in Sayre at 1:43 A.M., dodging June bugs. RAAM photographer Dave Nelson pushed a small sound boom my way for a talk. He expected to find me grinning away in the lead, singing "Oklahoma" just like I did in 1985. Instead, I was teary-eyed and wasted. I wasn't sad or depressed, I explained, just tired and emotionally drained after a tough day in the wind. At times like this, laughter or tears or a combination of both is a welcome release. I knew I'd be fine after a massage and sleep. I stopped five miles up the road, and bedded down for the night—all two hours of it!

Lee's nightly massages worked wonders on my tired legs, and the two-hour sleep breaks still seemed to be enough. When I got up from my third sleep break at 1,250 miles, I felt like a new woman. I was alert, focused, and ready to roll. The ABC entourage was also up and shooting film at 4:15 A.M. when I took off. The night was calm and my thoughts weren't distracted by the activity of the day. The pack behind me was stringing out: Kye was about an hour back, Sue about two, Georges three, Shelby four, and Rob was off the chart. Sue was staying even, but she wasn't gaining on me! I made the halfway point about midnight Thursday, only four and a half days out. Mom and Carol celebrated the occasion by making some paper lanterns that illuminated a short stretch of road so it looked like an airport landing strip. I was half a day ahead of my pace from last year, and I was feeling great!

As we rolled through Arkansas, my folks would occasionally get into the chase car and visit for a while. This was their first RAAM as well as their first cross-country trip, and they were enjoying it. One day Dad was beaming, telling me how friendly everyone was, and how flattered he was to sign an autograph at the general store. My

Photo by Carol Shanks

"Your road will be made smooth for you by good friends" was a fortune I got just before I left Berkeley for RAAM '86. Friends in Tennessee read about it in our newsletter and came out to greet me with this poster. Thanks, guys!

folks were great ambassadors. I almost never stopped at the time stations, I would just roll by shouting "Hello, thanks for the time station!" But Mom and Dad would stop with other crew members to visit with the volunteers, thanking them for their long hours and encouragement along the road. Mom and Pups were a big help and it was fun to have them along.

I was sticking to my sleep plan really well: ride until a couple of hours before dawn and then sleep for two hours. However, as I approached the Mississippi River Friday night, I got tired early. Since I had built a six-hour lead over Sue at that point, we tried a three-hour sleep break. It had a good effect and I charged across the Mississippi River in the predawn darkness to the theme from *Rocky*. While I slept, Sue closed to within three and a half hours, but by the next time station she had lost 45 minutes on me.

As Sue was chasing me into Tennessee, an incident occurred that wasn't covered on TV or anywhere else that I've seen. I only found out about it after the race was over. ABC had just finished filming Sue and their truck was pulling away. Rod Blackie, the camera assistant, lost his balance and fell to the road, striking his head on the pave-

The crew plans another celebration, this time at the Mississippi River. Back to front: John Tofield, Pups, Mom, Vance, and David Shanks.

Photo by Carol Shanks

ment. Sue got to him first. She got off her bike and found a seriously injured man bleeding from his mouth and ears and babbling incoherently. Sue is a trained nurse and immediately took charge, spending an hour on the roadside caring for him until an ambulance arrived. Then she got back on her bike, her jersey still bloodied from the ordeal, and continued riding. Sue is a class act.

Being Chased by a Class Act

I didn't know about Sue's roadside heroism, but I did know about her tenacity and will to win. I was starting to get tired, and I started worrying about Sue. I rode the last three days looking back over my shoulder. I had a very bad day on the Blue Ridge Parkway, only 230 miles, which shot a huge hole in daily average. Kye caught and passed me that night. Sue came from 12 hours back to only six and a half. I couldn't afford another day like that or Sue would be breathing down my neck! I managed to stabilize, but I was clearly very tired and digging down deep to maintain my pace.

I took my last sleep while closing in on Lancaster, Pennsylvania, 140 miles from the finish. When the crew got me up, I was in an unusual state. I was lucid and ready to ride, but I had somehow lost track of where I was and what I was doing. I knew I was about to achieve something I really wanted, but I really didn't know what it was. I tried to explain it to my crew at the time. I was very peaceful as I rode off in the darkness towards Atlantic City. It was a perfect moment, a moment of clarity.

Photo courtesy of Amy Smolens

I was thrilled when the officials let Jim and Pete Penseyres ride with me as I approached the boardwalk. They are two of my heroes.

Photo by Chris Kostman

Crossing that finish line in first place was a dream come true!

Winning

At dawn, as I rode through the rural hills of Pennsylvania, my normal consciousness returned and I realized that my thoughts the night before were no dream. Susan was seven hours back and I would clearly win in record time if I just kept pedaling. During the last few hours of the race my concept of time would alternately feel fast and slow. My mind would drift and I'd find myself reflecting on two previous races, hardly believing how far we had come.

I couldn't have done it without a great crew! Back, left to right: David Shanks, Lee Trampleasure, John Tofield, Ed Gould, Pups, Bob Fabry, Bindy Beck. Front: Matthew Mariolle, John Sparks, Vance Vaughan, Mom, and Carol Shanks.

Here's Diana Nyad interviewing me in 1986 at the finish in Atlantic City. It was great to finally make the transition from tourist to racer, from just making it across country to winning the race in record time.

ABC turned up to film the final miles. I was thrilled when the race officials allowed Pete and Jim Penseyres to accompany me for a few minutes as I approached the boardwalk. The actual finish was almost anticlimactic!

RAAM '86 Results:

OFFICIAL

1st: Pete Penseyres	8:09:47
2nd: Lon Haldeman	9:08:02
3rd: Matt Beerer	9:08:57
4th: Kye Waltermire	9:23:10
5th: Gary Verrill	10:05:27
1st: Elaine Mariolle	10:02:04
2nd: Sue Notorangelo-Haldeman	10:09:29

UNOFFICIAL
(more than 48 hours back)

Marvin Christy	11:10:19
Marty Horn	11:10:49
Bill DeBreau	11:23:59
Jim Mulligan	12:01:22
Bob Benorden	12:10:07
Wyatt Wood	12:14:40
Jim De Graffenreid	12:20:31

RAAM '86 Postscript

My story about 1986 left out much that was significant. I was vaguely aware that Mike Secrest fell while riding in second place. Mike broke his collarbone just outside Jonesboro, Tennessee, and had to give up chasing Pete. Since Lon Haldeman, who inherited second place, was almost half a day behind, that could have taken a lot of pressure off Pete. But Pete was racing the clock. Not just any clock, actually. The clock he was racing had Jonathan Boyer's face. Pete had taken umbrage at some condescending remarks Jonathan had made about ultramarathon cyclists the year before. Pete came out of retirement to race Jonathan, but Jonathan didn't return to defend his title. So Pete was riding to break Jonathan's record and even with the immediate pressure off, he demolished it.

After Sue's nursing duties, the race officials subsequently drove her an hour up the road to compensate her for the loss of time, a step we agreed with. Susan went on to finish in second place, bettering her own transcontinental record by five hours. The injured man was in the hospital in a coma for weeks, but has since fully recovered.

Shelby had a hard race. She faded behind Sue and after a while I stopped worrying about her. We were in Atlantic City waiting for her to arrive when we heard that she had fallen only 100 miles from the finish and was hospitalized with cracked vertebrae in her neck! She too, has subsequently recovered.

Casey Patterson proved she was someone to watch. She rode a strong first race, chasing the veterans until forced out by knee problems near Bald Knob, Arkansas, 1,758 miles into the race and only a day behind. Casey trained hard and came back to win RAAM '87 on the San Francisco to Washington, DC, course in 11 days, 21 hours.

I was very pleased with what my crew, my supporters, and I accomplished in RAAM '86. We won the race and we set a new record. I realized a dream that I had had since sitting on the fire fighters' truck in Atlantic City in 1984.

In many ways, 1986 was an easy race. I had no physical trauma and did moderately well staying on the bike. In fact, I never got off without good reason—sleep, clothing change, potty stop. I ate all my meals on the bike and I never stopped to sulk. I didn't listen to music

Photo by Carol Shanks

It was particularly special to win the same year as Pete Penseyres. He's always been a hero of mine.

Photo by Carol Shanks

John Marino, race director and founder of RAAM, presented my trophy.

the way I did in 1984 and 1985. I concentrated on my riding, keeping my speed up from time station to time station. This was especially useful since the 1986 course was essentially identical to the 1985 course and I could compare my times with the previous year's.

At the same time, I knew even as I stood at the finish line that it was possible to do better yet. I could train for more speed and use more aerodynamic technology, such as the riding position that Pete used. That was not to be in 1987. After three consecutive RAAMs I wanted a break and I wanted to try other kinds of racing. Will I ever race RAAM again? Sure—it's one hell of a ride!

RAAM: A TEAM SPORT

I couldn't have done RAAM without a lot of help. I am grateful to the following individuals and organizations:

Crews

Earle Young, '84: My first RAAM mechanic. He and I invented the "croissant wrench" to repair a stomach problem.

Lisa Bassett, '84: Lacking something to do over the summer, she answered our ad on the bike shop wall. A little more exciting than summer school could ever be, I imagine.

Gilly Furnivall, '85: A native of Kenya, I wish she would come back to visit us again. I promise I won't try to lock her into a van and drag her another 3,000 miles.

Helen Anrig and Frank Heer, '85: Two more members of our foreign legion. This Swiss couple wanted to see America, and they certainly got more than they'd bargained for.

Jaye Cook, '85: Coined the name "Mother Ship" for the RV. Our version of Felix Unger, Jaye made sure all the crew members cleaned up after themselves—well, he tried.

Scott Terriberry, '85: An accomplished cyclist himself, Scott has other talents. His guitar playing and singing in the wee hours made 2 A.M. in bug-infested Arkansas almost a pleasure.

John Tofield, '86: A crack mechanic, JT took care of my trusty steeds, keeping them in top condition through the most adverse circumstances.

David Shanks, '86: Always upbeat, and super in chase. A true "vidkid," he kept my mind occupied by singing TV theme songs with me.

Carol Shanks, '86: Another of the core chase crew. A real sweetheart and a heck of a photographer.

John Sparks, '86: Sparky is the man responsible for capturing all the gory details of behind-the-scenes crew life on Super-8 film. Some of that "up close and personal" stuff shocked even me!

Bob Fabry, '86: A champion crew chief. Bob always came up with the technical innovations that helped our crew be number one!

Bindy Beck, '86: A veteran of four RAAMs, Bindy is one of the best crew members around. An unbelievable stoker, Bindy gets an "A" in all categories!

Liz Vaughan, '84, '85: Her husband John is a rock musician, so Liz is a true "creature of the night." I could always count on her to be one of my best buddies in chase, no matter what the hour.

Jan Mariolle, '84, '85: My sister kept us all honest, whether we wanted her to or not. She also took beautiful photographs, which never fail to bring back RAAM memories!

Ed Gould, '85, '86: "Mr. Fix-it" was always there to take care of any and all mechanical difficulties that arose with our vehicles, which was no rare occurrence!

Lee Trampleasure, '84, '85, '86: Not only did our masseur extraordinaire keep my legs in perfect working order and able to turn the pedals clockwise, but he also tried to keep our political views counterclockwise—sufficiently left.

Matthew Mariolle, '84, '85, '86: He cleaned the bikes. He kept things light when the situation didn't seem that way. He kept his big sister's morale up when she was about to crumble. Did I say "big sister?" Matt, 15 years my junior, was nothing less than a big brother to me for three years on the road.

Ray Mariolle, '86: Dad and Mom finally came along to see what their crazy daughter was up to—and had a great time. Dad commanded the "Mother Ship." My proud father also stopped at the time stations to mingle with the townspeople. He was an extension of me, since I had other business to attend to.

Nancy Mariolle, '86: Mom did much more than wash my clothes and feed the crew—and those were mountainous jobs in themselves. A skillful spy, Mom kept us abreast of the competition and helped us pull out the big victory!

Vance Vaughan, '84, '85, '86: What can I say about Vance? He is the glue that held the whole operation together, from day to day, and from year to year. He *never* thought my dreams were impossible, even from the very start.

Sponsors

Bucci's and Le Clan Ordinaire, '85, '86
Calistoga, '84
Mavic, '84, '85, '86
Bernie Mikkelsen, '84
Grizzly Peak Cyclists, '84, '85, '86
Mt Xinu, '84, '85, '86
Munck, Benson, Skinner, & Wagner, '85
Northface, '85
The Palmers (Bill, Davis, Jaye, and the wine-country gang),
   '85
Shimano, '86
Specialized, '84
SportCare, '85
Unipro, '86
Univega, '85, '86
VeloSport Cyclery, '84, '85, '86
Vigorelli, '84, '85, '86
Western RV, '86
Yakima, '85, '86

Many friends, old and new, who contributed moral and material support.

A CLOSING THOUGHT

I have a three-dimensional relief map of the United States hanging on my kitchen wall. Sometimes, I'll stop and run my fingers over the surface, feeling the rough ridges of the mountain ranges, the ripple of the basin and range, and the smooth undulation of the plains. Occasionally, my eye will fall on a particular region and trigger a rush of emotion, color, and impression associated with adventures out on the road.

In many ways RAAM is a metaphor for life. There are no rehearsals and lots of surprises, as the peaks and valleys of many years of experience are collapsed into a week or so. For those of us who have been involved in RAAM, there are incredible moments that will always live in our hearts. For me, the greatest moments were those when we banded together, and simply mustered up the courage to move forward, however fast or slow, toward the horizon.

11
Women in Sports

"I've always wanted to equalize things for us. . . . Women can be great athletes. And I think we'll find in the next decade that women athletes will finally get the attention they deserve."

—Billie Jean King

The following interview with Diana Nyad, swimming champion and television sports commentator, was conducted by Michael Shermer. Diana Nyad, who is perhaps best known for her appearances on ABC's "Wide World of Sports" as a color commentator for such events as the Race Across AMerica, the Ironman Triathlon, the Iditarod, and the Western States 100, began her career in athletics as a long-distance swimmer. Her most celebrated swims include the lap around New York's Manhattan Island and the aquatic trek from the island of Bimini in the Caribbean to the American continent at Florida.

After an appearance on Johnny Carson's "Tonight Show" following the Florida swim, Diana received a phone call from ABC's Roone Arledge. Would she like to make an attempt at color commentating for ABC at a small, regional event in the Midwest? Diana refused, holding out for a more prestigious network position, and due to her boldness, she got it.

The Los Angeles-based Nyad has covered many events for ABC Sports, has published an exercise book, and is one of the most popular orators on the lucrative U.S. speaking circuit. Her delivery is powerful and emotional. Her description of Susan Notorangelo's life-saving

Photo courtesy of David Nelson/PIW

Diana Nyad covering the latest developments in the 1984 Race Across AMerica.

heroism during an accident in the 1986 RAAM left a large crowd near tears on the boardwalk in Atlantic City.

Diana can move an individual as well as an audience, and did so in a hotel room in Huntington Beach, California, the day before the 1986 RAAM was to begin. One gets the feeling that this is a woman who lives life to the fullest. Diana talks about women in sports and what it takes to get the most out of life.

Q: Twenty years ago, women just did not regularly participate in sports. Today you could almost call it an explosion. Women are getting involved. What's going on here?

A: Never in the history of mankind have women been so equal to men as now, equal in terms of using their own potential as humans—physically, emotionally, and intellectually. It shows in the job market, the executive boardroom, and it shows in the fact that women have to pull in some of that income to make a family work.

In the past the whole framework of the society has been so male dominated because, and this is the ironic thing, almost until this century we have always lived by "body." In prehistoric times you can understand the division of labor that existed, where it made sense for the woman to stay put and take care of kids and maintain the home. After all, someone had to go out on the hunt, and the best person for

that job was a man. In this century, however, with the advent of
machines and advanced technology, life became non-sex based, and
women could compete equally. If you and I go out for a job with the
same intellectual skills, it is likely our chances will be equal. But if
you and I had to arm-wrestle for the job, it is more likely you would
get the job. So now that the physical element has been removed from
our society, more women, and men too, actually, have the opportunity to become what they want to be within the society in terms of
jobs and leisure time. The irony is that because of this leisure time,
women are discovering the physical life through sports. Because of
their gender, they were never in the past able to experience the high
one can get from doing physical things. The high you get from going
into a weight room and seeing muscles develop is really exciting.

Most women I know who are just over thirty, which is very young,
thought that only men had biceps. They were so ignorant of the
muscular anatomy! The change is happening so quickly that today's
high school girls are completely removed from that lack of opportunity that the generation just before them experienced. People like
Cheryl Miller [basketball star], think that this has always been the
system, and they are on their way to making it in life.

**Q: Is it a striving forward in a self-fulfilling way, or is it a pushing
off against the bondage of a patriarchal society?**
    A: I think there was some of that in the late sixties and early
seventies. Take, for instance, the Billie Jean King/Bobby Riggs
match. That represented more to the average public. When someone
like my mother, who is uneducated as to sports and things physical,
saw that match, it meant to her that a woman can be in the same
arena as a man, and it's about time to fight back and get our own!

But we are past that at this point. I think that the average woman in
this decade doesn't go to the weight room or take up cycling or play
tennis because she wants to rebel against her husband or a male
society that has kept her down.

We are still animals—physical, pulsating beings that need physical
exercise. Just like a tiger that loses its fur and becomes neurotic when
locked in a cage, physically we are the same way. Women's suicides,
women's neuroses, women getting hooked on Valium—the old diary-
of-the-mad-housewife routine—had to do with lack of physical expression. Not competition, but expression. We have the chance for

physical expression now, and there is no going back. I've read some data recently indicating that we, as a society, are moving back away from the exercise explosion a bit, but I don't see this happening with women.

Q: *Are women sacrificing or postponing childbirth or other careers to become involved in sports, or are they trying to do both?*

A: The last study I saw showed that women are having children much later now. It is similar to a man's situation these days. People don't want to get married at the age of 21 just coming out of college. They don't know themselves very well, and they don't know what they want out of life. You have to do your own developing first, before you can help a child develop. Most of the women I know are waiting to have children until their late 30s and even into their early 40s. I'll be 37 this summer [1986] and I don't have a child yet, but I'll bet I do by the time I'm 43 or so. And it's not so risky anymore—there are ways to check for medical problems associated with birth at an older age.

There are plenty of examples of women having children and sports careers—Valerie Brisco-Hooks, Mary Decker-Slaney, and a lot of world-class athletes. They not only find that they can sandwich in the nine months of pregnancy and another few months of staying home to recuperate, but that there are some added strength levels that perhaps come from going through the childbirth experience. This is a study that will have to be conducted over the next 100 years because the phenomenon is just now starting.

Overall I would say that our society is becoming less gender-oriented. I don't mean styles and things of that nature. I'm talking about important things like where you get your money, where you work, and what you are allowed to do in your free time. Men and women are becoming much more equal in how they spend their time. So men and women of the same economic background wind up being lawyers and dishwashers, depending on what they can fight through.

The changes most men are going through now are very positive. Men are taking the natural childbirth classes and their fathers can't believe it! Most men in previous generations were taught that the only reason for physical expression was for competition. It was to beat the other guy, or beat the other team. That was the only reason for sports, and if you lost, you were nothing—you got absolutely nothing from the experience. Things are changing now. A lot of men I run with don't run to beat me, they run to experience exercise and nature. Men have made huge strivings in this direction and, in my opinion, have made as many changes as women.

People often ask me why I was so successful in getting backing for my swims in the '70s. I would admit that at least part of it was luck, but part of it was to my own credit. I went to the most intelligent sources and approached them in the right way. But more than anything, I think, what was happening was that I was a woman right at the time when sports were beginning to break down the Vince Lombardi ethic of winning is everything. We came to an ethic of sports where, if you pour your heart and soul into the event, you might be the last person in the New York Marathon, but you and your family will know what you put into that event, and *that* becomes an inspiring thing. People hear me say in my talks, "I wasn't an Olympic champion. All I want to do is to swim from Cuba to Florida, and I don't think there is another human being alive who can do it, male or female." It doesn't mean that I'm fast, but it shows that I have a lot of desire and believe in myself. And sponsors rallied around me because of that. There are lots of women AND men swimmers who are quite bitter about all the press I received for my long-distance swims. But my answer to them is: "You go down and swim from Bimini to Florida faster than I did."

Now there is a transition we can identify. Billie Jean King played Bobby Riggs in 1973, and that was male versus female. I set a world record in 1979 by swimming farther than any man or woman had ever swam, and it still stands today. In that six-year period, I think we got over the women-against-men attitude.

You will also notice that it is in the individual sports such as this race [the RAAM], the Western States 100, the Ironman Triathlon, marathons, 10Ks, and so forth that women are getting attention. Television coverage has improved dramatically for women in these sports to the point of almost equal time. And this is in spite of the fact that the competition level in the men's divisions of these events is so much deeper and stronger than in the women's, though this is changing rapidly.

Even in the major events such as Wimbledon, the women's division is receiving much more coverage than ever before, and the prize monies are becoming more equal. People are realizing that, to make a boxing analogy, a featherweight is no less an athlete than a heavy-weight. Women are physically different than men and need a different category.

Q: They have a different category in the RAAM, where there are two races, run concurrently, one for the men and one for the women. They take the same route across the country, they ride the same distance, and they receive equal prize money. But do you think, with distance as the great leveler, a woman could ever win the RAAM, or beat a man on a swim from here to Hawaii?

A: I don't think a woman could beat a man in the RAAM. There are too many hills and men have a better physical makeup for hill climbing. Swimming may be a different matter, though. I would have bet every penny I had that no man could have beaten me that day I swam from Bimini to Florida. However, if you were to line me up with the 10 best men swimmers in a race 10 miles long, I probably would have finished eighth, ninth, or tenth. That's because in a swim that distance (Bimini to Florida), at no time was strength or speed a factor. The difference in sexes is meaningless.

Q: You don't think that a woman will ever win the Ironman Triath-lon?

A: No, I don't think that's possible. It is too short. In a sport where strength is a factor, the very best woman will not beat the very best man. Michael Secrest will always beat Susan Notorangelo in the Race Across AMerica. Now, maybe if they cycled around the world it would be a different story!

Q: What is the motivation of athletes that have a need to achieve— not just the back-of-the-packers who are in there for the experience, but those at the front who want to win? Existentially, why do they compete?

A: I'll tell you my story, which I have a feeling is a similar story to many competitors. At age 10, I wrote an essay for my fifth-grade class on what I wanted to do with the rest of my life. My essay shows that I had a very clear sense that I knew I was going to die one day and probably—because of my genetic background, grandparents, parents and such—it would be in my 80s. That meant that at the age of 10, I only had 70 more years to go. In that span of time, was I going to do things well and really be alert and alive, or was I going to just glide through like most of the kids I saw in high school in Fort Lauderdale, Florida, who drank beer in the parking lots. I don't mean this to be judgmental either—people can do whatever they want under God's sky. But I knew for myself that I wanted to feel very alive. And when I got out there in that ocean and was swimming faster and farther than anyone I knew.

You know the moments I relish the most—and I swear this is true— the moments I relish the most were the moments about one to two minutes after the lowest point in the swim. There are lots of low and high points undulating throughout the whole experience, but when I would go through the worst hell—when I would be vomiting my guts out for 20 minutes, which is horrific thing in the ocean, when I would be so cold that my jaw was clenched shut; when I could barely move my limbs at all—when I could get by that worst hell, I would start feeding on myself. "You could do *that*?! I can't think of anybody who could do that!" I would be so impressed with myself that I would feel wonderously alive and would realize that THIS is why I do these swims. Not for the finish, though that has its own special experiences. I do them for the tough moments and getting through them. I like digging down inside myself. I don't *ever* want to be a coaster.

I do this in all ways, in all parts of my life, not just swimming—in relationships, work, everything. People think that now that I'm not in swimming I've lost all the black-and-white drama, but I say to them that it's all dramatic. Every single day can be dramatic if you make it that way. If you want everything out of life you will get it.

Q: Yes, even in such things as speaking to an audience. I have heard that your speaking engagements are quite moving.

A: I know plenty of world-class athletes who go on speaking tours during the off-season and make a lucrative career of speaking— maybe $10,000 an engagement—and on the way to the luncheon they mope in the back of the limo and complain that they don't want to speak to these stupid businessmen whom they have nothing in common with. And on the way back they say, "Ah, these suckers gave me $10,000 and I didn't prepare anything."

Not me! Occasionally I have the flu or something and I'd really rather be in my own home and not traveling to a little college in Illinois, but basically if someone is going to pay me $5,000 and sit there with wide-open eyes because they think I'm someone special and have done special things, then I'm going to give them every bit I've got. And it doesn't mean it has to be stern, sometimes it's soft, and sometimes it's self-deprecating. But if it's honest and genuine and they come out of it in tears or smiles and it makes a difference, wow, what a great feeling!

Q: Where did you get this attitude? Where does anyone get a need to achieve, as psychologists call it? From your upbringing, genetics, where? Some have got the need of achievement and some don't. Why is that?

A: I think it comes very early in life. Upbringing is very important. I remember my father brought me into the bedroom when I was 12 years old and he sat me down on the bed and he paced around the room and said, "I'm very, very concerned about you. It's been two years now, that you've been getting up at 4:30 in the morning every day of the year, Christmas and Thanksgiving included, riding your bicycle to swimming practice. You swim six hours a day and your mother has to pack your eyes in ice at night because they are red and swollen from the chlorine (before eye goggles). You don't know your brother and sister anymore. You don't go to church on Sunday. You don't go to birthday parties or movies. You tell us when to go to sleep in the house because you're going to be the world champion and we have to all shut up so you can sleep. And this just isn't normal. You're a fanatic. You're unstoppable. I don't think it's healthy, and we don't know what to do."

I stood up and I said, "That's right, Dad, and I'm going to continue just like this until I make that Olympic team." He said, "I knew you were going to say this. Did I really think I was going to change your mind with one little talk? Your mother and I have discussed this. We have cried about it. We have worried about it. We want to send you to the school psychologist. I called you in here to give you the key to the house because we can't live like this anymore. You're on your own."

Q: What did you do?

A: I took the key to the house! And I came and went as I pleased. In some ways I missed getting to know my brother and sister, and I'm trying to make up for it now, but I couldn't help it at the time. The peer group I was in was very oriented toward achievement. The Phi Beta Kappa, and the world records, and the like meant a lot to me then. I don't need that so much anymore. I used to need people's recognition. But I've learned a great deal in the television business. I've really been giving a lot of thought to what I am going to do with these last 40 years or so, and I want to make them all good.

I'm trying to become the person I admire. By my own standards. And I'm not ashamed of the fact that some of that includes money and a little recognition. But that's not what I go to sleep dreaming about, by any means.

Q: Did you have heroes when you were growing up?

A: Yes, do you know who my hero was? My hero was a nineteenth-century French author, a woman named George Sand. I've read every book she's ever written. She was a lover of Chopin in the 1850s in France. She wore men's suits. She left her husband and kids because it was the most boring thing that had ever happened to her. Not that I admire that, but she just came to the realization in her mid-20s that life was speeding by. Life was like going down a fast downhill course with trees, just speeding by, and if you wanted to get anything out of it you had to put the brakes on and focus. You have to decide what makes you happy and do it. It might not get you the most money, but if you can have your health together then you've got to do what makes you happy.

I have three close friends. One is a lover and two are friends. No matter what happens to me, every day of the year I call them and talk to them, no matter how briefly or where I am. I am so immersed in their three lives, and they are immersed in mine, that I put the dedication into these relationhips that you usually only find in sports and war. And even though I am gregarious and I meet new people and I like them, I don't strike up deep relationships anymore because I just want to be pure value and steadfast with those three people.

That's an analogy of how I go about things now. It won't get me anywhere in my career. I've been told that the reason I wasn't getting as far as I might at ABC, even though I have the talent, is that I wasn't at the right parties, and I didn't go to the right opening in New York City, with the right man on my arm. I guess I'll never make it then, because I'm not going to do it that way. I'll make it somewhere else, or I'll make it here, my own way. People are constantly telling me things like that, and I just continue doing what makes me happy.

Appendix 1
Gearing

One of the most difficult areas of cycling to master is the gearing system, particularly for those who don't think of themselves as mechanically minded. Bikes have different gearing systems, different size gears, different shift-lever locations, and so on. Some rear clusters have five speeds, most have six, but some even have seven. There are 1-speeds, 3-speeds, 5-speeds, 10-speeds, 12-speeds, 14-speeds, 15-speeds, 18-speeds, and 21-speeds. Do you need 21 gears? Aren't 12 speeds enough? What does it all mean?

Most people learn about gearing systems through experience alone. Experienced cyclists know that the shifter on the left side of the bike controls the front derailleur and the shifter on the right side controls the rear derailleur. A normal 12-speed bicycle has two chainrings connected to the pedals' crankarms, and a 6-speed gear cluster, or freewheel, on the rear wheel. The front derailleur shifts the chain from the little chainring to the big chainring and back. The rear derailleur shifts the chain up and down the six cogs, from the lowest to the highest gear and back. Thus, you have six choices of gears in the rear and two choices in the front, for a total of 12 gear alternatives.

The object of the drivetrain is to propel the bicycle forward under the power of the legs. On flat ground, this is relatively easy at low speeds, but as rolling hills and mountainous grades loom ahead on the road, you must shift gears according to your strength to negotiate the climb. The object of a gearing system is to allow you to maintain a fairly steady pedaling cadence. This can be easily calculated by counting the number of times one leg goes around in a complete circle in 10 seconds, then multiplying by six. Sixty revolutions per minute (RPM) is a slow to medium cadence. Eighty RPMs is a medium cadence. One hundred RPMs or more is a high cadence. It is generally agreed that for effective aerobic exercise, one should maintain a medium to high cadence, approximately 80–120 RPMs. This keeps the heart rate high and makes for a high-quality workout.

The gearing system becomes important in maintaining that steady cadence on a rolling or hilly course. If you begin to climb a hill and your cadence slows, shifting to a lower gear will restore your original cadence. When you begin to descend the hill and your speed increases dramatically, you will need to shift to a higher gear in order to keep pedaling. Once again, the object is to maintain a constant cadence.

Gears are classified by number of teeth. A "42" chainring has 42 teeth on it. A "14" cog is a gear on the freewheel with 14 teeth on it. Cyclists typically refer to their gears in these terms. One might say, "I was climbing in my 42 X 19, but it was so steep that I had to shift to my 21." This means the cyclist was riding in the 42-tooth chainring on the front and the 19-tooth cog in the back. Since the hill was steep, she had to shift to a lower gear, in this case the 21-tooth cog, in order to keep a reasonable cadence.

The more teeth there are on the front chainrings, the bigger or higher the gear. In the rear, the opposite is true. The more teeth the cog has, the smaller or lower the gear, so the easiest gear to pedal in would be the smallest chainring and the largest cog. The most difficult gear to pedal in would be the opposite—the big chainring and the smallest cog. When a cyclist is relating how hard and fast she was riding, she might say: "I was in my 52 X 13 and really hammering!"

Gearing systems are not sequential, although many novices mistakenly believe this to be so. Sequential design would mean that on a 12-speed bike, gears 1 to 6 would refer to the position of the chain on the small chainring, and the gears would just shift on the freewheel in the order 1–2–3–4–5–6. Gears 6 to 12 would then be the position of the chain on the big chainring, and the gears would simply shift down the freewheel 7-8-9-10-11-12. This couldn't be further from the truth.

Let's say your current gearing system is set up as follows: chainrings: 52 and 42; freewheel: 13, 14, 15, 17, 19, 21. The actual ranking from 1 to 12, or smallest to biggest gear, then, is:

1.	$42 \times 21 = 54.0$	7.	$42 \times 14 = 81.0$
2.	$42 \times 19 = 59.7$	8.	$52 \times 17 = 82.6$
3.	$42 \times 17 = 66.7$	9.	$42 \times 13 = 87.2$
4.	$52 \times 21 = 66.9$	10.	$52 \times 15 = 93.6$
5.	$52 \times 19 = 73.9$	11.	$52 \times 14 = 100.3$
6.	$42 \times 15 = 75.6$	12.	$52 \times 13 = 108.0$

With this gearing arrangement, shifting up through the gears from smallest to biggest requires 5 changes of the front derailleur and 11 changes of the rear derailleur. Obviously, this isn't as simple as most people believe. What if your gearing system isn't arranged in this manner? How can you objectively evaluate your own gearing system to decide on an appropriate gear? A gear ratio chart can aid you. The chart on page 338 plots number of teeth on the rear sprocket on the horizontal axis and number of teeth on the chainrings on the vertical axis. To find the number of gear inches, which will be the method of ranking the gears, correlate the chainring size with the cog size and read across the graph. For instance, a 42 chainring with a 21 cog is a 54-inch gear. From the explanation above, you would expect the 42×19 gear to be larger in inches. A quick check of the table shows it to be 59.7 inches—a larger gear.

Gear inches is a term that originated in the late 1800s when the "high-wheeler," or "ordinary" bicycle, was commonly used. Since the pedals were attached to the large front wheel and there was no chain or freewheel, the gear inches represented the diameter of that large wheel. An ordinary bike with a 54-inch gear had a front wheel that was 54 inches in diameter. In other words, the larger the wheel, the farther the bicycle would travel with each pedal stroke. The larger the wheel, the harder it would be to pedal up a hill. Thus a small gear or small wheel was needed for a hilly ride.

Translated into today's bicycle chains and freewheels, the distance you travel with each pedal stroke will depend on the circumference of the wheel and on the gear inches. To calculate the circumference of

GEAR RATIO CHART

Number of Teeth on Freewheel

Number of Teeth on Chainrings

	12	13	14	15	16	17	18	19	20	21	22	23	24	25	26	27	28
40	90.0	83.1	77.1	72.0	67.5	63.5	60.0	56.8	54.0	51.4	49.1	47.0	45.0	43.2	41.5	40.0	38.6
41	92.2	85.2	79.1	73.8	69.2	65.1	61.5	58.3	55.3	52.7	50.3	48.1	46.1	44.3	42.7	41.3	40.1
42	94.5	87.2	81.0	75.6	70.9	66.7	63.0	59.7	56.7	54.0	51.5	49.3	47.3	45.4	43.6	42.0	40.5
43	96.7	89.3	82.9	77.4	72.6	68.3	64.5	61.1	58.0	55.3	52.8	50.5	48.4	46.4	44.6	43.0	41.4
44	100.0	91.4	84.9	79.2	74.3	69.9	66.0	62.5	59.4	56.6	54.0	51.7	49.5	47.5	45.7	44.0	42.4
45	101.2	93.5	86.8	81.0	75.9	71.5	67.5	63.9	60.8	57.9	55.2	52.8	50.6	48.6	46.7	45.0	43.4
46	103.5	95.5	88.7	82.8	77.6	73.1	69.0	65.4	62.1	59.1	56.5	54.0	51.8	49.7	47.8	46.0	44.4
47	105.7	97.6	90.6	84.6	79.3	74.6	70.5	66.8	63.4	60.4	57.7	55.2	52.9	50.8	48.8	47.0	45.3
48	108.0	99.7	92.6	86.4	81.0	76.2	72.0	68.2	64.8	61.7	58.9	56.3	54.0	51.8	49.9	48.0	46.3
49	110.2	101.8	94.5	88.2	82.7	77.8	73.5	69.6	66.1	63.0	60.1	57.5	55.1	52.9	50.9	49.0	47.2
50	112.5	103.8	96.4	90.0	84.4	79.4	75.0	71.1	67.5	64.3	61.4	58.7	56.3	54.0	51.9	50.0	48.2
51	114.7	105.9	98.4	91.8	86.1	81.0	76.5	72.5	68.8	65.6	62.6	59.9	57.4	55.1	53.0	51.0	49.1
52	117.0	108.0	100.3	93.6	87.8	82.6	78.0	73.9	70.2	66.9	63.8	61.0	58.5	56.2	54.0	52.0	50.1
53	119.3	110.1	102.2	95.4	89.4	84.2	79.5	75.3	71.5	68.1	65.0	62.2	59.6	57.2	55.0	53.0	51.1
54	121.5	112.2	104.1	97.2	91.1	85.8	81.0	76.7	72.9	69.4	66.3	63.4	60.8	58.3	56.1	54.0	52.0
55	123.7	114.2	106.2	99.0	92.8	87.3	82.5	78.1	74.5	70.7	67.5	64.5	61.8	59.4	57.1	55.0	53.0
56	126.0	116.3	108.0	100.9	94.5	88.9	84.0	79.5	75.6	72.0	68.7	65.7	63.0	60.4	58.1	56.0	54.0

the wheel, multiply its diameter by pi (3.1416). A 27-inch wheel has a circumference of 84.82 inches. Thus, on a 27-inch ordinary bicycle, one pedal stroke would net you a distance of 84.82 inches, or a little over seven feet. To calculate how far you travel with each pedal stroke on a modern bicycle, multiply the number of gear inches (from Table 1) by pi. If you are in the 42 × 21 gear, you would multiply 54 by 3.1416 to get 169.65 inches, or 14.14 feet, traveled.

The gear chart should be used to adjust your bicycle's gears. If you are going on a training ride, a race, or a tour that is extremely hilly, you will need a gearing system that has low enough gear-inches to accommodate those climbs. Most of the adjusting can be done on the freewheel. Rarely would you switch the chainrings, as it is not as simple a task as replacing the rear wheel with a different freewheel.

For the most part, the more fit you are, the less variation is required between gears. Many competitive cyclists use a 52 × 42 chainring set up with a 13–21 freewheel structure. The 54-inch lowest gear can get a fit cyclist over most hills. The 52 × 39 chainring combination is also frequently used. In fact, Jonathan Boyer has boasted that he "straight-blocked" America in the RAAM in 1985, meaning he used a 13–18 freewheel, or one tooth difference between each gear.

Some cyclists like to use a slightly larger chainring. Some move up to a 53, particularly if they like to push big gears.

Occasionally one finds a chainring smaller than a 39. Tourists who carry heavy packs and mountain-bike racers frequently need a chainring as small as a 36 to reach a mountaintop. Some touring bikes even sport three chainrings (known as a "triple") to give extra gear options. Many, if not most, tandems have a triple chainring setup for those extra-big hills, which tandems are notoriously slow at climbing. An unusual setup for a tandem is to use index shifting with a 38-48-53 an elliptical chainring, and a 7 speed 13-14-15-17-19-21-23 cluster on the rear. It's a perfect combination for tandem riding, particularly if the stoker (the rider on the back) and driver are both strong riders.

Occasionally a 21-speed setup produces duplication of gears. For instance, a 52 × 28 is a 50.1-inch gear. A 42 × 22 is a 51.5-inch gear. The difference is so small that you could never distinguish between the two gears.

Experience and the use of the gear ratio chart on the opposite page will help you decide which system is best suited to your conditioning and cycling needs.

Appendix 2
A Glossary of Bicycle Jargon

Aerobic: An intense level of exercise during which oxygen needs are continuously satisfied and the exercise can be continued for long periods of time.

Aerodynamic: The action of the air passing over or through the cyclist and the bike. Increasing aerodynamic efficiency reduces the wind drag on the cyclist or bike, allowing for greater speed and less energy expenditure.

Amino acids: Amino acids are called the building blocks of life. Amino acids form proteins of two types: enzymes and structural proteins. Enzymes form the chemical actions of the cell. Structural proteins form the actual structure of the cell. There are 20 amino acids of which 11 are classified as "essential." Essential amino acids are not produced by the body and are obtained through food.

Anabolic steroids: Synthetic drugs that stimulate the protein building process (anabolic) in the body. They are used by athletes to build muscular strength, power, and size beyond the range of a "natural" training program. The negative side effects are well published and they are illegal in most sports, cycling in particular.

Anaerobic: Intense exercise endured even after the body can no longer dispose of the lactic acid produced and can no longer supply oxygen to the muscles. The exercise level is limited to a short period of time.

Anaerobic threshold: A level of exercise in which further increase in effort will cause more lactic acid to accumulate than can be readily eliminated.

Ankling: Dropping and raising the heels in an alternate fashion through a pedal stroke to improve power and efficiency.

ANSI: American National Standards Institute, an organized body for the purpose of testing products, for instance, bicycle helmets.

ATP (Adenosine Triphosphate): ATP is the chemical compound produced as a function of the transformation of food to muscular energy. Food is broken down into ATP, which is then stored in the cells of the muscles until use.

ATP-PC system: In anaerobic exercise (maximum effort for less than 10 seconds), ATP is produced by the breakdown of PC, or phosphocreatine.

Bicycle: A two-wheeled, non-motorized vehicle powered only by the rider, who pedals the bicycle to make it move. There are various types of bicycles designed for specific purposes, although the conventional drop-handlebar 10-speed, also called a racing bike, is probably the most recognizable. This "conventional" bicycle was originally designed for road racing and its chief characteristics are quick handling and stiff ride. A *road racer* is built for speed, and because it will cover varied terrain, it has derailleurs and brakes.

Track bicycles are built for speed and the special, near-perfect riding conditions of a track. Track bicycles have no derailleurs, only a *fixed gear*, and if they are set up for track racing, have no brakes. In many large American cities, bicycle messengers use track bikes modified with a front brake. The angles of a track frame, which are very steep, make it a fast-moving, fast-handling bicycle.

Touring bicycles are also drop-handlebar designs, but unlike either the road racer or track bike, touring bikes are designed for comfort and easy handling. These bicycles have wide-range derailleurs and brakes.

A relatively new design is the all-terrain bicycle (ATB), also known as the mountain bike or fat-tire bike. ATBs are designed and equipped to withstand the rigors of off-road riding, although because of the comfort of its upright riding position, a modified ATB, called the city bike, is popular with commuters and recreational riders. Similar to the ATB is the *BMX* (bicycle motocross) bike. BMXs are designed primarily for dirt-track racing; kids love them. These are great bikes for stunts, not so great for distance riding.

The *recumbent* is a two-wheeled bicycle designed to be ridden while in a prone or reclining position. These bikes have long wheel bases and sit very close to the ground.

Tandems are two-wheeled bicycles for two riders, one seated behind the other. The rider in the front is the driver or captain; the rider in the rear is the stoker. Tandems are usually made to order and so can be built to the riders' specifications and purpose.

Although all bicycles are human-powered vehicles, a bicycle that does not meet the racing requirements of either the USCF or NORBA because it is equipped with unapproved wind-resistance devices—fairings, wind shells, disk wheels—is known as a human-powered vehicle.

Bonking: When a cyclist completely runs out of energy. This is also known as "hitting the wall."

Calorie (kilocalorie): Technically, there are two types of calories—small and large. One thousand small calories equal one kilocalorie, which is a measure of heat, either in what the food provides or in how much energy the body uses. The vernacular use of the term calorie actually refers to kilocalorie. "Empty calories" contain no essential amino acids, vitamins, or minerals, and the term usually refers to processed foods such as candy bars, donuts, and so on.

Carbohydrates: Simple sugars and starches that provide a valuable source of muscle energy. They are found primarily in fruits, grains, potatoes, beans, breads, and pasta and are stored in the liver in the form of glycogen. The compound itself is simple and contains only carbon, hydrogen, and oxygen molecules.

Chainring: The rings attached to the crankset, which turn the chain.

Chondromalacia: A disintegration of cartilage surfaces in the knee due to improper tracking of the kneecap or to extreme overuse. Symptoms are deep knee pain and a crunching sensation during bending. Surgery is frequently recommended.

Cleat: A slotted, wedge-shaped fitting of metal, plastic, or another durable material that is fastened to a cycling shoe sole so the shoe will remain clamped to the pedal during riding.

Clinchers: "Conventional" tires with a separate inner tube.

Cluster: Also known as the freewheel or block, it is the series of gear cogs attached to the hub of the rear wheel that the chain wraps around.

Cog: A gear of a freewheel, of which there are usually 5, 6, or 7.

Complete protein: A protein food such as eggs, cheese, milk, and meat, that contains all 11 of the essential amino acids.

Cramping: Contraction of muscles due to loss of potassium and other minerals during excessive exercise and sweating.

Criterium: A multi-lap, short- to medium-distance race from 25 to 75 miles, conducted on a "closed," usually flat course no more than one to four miles. These are excellent spectator races as the riders can be easily seen and the pace is fast with many sprints for special lap prizes called *primes.*

Derailleur: The mechanism for shifting gears by moving the chain from one cog or chainring to another. There are two on a bike, front and rear.

Drafting: To ride in the slipstream or air pocket of another rider, greatly reducing the amount of energy needed by the following cyclist. Distances for drafting vary from two inches to 30 meters, depending on the speed and wind conditions. Drafting is the key to strategy in road and track racing. Drafting is not usually allowed in ultramarathon cycling events.

Drops: On a conventional "road" bicycle, the part of the handlebar below the brake hoods that curves down and usually runs parallel to the ground. (Also see *tops.*)

Echelon: A line of cyclists either single or double file, taking orderly turns at the lead in order to break the wind for the riders behind. A "pull" at the front lasts from a few seconds to a few minutes.

Ergogenic aids: Any stimulant or artificial aid to increase athletic performance. Most are illegal for competition. In small doses some are legal, such as the levels of caffeine found in coffee. "Blood doping" refers to a natural ergogenic aid that is now considered illegal for most competition.

Ergometer: An indoor, stationary bicycle device with adjustable pedal resistance used for training and physiological testing.

Fairing: Any object designed to lower wind resistance when attached to a bike.

Fartlek: A Swedish word meaning "speed play" that refers to training in intervals of alternate periods of sprinting and resting, with no structure for time; e.g., sprinting for city-limit signs, telephone poles, etc.

Fast-twitch muscle fiber: Muscular fibers with two to three times the contraction speed and power of *slow-twitch fibers.*

Feeding: When riders are fed during a race either from a moving vehicle or from the side of the road. Liquids are passed via a water bottle while food is handed up in a *musette bag.* In road races there are usually designated feed zones or times, whereas in ultramarathon races feeding is undertaken at the rider's request.

Fixed gear: A wheel with a single cog "locked" in place, allowing only that cog to be used. Also known as a single-gear bicycle, no coasting or "freewheeling" is possible. When the pedals are turning, the wheel is turning and the bicycle is moving. Essentially, when the rider stops pedaling, the bicycle will stop moving. There are no derailleurs on a fixed-gear bicycle, which is the type of bicycle used in track-racing events.

G.A.B.R.: The Great American Bike Race, the original name of the Race Across AMerica.

Glucose: When carbohydrates in the bloodstream are converted into glycogen, the resulting sugar is *glucose.* The body uses it to form fat or, when oxidized, to form carbon dioxide and water. Glucose is essential to the functions of the brain and nervous system.

Glycolysis: The process of breaking down glucose into ATP.

Hardshell helmet: This type of helmet is usually constructed of a hard plastic shell with a compressed polystyrene or Styrofoam liner. This helmet passes the ANSI Z90.4 crash tests and is recommended for use in competition, touring, and commuting.

Hemoglobin: The pigment in red blood cells that contains iron, allowing the cells to carry oxygen from the lungs into the cells and tissues of the body.

Hoods: The rubber coverings over the brake levers on drop-handlebars, they provide improved grip.

Hooks: The section of the handlebars on a track bike approximating the *drops* or curved section found on a road bicycle with drop-handlebars. Track, or *piston*, bars have almost no straight sections. The highly curved drops look like hooks.

Human-powered vehicle: Any vehicle, bicycle or otherwise, powered solely by a person or persons. These vehicles are usually enclosed in an aerodynamic structure or envelope that surrounds the rider.

Incomplete protein: A protein such as the one found in grains and vegetables, that lacks one or more of the essential amino acids necessary to maintaining good health. Many vegetarians are faced with the problem of getting all 11 essential amino acids and must take them in supplemental form.

International Human-Powered Vehicle Association (IHPVA): The IHPVA is the sanctioning body for competition among human-powered vehicles.

JMO: The John Marino Open, which is the qualifier for entering the Race Across AMerica. It is named after the founder of ultramarathon racing, John Marino.

Lactic acid: A byproduct of anaerobic exercise that accumulates in the muscles and causes pain and fatigue.

LSD: Long steady distance used for building endurance and a base of miles by riding at an even pace for several hours without intervals of speed or rest.

Motorpace: Riding behind a motorcycle or small car that breaks the wind, allowing the cyclist to accomplish a faster, more intense workout.

Musette bag: A cloth bag packed with food used for feeding cyclists during a long road race.

Myoglobin: The muscle's counterpart to the blood's hemoglobin, myoglobin is responsible for oxygen transport and storage in muscle tissue.

Orthotics: Custom-made supports worn in shoes for arch defects and other biomechanical imbalances in the feet or legs.

Overgear: Using a gear that is too big for the cyclist's conditioning level or for the prevailing terrain and wind conditions.

Overtraining: Extreme fatigue caused by exercising at a level beyond the body's capabilities. It is related to stress.

Oxygen debt: The amount of oxygen that needs to be consumed during exercise in order to "pay back" the deficit incurred by the muscles in anaerobic work.

Pace line: A single or double file of riders who take turns riding in front. See *echelon.*

Peak: A brief period of time when the body and mind are at their maximum performance level.

Quadriceps: The large muscles in front of the femur bone or thigh; usually well-developed in cyclists.

RAAM: The Race Across AMerica, the longest and most prestigious ultramarathon cycling event in the world. It is a 3,000-mile, non-stop bike race from the Pacific Ocean on the west coast of California to the Atlantic Ocean on the east coast of New Jersey or New York. It spans 8 to 14 days, and once the clock has started, it doesn't stop until the rider reaches the designated finish line on the East Coast. The event is owned and trademarked by John Marino, Michael Shermer, Lon Haldeman, and Robert Hustwit.

Recumbent: A bicycle of diverse design to be ridden while in a prone or recumbent position.

Road rash: Skin abrasion caused by a fall on pavement.

Rollers: An indoor training device that the bicycle balances on. It has one roller under the front wheel and two rollers under the rear wheel. Pedaling at medium to high cadence is required to maintain balance.

Rolling a tire: When a tubular tire is not glued on the rim properly, it can roll off the rim when under pressure, such as when turning a corner, causing a cyclist to crash.

Set: A specific number of repetitions in a weight-training program.

Sew-ups: See *tubulars.*

Side-by-side: A bicycle for two riders who ride next to each other as opposed to one in front of the other.

Silks: Silk sew-ups or tubulars—constructed with silk threads in the casing, making the tire very light and expensive.

Slipstream: The portion of moving air behind one rider that enables following riders to draft.

Slow-twitch muscle fiber: Fibers that contract two to three times slower than *fast-twitch fibers* and have less power, but greater endurance.

Solo/unpaced: A UMCA category that most ultramarathon cycling events are held under—a single cyclist on a conventional bicycle, riding without drafting.

Speed work: Doing intervals, fartleks, and motorpacing for fast training.

Spinner: A rider who pedals with a high cadence in a low (very easy to pedal) to medium gear. Spinning is recommended for recovery rides after races and to develop good form on the bike.

Spinning: Fluid, high-RPM pedaling in low to medium gears.

Sprint: A short burst of speed by group of racers trying to reach the finish line first.

Sprinters' hill: A short, steep hill that can be climbed quickly while out of the saddle, and body weight and muscular bulk don't hinder the rider from climbing.

Stage race: A series of different types of individual races—time trials, criteriums, and road races—all combined into one event that lasts a number of days. Each stage of the race presents cyclists with opportunities to gain scoring advantages and it is quite possible for a racer to win the entire event without taking first place in any single stage of the race. The winner is the rider with the least accumulated time for the entire event. The longest stage race is the world-famous Tour de France, spanning 2,300 to 2,600 miles over three weeks. The Coors International Bicycle Classic and the Ore-Ida Women's Challenge are the largest and most prestigious stage races in the United States.

Straddle height: The distance from the ground to the top of the top tube.

Straight block: A freewheel with cogs that increase in size in one-tooth increments, used primarily for racing.

Streamlined: Bicycles designed with full fairings to reduce wind resistance to a minimum.

Suppleness: Loose, smooth leg muscles of a quality that allow the cyclist to pedal with power and speed.

Support crew: A team of people who provide assistance to a cyclist. They may provide food, water, clothing, massage, moral support, directions, medical aid, and advice—virtually anything other than actual assistance to the cyclist in moving the bicycle.

Support vehicle: A vehicle that is driven and staffed by the support crew. This vehicle may be a motorcycle, car, van, truck, or motor home.

Time trial: A race against the clock. Drafting is not allowed.

Tricycle: A three-wheeled cycle with two of the wheels in the rear. There are tricycle races in Europe in both road racing and ultramarathon racing.

Tubulars: Tubulars, or sew-ups are constructed with intertube "sewn-up" inside the tire so that the tire-tube combination is a single unit.

Ultramarathon cycling: The word "ultra" refers to the surpassing of a specific limit or range, exceeding what is common, moderate, or proper. The word "marathon" is defined as a long-distance race, a contest of endurance. Ultramarathon cycling is riding a bicycle a distance considered to be beyond moderate or common human limits in the shortest time possible. The exact distance and elapsed time will vary. The characteristics of the event, such as terrain, weather conditions, distance, along with the age and physical condition of the competition, must be taken into consideration. Besides RAAM, other major ultramarathon events include the Seattle to San Diego course, the Miami to Maine course, the Spenco 500, the British Land's End-to-John O'Groat's course, the Bicycle Across Missouri, and the Paris-Brest-Paris race in France.

Vital capacity: The total volume of air that is expelled following full inspiration, in which the subject is forced to blow into a machine that measures precisely the amount of air intake, output, and residual. In conjunction with a max VO_2 measure, the athlete can calculate exactly how much oxygen is being utilized and how much is residual.

Vitamins: Commonly mistaken as sources of energy, vitamins are biochemical substances that act as regulators of metabolic processes and play a role in "energy transformation." Most sports medicine experts feel that most vitamins can be obtained from a well-balanced meal and that resorting to mega-vitamin therapy will not increase athletic performance.

VO_2 max: The maximum amount of oxygen a person can transfer from the lungs to the cardiovascular system in one minute. It is generally predetermined genetically, though improvements can be made through a serious exercise program. It is considered a good indicator of potential for aerobic sports such as cycling.

Wheelsucker: A derogatory word for a cyclist who refuses to take a turn at the front of the pack or breakaway group.

Wind drag: A term in aerodynamics referring to the resistance produced by moving air. Also called *wind resistance.*

Wind foil: An object attached to a bike that is designed to lower wind resistance.

Wind resistance: A term in aerodynamics referring to the resistance produced by moving air.

Z–90.4: Refers to the test set by ANSI for bicycle helmets.

Appendix 3
Bicycle Periodicals

The following is a list of bicycle periodicals, both consumer and trade, as well as other periodicals that are related to the sport or frequently cover cycling events. Trade magazines, which are for "the trade" (for retailers), not consumers, are indicated as such. The trade magazines are an excellent source for taking a pulse on the cycling industry—what's hot and what's not—particularly in bike shops.

American Bicyclist and Motorcyclist (Trade)
80 Eighth Avenue
New York, NY 10031

Bicycle Business Journal (Trade)
Quinn Publications, Inc.
4915 West Freeway
PO Box 1570
Fort Worth, TX 76107

Bicycle Dealer Showcase (Trade)
1700 E. Dyer Road
Santa Ana, CA 92713

Bicycle Guide
711 Boylston Street
Boston, MA 02116

Bicycle USA
League of American Wheelman, Inc.
6707 Whitestone Road, Suite 209
Baltimore, MD 21207

Bicycling
33 E. Minor Street
Emmaus, PA 18049

Bicycling News Canada
101-1281 W. Georgia Street
Vancouver, BC, Canada V6E 3J7

California Bicyclist
1149 Folsom Street
San Francisco, CA 94103

City Sports
PO Box 3693
San Francisco, CA 94119

Cycling
Currey House, 1 Thrawley Way
Sutton, Surrey SMA 4QQ
England

Cycling U.S.A.
1750 E. Boulder
Colorado Springs, CO 80909

Cyclist
20916 Higgins Court
Torrence, CA 90501

Mountain Bike
Back Country Publications
PO Box 989
Crested Butte, CO 81224

Mountain Bike Action
10600 Sepulveda Boulevard
Mission Hills, CA 91345

Mountain Bike for the Adventure
33 East Minor
Emmaus, PA 18049

Mountain Biking
7950 Deering Avenue
Canoga Park, CA 91304

Outside
1165 N. Clark Street
Chicago, IL 60610

Southwest Cycling
301 West California, #201
Glendale, CA 91203

Velo-News
67 Main Street, Suite 42
PO Box 1257
Brattleboro, VT 05301

Winning: Bicycle Racing Illustrated
1127 Hamilton Street
Allentown, PA 18102

RELATED PERIODICALS

Action Sports Retailer (Trade)
31652 Second Avenue
South Laguna, CA 92677

Athletic Journal (Trade)
1719 Howard Street
Evanston, IL 60202

Fit
1400 Stierlin Road
Mountain View, CA 94043

The Melpomene Report
Melpomene Institute for
Women's Health Research
2125 E. Hennepin Avenue
Minneapolis, MN 55416

MS.
Fairfax Publications
One Times Square
New York, NY 10036

New Woman
215 Lexington Avenue
New York, NY 10016

The Runner
One Park Avenue
New York, NY 10016

Runner's World
Rodale Press
33 E. Minor Street
Emmaus, PA 18098

Running News
PO Box 2822
La Jolla, CA 92038

Self
9100 Wilshire Boulvevard
Beverly Hills, CA 90212

Shape
21100 Erwin Street
Woodland Hills, CA 91367

Sierra
730 Polk Street
San Francisco, CA 94108

Sport
119 W. 40th Street
New York, NY 10018

Sportstyle (Trade)
Fairchild Publications, Inc.
7 E. 12th Street
New York, NY 10003

Triathlete
1127 Hamilton Street
Allentown, PA 18102

The Sporting Goods Dealer (Trade)
1212 N. Lindbergh Blvd.
St. Louis, MO 63166

Sports Merchandiser (Trade)
1760 Peachtree Road NW
Atlanta, GA 30357

Sports Retailer (Trade)
1699 Wall Street
Mt. Prospect, IL 60056

Women's Sports and Fitness
809 S. Orlando Avenue, Suite H
Winter Park, FL 32789

Appendix 4
Bicycle Associations

American Youth Hostels, Inc.
(AYH)
National Offices
PO Box 37613
Washington, DC 20013-7613

Bikecentennial
Bicycle Travel Association
PO Box 8308-S
Missoula, MT 59807-9988
(406) 721-1776

Canadian Cycling Association
333 River Road
Vanier, Ottawa, Canada K11
8B9

International Human-Powered
Vehicle Association (IHPVA)
PO Box 51255
Indianapolis, IN 46251

International Mountain
Bicycling Association (IMBA)
PO Box 2007
Saratoga, CA 95070-0007
(408) 741-5254
(619) 387-2757

International Randonneurs
Old Engine House #2
727 N. Salina Street
Syracuse, NY 13208
(315) 471-2101

League of American Wheelmen
(LAW)
6707 Whitestone Road, Suite 209
Baltimore, MD 21203
(301) 944-3399

National Off-Road Bicycle
Association (NORBA)
PO Box 1901
Chandler, AZ 85244

Professional Racing
Organization (PRO)
1524 Linden Street
Allentown, PA 18102

Ultra-Marathon Cycling
Association
4790 Irvine Boulevard, #105-111
Irvine, CA 92714
(714) 544-1701

United States Cycling Federation
(USCF)
1750 E. Boulder St.
Colorado Springs, CO 80909
(719) 578-4581

Triathlon Federation USA
PO Box 1963
Davis, CA 95617
(916) 757-2831

Washington Area Bicycle
Association
1332 I Street NW
Washington, DC 20005

Women's Cycling Network
PO Box 73
Harvard, IL 60033

Women's Mountain Bike and
Tea Society (WOMBATS)
Box 757
Fairfax, CA 94930

Appendix 5
Selected Bibliography

American College of Sports Medicine. *Guidelines for Exercise Testing and Prescription*. 3rd ed. Philadelphia: Lea & Febiger, 1986.

Anderson, Robert. *Stretching*. Box 1002, Englewood, CO 80110: 1975.

Apple, David, and John Cantwell. *Medicine for Sport*. Chicago: Year Book Medical Publishers, 1979.

Bailey, Covert. *Fit or Fat?* New York: Houghton Mifflin, 1977.

Bailey, Covert. *The Fit or Fat Target Diet*. New York: Houghton Mifflin, 1984.

Ballantine, Richard. *Richard's Bicycle Book*. New York: Ballantine Books, 1982.

Bicycling magazine et al. *Bicycle Repair*. Emmaus Pa.: Rodale Books, 1985.

Borysewicz, Edward. *Bicycle Road Racing*. Brattleboro, Vermont: Velo-news, 1985.

Briggs, George, and Doris Calloway. *Nutrition and Physical Fitness*, 11th ed. New York: Holt, Rinehart, and Winston, CBS College Publishing, 1984.

Brody, Jane. *Jane Brody's Good Food Book*. New York: W. W. Norton and Co., 1985.

————. *Jane Brody's Nutrition Book*. New York: W. W. Norton and Co., 1983.

Brooks, George A., and Thomas D. Fahey. *Fundamentals of Human Performance*. New York: Macmillan Publishing Company, 1987.

Burke, Edmund. *Toward an Understanding of Human Performance*. Ithaca, NY: Movement Publications, 1977.

355

———. *Science of Cycling*. Champaign, Ill.: Human Kinetics Publishers, Inc., 1986.

———. *The Two-Wheeled Athlete*. Brattleboro, Vermont: Velo-news, 1986.

———. *Inside the Cyclist*. Brattleboro, Vermont: Velo-news, 1984.

Cavanagh, Peter. *The Physiology and Biomechanics of Cycling*. New York: John Wiley & Sons, 1978.

Chernin, Kim. *The Obsession: Reflections on the Tyranny of Slenderness*. New York: Harper & Row, 1982.

———. *The Hungry Self: Women, Eating and Identity*. New York: Times Books, 1985.

Clark, Nancy. *The Athlete's Kitchen*. New York: Bantam, 1987.

Clark, Nancy. "Body Fat Measurement: Fat or Fiction?" *Cycling USA*. (1986): 10.

Colligan, Doug, and Dick Teresi. *The Cyclist's Manual*. New York: Sterling Publishing Co., 1981.

Cordellos, Harry. *Breaking Through*. Mountain View, Calif.: Anderson World, 1981.

Costill, David. *A Scientific Approach to Distance Running*. Los Altos, Calif.: Track and Field News, 1979.

Cuthbertson, Tom. *Anybody's Bike Book*. Berkeley, Calif.: Ten-Speed Press, 1984.

———. *Bike Tripping* Berkeley, Calif.: Ten-Speed Press, 1972.

de la Rosa, Denise, and Michael Kolin. *The Custom Bicycle* . Emmaus, Penn.: Rodale Press, 1979.

Downing, George. *The Massage Book*. Berkeley, Calif.: Bookworks, 1974.

Faria, Irvin. *Cycling Physiology for the Serious Cyclist*. Springfield, Ill.: Charles C. Thomas, 1978.

Festa, Susan. "That Time of the Month." *Women's Sport & Fitness* (August 1987): 29-31.

Fleck, Steven, Ph.D. "Body Composition of Elite American Athletes." *The American Journal of Sports Medicine* (– 1983): 398-403.

George, Barbara. *Ten Years of Championship Bicycle Racing. 1972-1981*. Brattleboro, Vermont: Velo-news, 1983.

Goulart, Frances. *Eating to Win: Food Psyching for the Athlete*. New York: Stein and Day, 1978.

Gross, Albert. *Endurance*. New York: Dodd, Mead & Co., 1986.

Grosser, Morton. *Gossamer Odyssey*. Boston, Mass.: Houghton Mifflin Company, 1981.

Harris, Dorothy V. and Harris, Bette. *The Athlete's Guide to Sports Psychology: Mental Skills for Physical People*. Champaign, Ill.: Leisure Press, 1984.

Herrigel, Eugen. *The Method of Zen* New York: Vintage Books, Random House, 1974.

————. *Zen in the Art of Archery.* New York: Vintage Books, Random House Inc., 1971.

Howard, John. *The Cyclist's Companion.* Brattleboro, Vermont: Stephen Green Press, 1984.

Howard, John, Albert Gross, and Christian Paul. *Multi-Fitness.* New York: Macmillan, 1985.

Klafs, Carl, and M. J. Lyon. *The Female Athlete: A Coach's Guide to Conditioning and Training.* St. Louis, Mo.: C. V. Mosby, 1978.

Kleeberg, Irene. *Bicycle Touring.* New York: Franklin Watts, 1975.

Leete, Harley. *The Best of Bicycling!* New York: Trident, 1970.

LeMond, Greg, and Kent Gordis. *The Complete Book of Bicycling.* New York: Putnam, 1987.

Lincoln, A. *Food for Athletes.* Chicago: Contemporary Books, 1979.

Mackenzie, Jeanne. *Cycling.* Oxford, England: Oxford Small Books Press, Oxford University Press, 1981.

Marino, John. *John Marino's Bicycling Book.* Los Angeles: J. P. Tarcher, Inc., 1981.

Matheny, Fred. *Beginning Bicycle Racing.* Brattleboro, Vermont: Velo-News, 1981.

McCullagh, James C. *American Bicycle Racing.* Emmaus, Penn.: Rodale Press, 1976.

The Melpomene Institute. "Women's Issues in Exercise and Fitness," *Fitness Management* (May/June 1987): 17-19, 58-59.

Merckx, Eddy. *The Fabulous World of Cycling.* Belgium: Andre Grisard, 1982.

Miner, Valerie and Longino, Helen. *Competition: A Feminist Taboo?* New York: The Feminist Press, 1987.

Mirkin, G., and Hoffman, M. *The Sports Medicine Book.* Boston: Little, Brown & Co., 1978.

Mohn, Peter. *Bicycle Touring.* Mankato, Minn.: Crestwood House, 1975.

Orbach, Susie. *Fat Is a Feminist Issue.* New York: Berkeley Books, 1978.

Orlick, Terry. *Psyching for Sport.* Champaign, Ill.: Leisure Press, 1986.

————. *In Pursuit of Excellence.* Champaign, Ill.: Human Kinetics, 1980.

Plas, Rob Van der. *The Bicycle Touring Manual.* San Francisco, Calif.: Bicycle Books, 1987.

Puhl, Jacqueline L., and C. Harmon Brown, eds. *The Menstrual Cycle and Physical Activity.* Champaign, Ill.: Human Kinetics Publishers, Inc., 1986.

Rakowski, John. *Adventure Cycling in Europe.* Emmaus, Penn.: Rodale Press, 1981.

Reynolds, Bill. *Complete Weight Training Book.* Mountain View, Calif.: World Publications, 1976.

Reynolds, Gretchen. "Fast and Feminine." *Bicycling* magazine (August 1987): 53–55.

Savage, Barbara. *Miles from Nowhere.* Seattle: The Mountaineers, 1983.

Schwarz, Jack. *Voluntary Controls for Creative Meditation.* New York: E. P. Dutton, 1978.

Schwarzenegger, Arnold. *Encyclopedia of Modern Bodybuilding.* New York: Fireside Press, Simon & Schuster, Inc., 1985.

Shermer, Michael. *Sportcycling.* Chicago: Contemporary Books, Inc., 1985.

———. *Cycling, Endurance, and Speed.* Chicago: Contemporary Books, Inc. 1987.

Simes, Jack. *Winning Bicycle Racing.* Chicago: Contemporary Books, Inc., 1976.

Sloane, Eugene. *The Complete Book of Cycling.* New York: Trident, 1970.

———. *Complete Book of All-Terrain Bicycles.* New York: Simon & Schuster, 1985.

Smith, N. J. *Food for Sport.* Palo Alto, Calif.: Bull Publishing, 1976.

Smith, Robert A. *A Social History of the Bicycle.* American Heritage Press, 1972.

Straub, William. *Sports Psychology: An Analysis of Athletic Behavior.* Ithaca, NY: Movement Press.

Sutherland, Howard. *Sutherland's Handbook for Bicycle Mechanics.* Berkeley, Calif.: Sutherland, 1974.

Tinley, Scott. *Winning Triathlon.* Chicago: Contemporary Books, 1986.

———. *All About Bicycle Racing.* Mountain View, Calif.: World Publications, 1975.

———. *Food for Fitness.* Mountain View, Calif.: World Publications, 1975.

Ullyot, Joan. *Running Free: A Book for Women Runners and Their Friends.* New York: Putnam, 1982.

Urrutia, Virginia. *Two Wheels & a Taxi.* Seattle: The Mountaineers, 1987.

Velo-News Editors (Contributors: Fred Matheny, Stephen Grabe, Andrew Buck, and Geoff Drake). *Weight Training for Cyclists.* Brattleboro, Vermont: Velo-news, 1986.

Wells, Christine. *Women, Sport & Performance: A Physiological Perspective.* Champaign, Ill.: Human Kinetics Publishers, Inc., 1985.

Whitt, Frank and Wilson, David Gordon. *Bicycling Science.* Cambridge, Mass.: The MIT Press, 1974.

Appendix 6:
Women's Cycling Records

UCI (Union Cycliste International)
WORLD AMATEUR CHAMPIONSHIP MEDALISTS
FROM THE UNITED STATES*

Year	Location	Event	Place	Name
1969	Brno, Czech	Road	1	Audrey McElmury
1972	Marseille, France	Sprint	3	Sheila Young
1973	San Sebastian, Spain	Sprint	1	Sheila Young
1974	Montreal, Canada	Sprint	2	Sue Novara
1975	Liege, Belgium	Sprint	1	Sue Novara
			3	Sheila Young
		Pursuit	2	Mary Jane Reoch
1976	Mendrisio, Italy	Sprint	1	Sheila Young
		Sprint	2	Sue Novara
1977	San Cristobal, Venice	Sprint	2	Sue Novara
		Road	2	Connie Carpenter
1978	Munich, Germany	Sprint	2	Sue Novara
1979	Amsterdam, Netherlands	Sprint	3	Sue Novara
1980	Sallanches, France	Road	1	Beth Heiden
1980	Besancon, France	Sprint	1	Sue Novara

*Reprinted from the United States Cycling Federation 1988 Rule Book.

Year	Location	Event	Place	Name
1981	Prague, Czech	Road	3	Connie Carpenter
1981	Brno, Czech	Sprint	1	Sheila Young-Ochowicz
1982	Leicester, England	Sprint	1	Connie Paraskevin
		Sprint	2	Sheila Young-Ochowicz
		Pursuit	1	Rebecca Twigg
			2	Connie Carpenter
1983	Altenrhein, Switzerland	Road	2	Rebecca Twigg
1983	Zurich, Switzerland	Pursuit	1	Connie Carpenter
			2	Cindy Olavarri
1983	Zurich, Switzerland	Sprint	1	Connie Paraskevin
1984	Barcelona, Spain	Sprint	1	Connie Paraskevin
		Pursuit	1	Rebecca Twigg
1985	Bassano del Grappa, Italy	Sprint	2	Connie Paraskevin
		Pursuit	1	Rebecca Twigg
			2	Peggy Maass
1986	Colorado Springs, Colorado	Sprint	3	Connie Paraskevin
		Pursuit	2	Rebecca Twigg-Whitehead
		Road	2	Janelle Parks
1987	Vienna, Austria	Pursuit	1	Rebecca Twigg-Whitehead
			3	Melinda Mayfield
		Sprint	3	Connie Paraskevin Young
		Team Time Trial	2	Leslee Schenk, Susan Ehlers, Jane Marshall, Inga Benedict
1987	Bergamo, Italy	Jr. Sprint	1	Janie Eickhoff
		Jr. Pursuit	1	Janie Eickhoff

OLYMPIC MEDALISTS

Year	Location	Event	Place	Name
1984	Los Angeles, California	Road Cycling (first time held for women)	Gold / Silver	Connie Carpenter-Phinney / Rebecca Twigg
1988	Seoul, Korea	Match Sprint (first time held for women)	Bronze	Connie Paraskevin-Young

UCI WORLD RECORDS*
Indoor Track

STANDING START

1 km	1:08.247	E. Salumyae (URS), Moscow, 19 Aug. 84
3 km	3:49.646	J. Longo (FRA), Paris Palais-Omnisport, 17 Nov. 85
5 km	6:22.713	J. Longo (FRA), Paris Palais-Omnisport, 15 Nov. 85
10 km	13:29.395	J. Longo (FRA), Paris Palais-Omnisport, 7 Nov. 86
20 km	26:58.157	J. Longo (FRA), Paris Palais-Omnisport, 7 Nov. 86
100 km	2:37:16.578	E. Menuzzo (ITA), Milan ITA-Vigorelli Std, 18 May 85
1 hr	44.718 km	J. Longo (FRA), Paris Palais-Omnisport, 7 Nov. 86 (0-600 m Track Altitude)
3 km	3:43.490	J. Longo (FRA), Paris-Fra, 14 Nov. 86

FLYING START

200 m	11:489	E. Salumyae (URS), Moscow-Olympic Velo., 8 July 86
500 m	30.834	N. Kruchelnitskaya (URS), Moscow-Olympic Velo., 4 Feb. 87
1 km	1:09.007	G. Tsareva (URS), Moscow-Olympic Velo., 10 Jun. 80

Outdoor Track

STANDING START

1 km	1:14.249	E. Salumyae (URS), Tachkent, URS-Velo., 17 May 84
3 km	3:49.780	R. Whitehead (USA), Barcelone, ESP-Velo., 29 Aug. 84
5 km	6:41.75	A. Jone (GBR), Leicester, GBR-Saffron Lane 31 Jul. 82
10 km	13:30.055	J. Longo (FRA), Colorado Springs, USA-7-Eleven Velo. 20 Sept. 86
20 km	26:55.611	J. Longo (FRA), Colorado Springs, USA-7-Eleven Velo. 20 Sept. 86
100 km	2:31:28.374	F. Galli (ITA), Milan, ITA-Vigorelli Std, 18 Aug. 85
1 hr	44.77028 km	J. Longo (FRA), Colorado Springs, USA-7-Eleven Velo. 20 Sept 86 (600 m and Higher Track Altitude)
1 hr	43.58789 km	J. Longo (FRA), Milan, ITA-Vigorelli Std, 29 Sept 86 (0-600 m Track Altitude)

FLYING START

200 m	11.383	I. Gautheron (FRA), Colorado Springs, USA-7-Eleven Velo., 16 Aug. 86
500 m	30.59	I. Gautheron (FRA), Alcides Nieto Patino, Col-Velo. 14 Sept. 86
1 km	1:10.463	E. Salumyae (URS), Tachkent, URS-Velo., 15 May 84

*Reprinted from the *United States Cycling Federation 1988 Rule Book*.

USCF
UNITED STATES NATIONAL RECORDS*

TRACK TIME TRIAL, FLYING START
200 m   11.393   Connie Paraskevin, Colo. Springs, CO, 5 July 85
500   Rebecca Twigg-Whitehead, Colo. Springs, Colo., 16 Aug. 86
1000   (not established)

TRACK 1 KILOMETER TIME TRIAL
Senior   1:14.04   Rebecca Twigg, Trexlertown, PA, 8 Aug. 84

TRACK 3 KILOMETER TIME TRIAL
Senior   3:45.02   Rebecca Twigg, Barcelona, Spain (World Champ.), 30 Aug. 84
Sr. 35   4:08.40   Susan Barton, Colo. Springs, CO, 27 Sept. 85

TRACK TIME TRIAL
5 km   7:17.47   Carol Lewnau, Indianapolis, IN, 19 Sept. 87
10   14:38.71   Carol Lewnau, Indianapolis, IN, 19 Sept. 87
20   29:32.21   Carol Lewnau, Indianapolis, IN, 19 Sept. 87
1 hour   40.116 km   Carol Lewnau, Indianapolis, IN, 19 Sept. 87
50   1:15:38.92   Carol Lewnau, Indianapolis, IN, 19 Sept. 87
100   (not established)

ROAD 20 KILOMETER TIME TRIAL
Junior   29:52.90   Linnea Lindgren, Moriarty, NM, 15 Sept. 85
Sr. 65   40:33.93   Martha Hanson, Elberta, UT, 13 July 87

ROAD 40 KILOMETER TIME TRIAL—This is actually a 25-mile record (40.233 km)
Senior   55:46.71   Jane Marshall, Moriarty, NM, 13 Sept. 86
Sr. 30   55:53.53   Jane Marshall, Moriarty, NM, 7 June 87
Sr. 35   58:09.7   Judy Layton, Sierraville, CA, 16 June 84
Sr. 40   58:09.7   Judy Layton, Sierraville, CA, 16 June 84
Sr. 45   1:06:41.1   Joan Paul, Tallahassee, FL, July 83
Sr. 50   1:06:14.8   Joan Paul, Moriarty, NM, 13 Sept. 86
Sr. 55   1:12:32.7   Emily DeLuca, Elberta, UT, 13 July 87
Sr. 60   1:16:45.3   Martha Hanson, Tallahassee, FL, July 83

BORDER-TO-BORDER
Individual   (not established)
Team of 2   (not established)
Team of 4   (not established)

TRANSCONTINENTAL
Individual   (not established)
Team of 2   (not established)
Team of 4   (not established)

*Reprinted from the *United States Cycling Federation 1988 Rule Book.*

UMCA
ULTRA-MARATHON RECORDS**
Solo Transcontinental Records

Southern Route
Ann Kovich   14-14-54***
Santa Monica, CA–New York City, NY
6/82

Susan Notorangelo   11-16-15
Santa Monica, CA–New York City, NY
2,960 miles
7/83

Susan Notorangelo   10-14-25
Huntington Beach, CA–Atlantic City, NJ
3,120 miles
7/85

Elaine Mariolle   10-02-04
Huntington Beach, CA–Atlantic City, NJ
3,107 miles
7/86

Northern Route
Casey Patterson   11-21-15
San Francisco, CA–Washington, DC
3,117 miles
7/87

Tandem Transcontinental Records

Estelle Gray and Cheryl Marek   10-22-48
Santa Monica, CA–New York, NY
7/84

Cherrie Moore and Debbie Rocker   12-07-43
Huntington Beach, CA–Atlantic City, NJ
5/86

**Provided by the Ultra-Marathon Cycling Association
***(Days-Hours-Minutes)

Mixed Tandem Transcontinental Records

Sue Notorangelo and Lon Haldeman   10-20-23
Santa Monica, CA–New York, NY
2,927 miles
6/83

Sue Notorangelo and Lon Haldeman   9-20-07
Huntington Beach, CA–Virginia Beach, VA
2,800 miles
4/86

Seattle to San Diego

Elaine Mariolle   4-22-01
1,339 miles
5/85

Mixed Tandem, San Francisco to Los Angeles

Alice and John Watt   21-44 (hours-minutes)
394 miles
8/86

Santa Barbara to San Diego

Bindy Beck   13-00
222 miles
11/87

Twenty-Four Hour Ride

Susan Notorangelo   401.6 miles
5/82

Twenty-Four Hour Tandem Ride

Patty Brehlen and Patience Hutton   422.51 miles
9/86

Twenty-Four Hour Mixed Tandem Ride

Susan Notorangelo and Lon Haldeman   431.99 miles
5/83

El Tour de Tucson 24-Hour Record

Cheryl Campbell   258 miles
11/87

Appendix 7
United States Cycling Federation Velodromes

The following is a list of UCSF velodromes. For further information on the address, hours, etc., contact your local USCF District Representative. You can find out who your District Representative is through your local bike shop, local racing club, or by contacting the USCF office in Colorado Springs, CO (see Appendix 4: Bicycle Associations).

Alpenrose Velodrome
Portland, OR

Brown Deer Velodrome
Milwaukee, WI

Dick Lane Velodrome
East Point, GA

Dorais Velodrome
Detroit, MI

Encino Velodrome
Encino, CA

Lehigh County Velodrome
Trexlertown, PA

Madison Velodrome (portable)
Detroit, MI

Major Taylor Velodrome
Indianapolis, IN

Meadowhill Park Track
Northbrook, IL

Marymoor Park Velodrome
Redmond, WA

Penrose Velodrome
St. Louis, MO

San Diego Velodrome
San Diego, CA

Santa Clara County Velodrome
San Jose, CA

Shakopee Velodrome
Shakopee, MN

Siegfried Stern Velodrome
Flushing, NY

7-Eleven Velodrome
Colorado Springs, CO

Washington Park Bowl
Kenosha, WI

California State University
Dominguez Hills
Carson, CA

Index

ACI, 29
Aerobic exercises, 73
Aerolite, 13
Aero spokes, 14
Age, as factor in cycling, 164
Alcohol consumption, 175
Allen, Mark, 250
All-terrain bicycle, 195
Almanac, 130
Alsop, 50
Alternating V-ups, 100
Aluminum, as frame material, 10
Amenorrhea, 70, 74–75
American National Standards
    Institute, 29
American Youth Hostels, Inc. (AYH),
    121, 126–27, 138
    publications of, 127
Anderson, Julie, 270, 277
Anemia, 72
Anrig, Helen, 282, 323
Anthony, Susan, 1

Anybody's Bike Book (Cuthbertson),
    49, 62
Arch pain, 24, 36
Arledge, Roone, 326
*Arnold Schwarzenegger's
    Encyclopedia of Modern
    Bodybuilding*, 108
Athlete's Guide to Sports Psychology
    (Harris), 82
Athlete's Kitchen, The (Clark), 80
Automobile, bike racks for, 43
AYL Handbook, 127

Back, problems with, 28, 83–84
Back hyperextensions, 94
Bags, 41
Bailen, 29
Bailey, Covert, 72, 73, 81
Bassett, Lisa, 260, 264, 269, 277, 323
Beck, Bindy, 314, 319, 323
Beerer, Matt, 310, 322
Bell, 29

Bench press, 92
Benes, Cindy, 280
Benorden, Bob, 322
Berryman, Scott, 188
Bib shorts, 35
Bicycle(s)
  basic skills in handling, 55-59
  early popularity of, 1-2
  equipment for, 11-17, 40-41, 59-62
  frame geometry for, 8-10
  frame materials, 10
  maintenance of, 49-55, 62, 124
  reemergence of, 2-3
  types of, 4-5
  and women, 1-3
Bicycle associations, 353-54
Bicycle clubs, 148
Bicycle commuting, 131-43
  arrival, 133-34
  choosing a route, 133
  equipment for, 132-33
Bicycle periodicals, 350-52
Bicycle racing, 146-47
  associations for, 147
  events in, 148-55
  training for, 169-70
  women in, 165-66, 181-83, 185,
    189, 190-91
Bicycle Repair Book, The, 49, 62
Bicycle Road Racing (Borysewicz),
    68, 194
Bicycle touring, 118-21
  resources for, 126-30
  world, 122-26
Bicycle USA, 130
Bicycling Safety on the Road, 143
Bicycling to Work, 143
Bikecentennial, 120, 121, 127
  publications of, 127-28
Bike racks, for automobiles, 43
Bike Report, 128
Birth control, 75
Blackburn Trackstand windtrainer,
    42
Blackie, Rod, 316

Bladed spokes, 14
Blood pressure, 69
Bly, Nelly, 1
Body fat, ideal percent of, 163
Body image, 63-65
Borysewicz, Eddie, 68, 172, 194
Boswell, Grant, 240
Boyer, Jonathan, 284, 285, 288, 293,
    296, 299, 303-4, 320, 338
Brakes, 15
Brancale, 29
Braun, Cyndy, 114
Breathing, as part of weight
    training, 86
Brice, Fanny, 63
Bridgestone, 21
Brink, Patty, 33
Brisco-Hooks, Valerie, 329
Brown, Madeline, 64
Bucci, 280
Burden, Dan, 128
Burden, Lys, 128
Burke, Edmund, 71
Buttocks, problems with, 25-26

Cadence, 12, 40-41, 57
Calf raises, 91
California Bicyclist, 111
Caliper brakes, 15
Callaway, Dwight, 299
Camardo, Paul, 280
Campagnolo, 8, 13
Canins, Maria, 77, 178, 179, 199
Cannondale, 21
Carbon fiber, as frame material, 10
Carpenter-Phinney, Connie, 144,
    145, 146, 159, 168, 177, 188, 212
Cat-Eye, 132
Centurion, 21
Century rides, 73, 115-18
  tips for enjoying, 25-26, 116-17
  tips for group riding, 117-18
Chain, cleaning of, 50
Chair leg raises, 101
Chamois, 34-35

Chapman, Tally, 299
Charameda, Laura, 156
Chico Wildflower Century, 115
Cholesterol check, 69
Christy, Marvin, 322
City Sports, 111
Clark, Nancy, 74, 80
Claus, Sarah, 31, 39
Clifton, Eric, 305
Clifton, Shelby, 305
Clinchers, 13–14, 40
Clothing, 30–32, 85–86
    for bicycling, 123–24
    for bike touring, 123–24
    fabrics for, 32–34
    fit of, 32
    foul-weather gear, 38–39
    gloves, 26–27, 37–38
    jerseys, 35–36
    shoes, 13, 24–25, 36–37
    shorts, 30–31, 34–35
    for weight training, 85–86
Club riding, 111–13
Coles, Michael, 284
Colnes, Andrea, 119
Colnes, Barry, 119
Comfort, 24–28
Commuting, bicycle. *See* Bicycle
    commuting
*Competition Among Women: A
    Feminist Forum* (Longino and
    Miner), 82
Complete Book of Bicycling
    (LeMond), 194
Computers, 40–41
Concentration curls, 97
Concor America, 16
Cook, Jaye, 323
Coors Classic, 155, 213–14
Cotton fabric, for clothing, 33
Crankarms, 13
Cranks, 13
Criteriums (USCF), 151
Crunches, 99
Cuthbertson, Tom, 49, 62

Cycling. *See* Bicyling
Cyclists' Yellow Pages, 127–28
Cyclocross (USCF), 151

Daily journal, keeping, 65–66
Davis Bike Club, 112
Davis Double Century, 112
DeBreau, Bill, 322
Decker-Slaney, Mary, 329
Defensive driving, 48
Dembling, Arthur, 280
Denman, Rick, 196
Derailleurs, 4, 11–12
Diet, 72–73, 174–75
Disk wheels, 14
Docter, Sarah, 146, 166
Downhill riding, 57–59
Drafting, 118, 150
Dubois, Blanche, 44
Dukes, Caroline, 113
Dukes, Charles, 113
Dukes, Jean, 113
Dukes, Sara Beth, 113

Edwards, Sally, 250
Effective Cycling (Forrester), 49, 62,
    143
Electro-impedence, 70–71
Elliot, Jim, 278
Endurance cycling, 206, 238, 239–40
    Ironman triathlon, 206–7, 206–7,
        236–38, 331
    Race across America (RAAM), 146,
        204–8, 251–322, 330–31
Epperson, David, 286, 314
Equipment, for mountain bicycling,
    202
Ernst, Joanne, 74, 207, 235–48
Exercise, 72–73

Fabrics, for clothing, 32–34
Fabry, Ben, 290
Fabry, Bob, 282, 314, 319, 323
Fasting, 72
Fat, estimating percent, 70–71

Feet, problems with, 24–25
Feld, Joel, 267, 270
Fenders, 38
Fisher Mountain Bikes, 21
Fit, for clothing, 32
Fit Kit, 17
Fit or Fat (Bailey), 72, 81
Flat tire, changing, 50–55
Fletcher, Ellen, 132, 134, 136–43
Fletcher, Jeff, 138
Fletcher, Linda, 138
Fletcher, Terry, 138
Forrester, John, 49, 143
Frame geometry, 8–10
Frame materials, 10
Fuji, 21
Furnivall, Gilly, 282, 283, 297, 323

Galli, 8
Gear inches, 337
Gears, 11–12, 124, 335–39
Gillis, Rob, 299, 315
Giro Kiwi, 29
Gloves, 26–27, 37–38
Good Roads Movement, 129
Gore-Tex, for clothing, 34, 38
Gould, Ed, 314, 319, 324
Goursolle, Kitty, 207, 253, 255
Graffenreid, Jim De, 322
Graphic, 128
Grates, 56
Gray, Estelle, 208, 214–23
Greater Arizona Bicycling
    Association, 110
Grizzly Peak Cyclists, 112
Group riding, tips for, 117–18

Haas, Deb, 306, 308
Haldeman, Lon, 132, 147, 208, 209,
    213, 219, 220–21, 226, 257, 270,
    288, 304, 310, 314, 320, 322
Handlebar height, adjusting, 23
Handlebars, 16–17
Hands, problems with, 26–27

Harris, Dorothy, 82
Harris, Madonna, 155
Harse, Debra, 49, 122–26
Hayden-Clifton, Shelby, 254, 256,
    258, 265, 278, 283, 284, 285, 286,
    291, 292, 293, 298, 299, 306, 309,
    310, 312, 313, 314, 315, 320
Headway, 81
Heart rate
    measuring, 174
    training, 67–69
Heart rate monitors, 40–41, 68–69
Heer, Frank, 323
Heiden, Beth, 145, 146, 166, 188
Heiden, Eric, 166, 182
Helaouet, Georges, 312, 315
Helmets, 29–30, 203
Hepburn, Katharine, 206
Herr, Frank, 282, 290
Herrigel, Eugene, 82
Hills, climbing, 57–58
Hinault, Bernard, 182
Hines, Pat, 255, 257, 262, 265, 271,
    275, 278, 305
Horn, Marty, 322
Hot foot, 24–25
Human Powered Transit
    Association, Inc. (HPTA), 143

Individual Time Trial (USCF), 151
International Mountain Bicycling
    Association (IMBA), 204
International Randonneurs, 249
Interval training, 68
Ironman triathlon, 206–7, 236–38,
    331

Jaffee, Lynn, 64
Jerseys, 35–36
John Marino Open (JMO), 207, 226,
    253, 305
Johnson, Brooks, 240
Julian, Leslie, 280

Kearney Lighting System, 132

Keller, Helen, 195
King, Billie Jean, 326, 328, 330
Kish, Rob, 299
Knees, problems with, 27
Kreitler, 43
Krueger, Steve, 269, 288, 290, 293, 299
Kyle, Chet, 30, 32

Lampley, Jim, 259, 267, 306
Lat pull-downs, 93
Lazer, 29
League of American Wheelmen (LAW), 45, 62, 121, 129
 activities and services of, 129
 publications of, 130
Lean body mass (LBM), 69-70, 72
Lee, Valerie, 77, 268, 269, 294, 314
Leg bands, 140
Leg curl, 89
Leg extension, 88
Leg press, 90
LeMond, Greg, 58, 68, 194
Lessing, Doris, 197
Lights, 41, 132-33, 140
Lindbergh, Anne Morrow, 109
Living room, riding in your, 42-43
Longino, Helen, 82
Longo, Jeannie, 12, 58, 149, 155, 178, 184
Look, 13
Lycra, for clothing, 30-31, 34, 36

Maillard, 8
Manno, Tony, 280
Marek, Cheryl, 208, 214-23, 225, 231
Marino, John, 147, 207, 261, 278, 307, 321
Mariolle, Elaine, 226, 227, 242, 259, 273, 278, 299, 307, 322
Mariolle, Janice, 277, 283, 290, 292, 294, 295, 324
Mariolle, Matthew, 260-61, 263, 277, 290, 291, 294, 295, 314, 319, 324
Mariolle, Nancy, 282, 324

Mariolle, Ray, 324
Markleeville Death Ride, 253
Massage, 108
Massage Book, The, 108
Match sprint (USCF), 152-54
Mavic, 8, 13
McElmury, Audrey, 144
Media coverage, 200, 219, 244, 330-31
Meister, Sandy, 156
Melpomene Institute for Women's Health Research, 64, 74, 75, 80
Melpomene Report, 80
Men
 comparing with women, 77-80
 fitting bicycle to, 18-21
Menstrual period, and cycling, 74, 193
Method of Zen, The (Herrigel), 82
Military press, 95
Miller, Cheryl, 328
Miner, Valerie, 82
Mirrors, 41
Miyata, 21
Modolo, 17
Monarch, 29
Moses, Edwin, 246
Motorpacing, 173
Mountain bikes, 5, 17
Mountain biking, 195-200
 equipment for, 202-3
 resources on, 204-5
 tips for, 201
 training for, 204
Mulligan, Jim, 322
Murdoch, Iris, 131

National Off-Road Bicycle Association (NORBA), 147, 196, 200, 204
Navratilova, Martina, 246
Neck, problems with, 27-28
Neil, Sara, 22, 50, 156
Nelson, Dave, 315
Nelson, Martha, 64
Nike, Phil, 244

Nishiki, 21
Notorangelo-Haldeman, Susan,
208-14, 219, 220-21, 223, 254,
255, 256, 257, 265, 269, 272, 278,
283, 284, 285, 286, 291, 293, 298,
299, 300, 304, 305, 306, 307, 308,
309, 312, 313, 315, 316, 317, 320,
322, 326-27, 331
Novara-Reber, Sue, 71, 75, 76, 144,
145, 157, 158-66, 182, 190
Novice series, 113-15
Nyad, Diana, 79, 267, 270, 272,
286-87, 309, 319, 326-34

Olavarri, Cindy, 73, 84-85, 103
One-Kilometer Time Trial (USCF),
154
Ore-Ida Women's Challenge, 155, 156
Osteoporosis, 70, 72
Overtraining, 73, 170

Palo Alto Bicycles, 21
Panniers, 41
Paraskevin-Young, Connie, 145, 149,
154, 159, 186-93
Patterson, Casey, 208, 224-35, 305,
306, 307, 320
Patterson, Charlie, 307
Patterson, Mary, 307
Peak, training to, 172
Pedals, 12-13
Penseyres, Jim, 288, 290, 299, 318, 319
Penseyres, JoAnn, 288
Penseyres, Penny, 288
Penseyres, Pete, 37, 132, 210-11, 228,
229, 257, 270, 271, 278, 288, 306,
308, 310, 318, 319, 320, 321, 322
Peugeot, 21
Phelan, Jacquie, 197-200, 205
Phillips, Wayne, 300, 312
Physical conditioning, for cycling,
173-74
Physiological testing, 69
Physiology, 78

Polypropylene, for clothing, 34
Position, maintaining comfortable,
55-56
Pregnancy, cycling during, 75-77,
164-65
Premenstrual syndrome (PMS), 74
Price, Nancy, 120
Professional league for women, 162
Professional Racing Organization
(PRO), 147
Pro-Tec, 29
Pulse
standing, 66-67
waking, 66-67
Pumps, 40

RAAM (Race Across America), 146,
207-8, 330-31
'84, 251-75
'85, 279-300
'86, 300-322
qualifying for, 254-56
Racks, 41
Railroad tracks, 56
Raleigh, 21
Rapitours, 120
Reach, adjusting, 23
Recreational riding, 109-10
bicycle touring, 118-19
century rides, 115-18
club riding, 111-13
getting involved, 111
novice series, 113-15
Recruitment programs, 161
Reflectors, 41, 133, 140
Repetitions, 87
Rich, Peter, 55
Riggs, Bobby, 328, 330
Road bikes, 5
Road hazards, 56-57
Road race (USCF), 149-51
Road turtles, 56
Rollers, 43, 172-73
Roosevelt, Eleanor, 251

Rose, Patty, 253

Saddle, 16
Saddle adjustments
  forward and backward, 22–23
  height, 21–22, 27
  reach, 23
Saddle tilt, 23
Saddle pads, 26
Saddle sores, 25
Safety, 132
  traffic, 45–48, 142–43
  for women, 49
Safety gear,for mountain bicycling,
  203
Sanyo, 132
Schuler, Tom, 188
"Scott" bars, 17
Seafirst Crown, 155
Seated rear flys, 98
Seat post, 16
Secrest, Michael, 257, 259, 265, 278,
  285, 288, 293, 296, 299, 306, 308,
  320, 331
Set-point theory, 71
Sew-ups, 13–14, 40
Sex discrimination, 213
Shanks, Carol, 314, 315, 319, 323
Shanks, David, 313, 317, 319, 323
Shermer, Michael, 143, 147, 168, 208,
  250, 257, 278, 284, 288, 293, 296,
  299, 326
Shimano, 8, 13
Shimmy, 59
Shoes
  for cycling, 13, 24–25, 36–37
  for weight training, 86
Shogun, 21
Shorter, Frank, 246
Shorts, 30–31, 34–35
Siple, Greg, 128
Siple, June, 128
Sirotniak, Ann, 156
Skinfold caliper, 71
Skinner, Linda, 251

Smolens, Amy, 31, 39, 277
Snell Foundation, 29
Spares, 40
Sparks, John, 319, 323
Specialized, 21
Spenco 500, 24
Spinning, 12, 57
Sponsorship, problem of, 157,
  161–62, 200, 219
Sport Cycling, 143
*Sport Cycling and Cycling:
  Endurance and Speed* (Shermer),
  250
Sports Medicine, Inc., 74
Sports testing, 69
Sprinting, 150–51
Stage races, 154–55, 179–80
Stair climbing, 169–70
Standing pulse, 66–67
Stationary bikes, 42–43, 172–73
Steel, as frame material, 10
Stems, 16–17
Sterling Cycle, 21
Strength training, benefit of, for
  women, 28, 83–84
Stress, 186
Stretching, 102
  technique for, 102–8
Sun-Tour, 8
Swisstex, 34, 36

Tamaro, Janet, 286
Tandem bike, 5
Tandem Club of America, 110
Team Time Trial (USCF), 151
Templin, Rob, 290, 293, 299, 310, 312
10-speed, 4–5, 5
  anatomy of, 7–8
  brakes for, 15
  frame for, 8–9
Terriberry, Scott, 283, 290, 294, 323
Terry, Georgena, 21, 158
Terry Precision Bicycles, 20
TeSelle, Davis, 282
Testosterone, 83

Third-world cycling, 123
Thompson-Benedict, Inga, 144, 155, 157, 177–86
Three-Kilometer Pursuit (USCF), 154
Thuemer, Petra, 79
Thule, 43
Tinley, Scott, 244, 250
Tires, 13–15
  changing flat, 50–55
  for mountain bicycling, 202
Tobey, Alan, 135
Tobey, Chandra, 31, 39
Tobey, Ruth, 31, 39, 134, 135
Tobin, Katrin, 155
Toeclips, Alice B. *See* Jacquie Phelan
Tofield, John, 311, 314, 317, 319, 323
Tour de France Féminin, 12, 154, 155, 213–14
Tour Finder, 130
Touring shorts, 35
Track bike, 5, 152, 202
Traffic, techniques in, 45–48
Traffic laws, 44–45
Traffic safety, 45–43, 142–43
Trail, Michael, 299
Trailers, 41
Training, 213
  for bicycle racing, 169–70
  for cycling, 168, 169–70, 174
  intervals in, 242
  for mountain bicycling, 204
  for triathlon, 241–42
  weight, 28, 84–101
Training diary, keeping of, 185–86
Training heart rate, 67–69
Training log, 172
Trampleasure, Calvin, 265–66, 269
Trampleasure, Lee, 255, 260, 263, 264, 265–66, 274, 290, 297, 312, 313, 319, 324
TransAmerica trail, 120
Transportation. *See* Bicycle commuting
Triathlon, 32, 240

clothing for, 32
Ironman, 206–7, 236–38, 331
training for, 241–42
Triathlon, 235, 236
Triathlon bikes, 17
Triathlon Federation USA, 249
Tricep press-down, 98
Tri-Flow, 50
20-Kilometer Points Race (USCF), 154
Twigg, Rebecca, 144, 154, 166–76, 184, 210

Ullyot, Dr. Joan, 75
Ultra-Marathon Cycling Association (UMCA), 147, 249
Ultra-marathon events, 206
Underwater weighing, 70
Union, 132
Union Cycle International (UCI), 146
United States Cycling Federation (USCF), 29, 147, 194
  road and track racing, 148–55
  support of, for women's cycling, 155–56
Univega, 21

Van Renterghem, Kay, 110
Van Renterghem, Rudy, 110
Vaughan, Liz, 263, 264, 289, 290, 324
Vaughan, Vance, 55, 253, 255, 256, 263, 266, 268, 273, 275, 277, 282, 287, 289, 292, 293, 314, 317, 319, 324
Velodrome, 152
Velo-Lux, 132
Verrill, Gary, 322
Vetta, 29
Vitus, 21
VO_2 (oxygen volume intake) test, 69, 163–64

Waking pulse, 66–67
Walden, Mike, 188
Wallace, Robert, 50

Waltermire, Kye, 224, 226, 274, 291,
    297, 299, 310, 312, 317, 322
Walters, Trica, 148
Warm-up activities, 85
Water bottles, 40
Weight, 69–72
    determining ideal, 71–72
    as factor in hill climbing, 58
    as factor in road racing, 5, 7
Weight belt, 86
Weight control, 72–73
    and cycling, 64
Weight training, 28, 83–84
    for advanced cyclists and racers, 87
    alternating V-ups, 100
    back hyperextensions, 94
    bench press, 92
    calf raises, 91
    chair leg raises, 101
    clothing for, 85–86
    concentration curls, 97
    crunches, 99
    lat pull-downs, 93
    leg curl, 89
    leg extension, 88
    leg press, 90
    military press, 95
    seated rear flys, 98
    sets and repetitions in, 87
    tricep press-down, 98
    warm-up activities for, 85
    working with an instructor, 87
Weight Training for Cyclists, 108
Weissmuller, Johnny, 79
Wells, Christine, 76, 78, 79, 82
Wheels, 13–15
Whitehead, Cindy, 201
Wind resistance, as factor in road
    racing, 5, 7–8, 150

Windshell, 38
Winterhalter, Karen, 306, 308
Women
    and bicycle racing, 165–66, 181–83,
        185, 189, 190–91
    and bicycle touring, 122–26
    comparing with men, 77–80
    and cycling, 1–3
    fitting bicycle to, 18–21
    and hints for traveling alone, 123
    safety for, 49
    in sports, 326–34
    strength training for, 83–84
    training for, 213
    weight training for, 83
Women, Sport & Performance: A
    Physiological Perspective (Wells),
    76, 78, 82
Women's Cycling Network, 82, 250
Women's cycling teams, 157
Women's Mountain Bike and Tea
    Society (WOMBATS), 82, 204–5
Women's Sports & Fitness Magazine,
    81, 121
Women's Sports Foundation (WSF), 81
Wood, Wyatt, 322
Wong, Bonnie, 228
World Adventure, 127
World traveling, by bicycle, 122–26

Yakima, 43
Young, Claire, 188
Young, Earle, 260, 263, 266, 277, 323
Young-Ochowicz, Sheila, 77, 145,
    159, 165, 188, 190

Zack, Sally, 156
Zen in the Art of Archery (Herrigel),
    82

About the Authors

Elaine Mariolle lives in Berkeley, California. Active in cycling since 1983, she is an adventurer and racer. Elaine has competed in the Race Across AMerica three times (1984, 1985, and 1986) and has been featured on ABC's "Wide World of Sports." In 1986 she won the RAAM, setting a new transcontinental record for women. Elaine does some touring in the off-season and regularly competes in USCF races.

Elaine holds a degree in geography from the University of California at Berkeley. She was accepted to graduate school in business but declined the offer in order to race bicycles. Elaine frequently travels around the country giving presentations and motivational talks to a variety of groups, from bicycle clubs to professional organizations.

In addition to cycling Elaine also enjoys reading, music, film, and schmoozing with friends.

Michael Shermer is an assistant professor of psychology at Glendale Community College. He has a bachelor's degree in psychology from Pepperdine University and a master's degree in psychology from California State University, Fullerton. He has published articles in psychological journals as well as presented papers at professional psychological conventions.

377

His area of specialty is motivation and goal orientation, and he is particularly interested in the psychology of individuals who push themselves to their physical and mental limits.

Shermer frequently lectures to audiences around the United States on psychology, health and fitness, and his world-record rides.

He has written many articles for bicycle and health-related magazines, and he was editor of a bicycle trade publication for three years. He frequently writes articles for bicycle magazines and is currently a monthly columnist for *Cyclist* magazine. Michael has produced a 20-minute color documentary film on the 1981 Seattle-to-San Diego ride. He has appeared on ABC's "Wide World of Sports" in 1982, 1983, 1984, and 1985 in their coverage of the Race Across AMerica.

Michael, along with John Marino, Lon Haldeman, and Robert Hustwit, is an owner and director of the Race Across AMerica. In 1980 he and Marino founded the Ultra-Marathon Cycling Association, for the advancement of the sport of endurance riding. Michael also has a partnership in a bicycle shop, Shermer Cycles of America, in Arcadia, California.

Shermer has participated in the Ironman Triathlon, the Spenco 500 twice, and the Race Across AMerica in 1982, 1983, 1984, and 1985, taking third place twice. He currently holds records for cycling from Seattle to San Diego, Miami to Maine, and San Francisco to Los Angeles.

He is the author of *Sport Cycling* and *Cycling: Endurance and Speed.*